Symbol	Explanation	
¶ tr	Paragraph needs tr[...]	
Org	Organization weak	
Pass	Passive voice	127–129
Pro	Pronoun-antecedent unclear	138–143
Prf	Proofread	211–213
p	Punctuation needed	171, 202–204
.	Period needed	167–168
?	Question mark needed	169–171
!	Exclamation point needed	170–171
,	Comma needed	175–181
;	Semicolon needed	181–184
:	Colon needed	186–187
" "	Quotation marks needed	191–194
'	Apostrophe needed	197–198
. . .	Ellipses needed	195–197
[ ]	Brackets needed	195
—	Dash needed	187–188
-	Hyphen needed	200–202
( )	Parentheses needed	189–191
Rep	Unnecessary repetition	99–101
Run	Run-on sentence	116–117
Sxl	Sexist language inappropriate	226–228
Shft	Shift in tense, person, or number	145–147
Sp	Spelling is incorrect	213–216
Split	Split infinitive	129–130
Style	Style is inappropriate	223–225
S-V agr	Subject-verb do not agree	133–138
Sub	Subordination needed	114–116
Thesis	Thesis weak	51–53
Tone	Tone is inappropriate	225–226
Trans	Transitions weak	80–81, 216–220
Ts	Verb tense incorrect	133–138
Und	Underlining needed	198–199
Usg	Usage inappropriate	156–158
Var	Vary sentence structures	223–225
Word	Word choice inappropriate	154–156
Wdy	Wordy	95–97

Concise Process Handbook

Dennis M. Clausen University of San Diego

Concise Process Handbook

McGRAW-HILL BOOK COMPANY

New York St. Louis San Francisco Auckland Bogotá Hamburg
Johannesburg London Madrid Mexico Milan Montreal New Delhi Panama
Paris São Paulo Singapore Sydney Tokyo Toronto

CONCISE PROCESS HANDBOOK

Copyright © 1987 by McGraw-Hill, Inc. All rights reserved.
Printed in the United States of America. Except as permitted under the United States Copyright Act
of 1976, no part of this publication may be reproduced or distributed in any form or by any means,
or stored in a data base or retrieval system, without the prior written permission of the publisher.

1 2 3 4 5 6 7 8 9 0   KGPKGP   8 9 4 3 2 1 0 9 8 7

ISBN 0-07-011287-8

This book was set in Times Roman by Monotype Composition Company.
The editors were Emily G. Barrosse and James R. Belser; the designer was Joan Greenfield;
the production supervisor was Phil Galea.
Arcata Graphics / Kingsport was printer and binder.

The author wishes to thank the following for permission to quote from the materials listed:

F. Scott Fitzgerald, *The Great Gatsby,* copyright 1925,
Charles Scribner's Sons; Copyright renewed 1953 by Frances
Fitzgerald Lanahan. Courtesy of Charles Scribner's Sons.

From *One Flew Over the Cuckoo's Nest,* by Ken Kesey.
Copyright © 1962 by Ken Kesey.
Reprinted by permission of Viking Penguin, Inc.

From *The Fire Next Time* by James Baldwin.
Copyright © 1962, 1963 by James Baldwin.
Reprinted by permission of Doubleday and Company, Inc.

From *The Poet in America 1650 to the Present* by Albert Gelpi.
Copyright © 1973 by D. C. Heath and Company.
Reprinted by permission of D. C. Heath and Company.

From *The Poetry of Robert Frost* edited by Edward Connery Lathem.
Copyright 1930, 1934, 1939 © 1969 by Holt, Rinehart and Winston.
Copyright © 1958, 1962 by Robert Frost. Copyright © 1967 by
Lesley Frost Ballantine. Reprinted by permission of Henry Holt
and Company.

"Sinclair Lewis" by Mark Schorer.
Copyright © 1961 by Mark Schorer.
Reprinted by permission of Brandt and Brandt Literary Agents, Inc.

Library of Congress Cataloging-in-Publication Data

Clausen, Dennis M.
  Concise process handbook.

  Includes index.
   1. English language—Rhetoric—Handbooks, manuals,
etc. 2. English language—Grammar—1950–   —Handbooks, manuals, etc. I. Title.
PE1408.C524 1987   808'.042   86-21030
ISBN 0-07-011287-8

About the Author

Dennis M. Clausen, professor of English at the University of San Diego, received his B.A. and M.A. from the University of Minnesota and his Ph.D. from the University of California, Riverside. He has directed writing programs at both the University of California and the University of San Diego, and he has received several distinguished-teaching awards for his work in writing courses. A published novelist, who has been reviewed by *Publishers Weekly* and other such national publications, he is, "like everyone else in California, the author of several screenplays, most of which have been banished to the closet." He has also authored numerous editorials, other newspaper articles, and another text entitled a *Concise Process Workbook.*

His background and hobbies reflect a diverse range of interests; although teaching is his passion, he has worked in tax advising, journalism, woodworking, and automobile mechanics. As a former college athlete, he has an active interest in almost all sports, and he enjoys reading articles from several other academic disciplines—especially astronomy and history. This diverse background reflects his belief that "a serious writer should not search for a comfortable niche in life but rather should move around a bit and write about a variety of human experiences."

*"A word that breathes distinctly
Has not the power to die . . ."*

—Emily Dickinson

Contents

Preface

To the Teacher

In the spring of 1984, when several of my colleagues and I were reviewing books for the next academic year, we began to share ideas on what we were looking for in a text for freshman- and sophomore-level writing courses. Over the next few weeks, as we reviewed more and more books on writing, we even established a rough list of priorities for such a text.

Our general impression was that, although many of the existing texts clearly had their respective strengths, their priorities were not always our priorities as classroom teachers of writing. For example, comprehensiveness of coverage and formal academic tone were exceedingly low on our list of priorities. In fact, through experience we knew that these priorities could actually work against the goals of our respective writing courses, goals that were primarily to motivate our students to become more involved in the writing and editing process.

Over the next few months, we talked more and more about our own priorities for a text for freshman- and sophomore-level writing courses. In time, we developed a general consensus of opinion that such a text should be motivational, unintimidating, and, above all else, written in a style that was accessible to our students. Furthermore, for successful classroom implementation, we agreed that such a text should incorporate much common sense in terms of what students did and did not need to know about writing and editing, solid practical advice on the writing and editing process, and occasional humor to lighten the tone and provide meaningful examples for our students.

Indeed, many of the examples in the *Concise Process Handbook* were written by students who were encouraged to deliberately parody ineffective writing. Also, the quotations that parody the principles of English grammar in Parts II and III of this text frequently come directly from student journals.

The way many of the existing texts addressed themselves to the issue of English grammar also seemed to us to be somewhat impractical. We were not, for example, ready to dispense with the teaching of grammar altogether. But, at the same time, we were not prepared to teach a comprehensive grammar in our writing courses. A basic English grammar was, for us, an indispensable editing tool, one that was an essential part of any composition course. However, we were convinced that these grammatical principles could be taught most effectively with a minimum of technical jargon and terminology. Furthermore, we were equally convinced that these grammatical principles should be taught within the context of writing and editing as *process.*

Finally, we concluded that an effective writing text should incorporate the advice of James Moffet, Mina Shaughnessy, Peter Elbow, and others—namely, that "there is only one way for students to learn how to write, and that is by writing." Because we all believed so strongly in this advice, we agreed that an effective text would have to be one that was compatible with those courses in which students devote most of their time to writing and editing—and not simply *talking* about writing and editing.

The *Concise Process Handbook* and its companion text, the *Concise Process Workbook,* were the results of those many hours of deliberation and brainstorming. The texts were written primarily for those basic-writing, freshman English, and other courses that require a series of short expository essays. However, the *Handbook* also contains sufficient footnoting and bibliographical information to be a valuable resource tool in courses that require a single term or research paper. There is also a sample research paper and supporting instructional materials in "Appendix A" of the *Handbook* to assist instructors who are teaching such courses.

Still, the emphasis in the *Handbook* is on *writing* skills and not *research* skills. For this reason, the text will prove especially valuable to those teachers and professors who believe students can benefit most by going through the writing and editing process as many times as possible in a given course or semester.

The *Concise Process Workbook* provides supplemental lessons and exercises that parallel and reinforce the instructional materials available in the *Handbook*. Like the *Handbook*, the *Concise Process Workbook* is written in a style that is accessible to students. Furthermore, the *Workbook* contains exercises that are designed so that they do not demand constant supervision by the teacher or professor. For this reason, the exercises in the *Workbook* are conducive to various writing-workshop activities, independent study, and, of course, more traditional classroom activities. In sum, the *Concise Process Handbook* and the *Concise Process Workbook* have been designed to provide a sensible and practical instructional support system for professors and teachers who teach basic writing and/or introductory writing and literature courses.

Acknowledgments

Although many individuals have contributed immensely to the writing and editing of this text, a very special thank you must be extended to Emily Barrosse and James Belser for their patient and knowledgeable editorial assistance. Professors Eddie Goodson of New River Community College, Pamela Bourgeois of California State University at Northridge, Bob Esch of the University of Texas at El Paso, and Edward A. Kline of Notre Dame University reviewed the various drafts of this manuscript and provided valuable professional advice on ways to improve the text. My colleagues in the University of San Diego's English Department, especially Professor Ron Hill, have been most encouraging and supportive. The students at the University of San Diego, especially those in my writing courses, have in a very real sense helped to "co-author" this text. Their generosity, intelligent insights into the early drafts of this text, and good-humored contributions have been greatly appreciated. Finally, I would like to thank my wife Alexa, who has been my partner in this and all other writing projects. Without her generous assistance, this text would undoubtedly still be in the planning stages.

Dennis M. Clausen

To the Student

This is your book. It is written for you, not for anyone else. And it is meant to be your *partner* in the writing process. It is not meant to be another critic who is concerned only with misspelled words, inappropriate punctuation, and other grammatical oversights (although these are important considerations, as we shall see later in this text).

Furthermore, this text is written by someone who admittedly continues to struggle with the writing process, someone for whom mastery of the writing and editing process has not, and does not, come easily. I continue to make mistakes, sometimes terribly embarrassing mistakes that undermine much of what I am trying to say. Indeed, I can safely say that I have, on numerous occasions, made every writing mistake that I discuss throughout this text. In fact, many of the examples I use to illustrate ineffective writing came, at one time or another, from my own pen.

Since writing has always been a struggle for me, I learned very early that I would have to develop a system to accomplish what some writers seemed to do naturally and effortlessly. It was very clear to me that I was not the Ted Williams, Rod Carew, or George Brett of the writing world. I was, at best, a .250 hitter who felt he just might be able to bat .300 if he worked hard and approached the whole craft of writing systematically. Furthermore, I also knew I would have to develop a sense of humor about my own writing inadequacies, or else I would be devastated when other people pointed out my errors and oversights to me.

So, if I were to give you some early advice, it would be not to worry too much about making mistakes. Everyone who writes makes mistakes (although, of course, we should try to learn from these mistakes). Second, try to develop a sense of humor about the whole subject of writing and editing. A sense of humor is a marvelous defense against the natural tendency to be defeated by one's mistakes. And finally, try to remove the "mystique" of writing from your mind. Remember, it is the exceedingly rare individual who is a "born writer"; most people acquire the skill through constant practice.

Although analogies can be misleading, learning to write is not all that different from learning to swing a baseball bat, plant a garden, build a house, and so on. Writing involves a process of trial and error through which writers learn, over a period of time, to generate sentences and paragraphs more effectively and systematically.

Also, undoubtedly the term "grammar" conjures up strange and nightmarish visions for you. You probably envision a seemingly endless list of rules that must somehow be memorized before you can even begin to write. But nothing could be further from the truth. Many of the world's finest writers have neither studied nor memorized a comprehensive English grammar (although most have acquired an instinctive knowledge of grammar through reading, writing, editing, and rewriting). Nonetheless, there are a few simple rules and guidelines that can help you navigate in the tricky waters of English composition.

The first and most important guideline is to remember that grammar is an *editing* skill, not a *writing* skill, and it is important only in the later stages of the development of the essay. If you are overly attentive to the rules of grammar too early in the writing process, you are likely to develop any of several forms of writer's block—anxieties that will make it extremely difficult for you to generate ideas effectively. Furthermore, you will be wasting time and energy editing sentences that may not even appear in the final draft.

It is sometimes helpful to remember that the writing stage can be further divided into two major areas: prewriting and writing. Prewriting involves any of several activities the writer can participate in to generate ideas for writing assignments. Writing involves the actual recording of these words and ideas on paper until the writer has created a rough draft. Similarly, editing can be further divided into two major areas: editing and rewriting. Editing is the process whereby the writer applies the principles of English grammar and rhetoric to identify and revise the major problem areas in the rough drafts. The final stage, rewriting, can actually require several new drafts, each one more polished than its predecessor, as the writer rewrites sentences and paragraphs that he or she has identified as grammatically incorrect or inconsistent. The importance of this stage is reflected in the writer's axiom, "Books are not written—they are edited and rewritten."

As will be illustrated frequently throughout this text, learning to write and edit systematically can save you much time and frustration. At the same time, remember that you are an individual with certain strengths and weaknesses. (In this respect, you are no different from the rest of us, even those of us who are teaching writing courses.) And, for this reason, you may occasionally have to modify the advice in this text to make it compatible with your own writing idiosyncrasies. If so, *be sure to check with your instructor first to make sure it is really in your best interests to make such adjustments*. If your instructor agrees with you, then you have already learned something about the writing and editing process—namely, that there is no one way for all of us to become effective writers. We can learn from others, but we must all eventually develop a system that is compatible with our own individual strengths and weaknesses.

Dennis M. Clausen

1

Prewriting
and Writing

A

Prewriting Strategies

Nothing is so uniquely human as the writing process. Other creatures that inhabit this earth can run faster, jump higher, and move quicker. But no other living thing can record messages on paper or stone surfaces, messages that can be read hundreds and thousands of miles or years removed from the person (or persons) who wrote them. That is the power of language; it enables individuals to extend the range of their influence well beyond the physical limitations of time and space.

The writing process, however, involves more than just the sending of messages across time and space. It involves the way human beings *discover, clarify,* and, finally, *express* meaning.

Why do we discover and clarify ideas as we write about them? Undoubtedly there are many very sophisticated answers to this question. But perhaps the most compelling reason is that writing involves our total intellectual, emotional, and psychological framework. Everything we are and have been, together with all of our experiences in life, are called into play during the writing process. Obviously, with so much of ourselves involved in the actual process of putting pen to paper, we are going to discover and clarify new ideas as we engage in the writing experience.

Indeed, this is why the writing process is so exciting and so thought-provoking. Although writing has much in common with many other human activities, it alone calls into play so much of our total personality and our values. It alone is capable of revealing so very much about both ourselves and the world around us. It is for this reason that many educators and writers have long maintained that "we don't truly understand an idea until we are required to write about it."

A 2

Clarify Meaning

Prewriting is that stage of the writing process in which the writer is concerned primarily with the discovery of and, to a lesser extent, the clarification of meaning.

1. Discover Meaning

We discover meaning through writing in the same way that we discover meaning through any other human activity—namely, through trial and error. For this reason, if we are afraid to make mistakes when we write, we are doomed from the start.

Do not be afraid to make mistakes during the prewriting stage of the writing process. In fact, remove the concept of error from your mind completely. There is nothing wrong with moving out into areas that you do not fully understand. There is nothing wrong with expressing ideas you do not fully comprehend. And there is nothing wrong with expressing ideas through a vocabulary that you have not yet fully mastered.

In fact, the only way to discover meaning is to make some false starts and take some positions that turn out to be unworkable. Indeed, without the courage to accept writing as a process of trial and error, very little effective prose would have been written over the past several centuries.

2. Clarify Meaning

The process of writing involves a natural evolution through which meaning is inevitably clarified at the same time that it is discovered. Indeed, our knowledge of any subject matter becomes more precise and detailed as we work with it for a period of time. Similarly, we can ponder our ideas for days and weeks, but it is only when we begin to talk about them or record them on paper that we truly learn to understand their subtleties.

At the same time, do not be too concerned with clarifying meaning at this stage of the writing process. The meaning will undoubtedly be clarified naturally through various freewriting and brainstorming activities. If not, there is plenty of time during the later stages of the writing and editing process to worry about precision and clarity of meaning.

This is not, of course, to suggest that prewriting activities should encourage fuzziness and ambiguity in the thinking process. It is, rather, to suggest that writers who are overly concerned with clarifying meaning at this stage will inevitably focus on smaller, less significant details, when they should be addressing the larger issues and concerns raised by the essay topic.

3. Identify Your Audience Immediately

An intelligent appraisal of your audience is necessary if you are to adopt effective strategies for whatever it is you are writing. Normally, writers of the typical college-level essay should avoid two extremes when they are appraising their respective audiences. First, they should avoid thinking of their audiences as friends and casual acquaintances, people for whom colloquialisms, slang, and occasional obscenities might be both amusing and appropriate. Second, they should avoid thinking of their audiences as stuffy, pretentious pseudoscholars who will only be impressed by "big words." In most cases, the audience for the college-level essay consists of reasonably educated men and women—not linguistic geniuses or professional grammarians—who recognize clear prose when they see it.

This is not, however, to suggest in any way that you should be overly concerned with the questions of tone, style, and vocabulary during the prewriting stage. To the contrary, these are issues that can be better addressed during the editing stage. But careful attention to your audience will provide immediate focus and direction for your essay even in its early, formative stages.

The best way to keep in touch with your audience is, of course, to meet with one of its members occasionally to talk about the essay you are writing. If this is impossible, as it frequently is in many writing classes, periodically try to imagine that your audience is sitting next to you while you talk your way through the essay. Or seek an ongoing exchange with some of your classmates, who can serve as convenient substitutes for your real audience. If practiced conscientiously, any of these methods will establish a much stronger sense of audience as you develop strategies for your writing project. And the stronger the sense of audience, the more likely you are to adopt appropriate and effective writing strategies.

(See also "Bring Your Audience Back into Focus," pages 28–29, "Check for Tone," pages 225–226, and "Avoid Sexist Language," pages 226–228.)

4. Write with Purpose and Conviction

If you are free to choose your own essay topic, choose one that means something to you. We all write better when we write with purpose and conviction. Furthermore, when we have something we truly want to say, most of us have less difficulty finding the appropriate words to express ourselves. Conversely, when we are indifferent about something, we all have problems generating appropriate sentences and paragraphs to express our thoughts and feelings.

If you cannot choose your own essay topic, try to formulate a thesis position to make it mean something to you. Again, the sense of purpose and conviction will make the writing of the essay much easier.

If you are required to write on a topic that means absolutely nothing to you, do not complain. This, too, can be a valuable writing experience. In our personal and professional lives, almost all of us will be called upon occasionally to write something simply because "it has to be done"—not because we have any strong feelings about the subject.

5. Try Freewriting

Freewriting is a prewriting activity many professional writers engage in to loosen up and to generate ideas. In this respect, freewriting is to the writing process what calisthenics is to various sporting activities. Both are necessary "warm-up exercises" for people who are about to engage in some strenuous activity.

During a typical freewriting exercise, the writer writes for 10 or 15 minutes without hesitating or pausing. The writer can simply tap into his or her "internal dialogue" and record those thoughts on paper, or else he or she can focus on the essay topic and record, in stream-of-consciousness fashion, everything that is associated with that topic. No attention whatever should be devoted to the details of sentence structure, punctuation, or spelling. The only guideline is that *the writing must be nonstop*. That is, the writer cannot pause for any reason whatever. If the writer has nothing to say, then the proper thing to do is to write, "I have nothing to say," until other ideas are generated through the simple act of recording words on paper.

There are at least five specific advantages to freewriting activities:

- As "warm-up exercises," they help to eliminate writer's block—the anxieties we all feel when we first confront a new writing assignment.

- They remove the ingrained and debilitating habit of editing prematurely. Since freewriting is a nonstop activity, it eliminates the obsessive need to *judge* ideas and expressions when one should be doing everything possible to *generate* them.

- They put the writer in touch with the deepest level of the subconscious mind, where one's strongest, most intuitive responses to an issue are found. In this respect, freewriting activities help the writer argue with purpose and conviction.

- Since the very purpose of freewriting exercises is to generate ideas, they help to produce the "volume of materials" necessary for the editing stage to be successful.

- They tend to improve on the writer's style, because the flow of thoughts is a natural reflection of the internal dialogue the writer carries on constantly with himself or herself.

All writers occasionally have the experience of not being able to generate ideas for a certain writing project. They may have read several newspaper articles on the issue, discussed it thoroughly with their friends, and pondered it for hours in the privacy of their rooms. Still, they feel they have nothing significant to contribute to the essay topic.

At these times, freewriting can be a godsend. When confronted by this dilemma, many writers sit down and, without pausing, write one or two pages on the assigned topic. They simply allow their responses to the topic to flow onto the paper in stream-of-consciousness fashion. Afterward, they sift through their prose, searching for the following:

- the one sentence that best summarizes their response to the essay topic. This becomes the basis for the *thesis position* (the main, controlling idea for the essay).

- three or four sentences that are capable of developing different aspects of this thesis position. These sentences become the basis for the various *topic sentences* in the body of the essay.

- lists of *supporting evidence* for all of the above.

A SAMPLE FREEWRITING EXERCISE

Essay topic: The effect of violence on American

life

    Violence in America has gotten out of hand.

Everywhere we look, there are examples of the

glorification of violence. This country is

obsessed with death and destruction. So much so

Thesis → that steps must clearly be taken to reduce the
possibility

amount of violence depicted, or America is doomed.

Topic →
sentence   On television, even the cartoons are violent. For
possibility

example, ''Tom and Jerry'' and ''Bugs Bunny'' seem *Evidence*

simple and innocent enough on the surface, but to

young children their antics are extremely prone to

violence. The evening news is even worse coming as *Topic*
                                                               sentence
                                                              possibility

it does at the baby-sitting hour, when parents

watch the death and destruction raging not only in

this country but elsewhere as well. Other   *Topic sentence possibility*

television shows that depict violence. ''All My

Evidence Children,'' ''Dynasty,'' and ''Dallas'' etc. all

glorify violence, ranging from rape to murder. If

this isn't bad enough, it is almost impossible to   *Topic sentence possibility*

find movies anymore where someone isn't mutilated,

gored, or tortured into submission. ''Taxi

Evidence Driver'' was a film watched by John Hinckley that

led him to try an assassination attempt on the

President of the United States. Another movie,

Evidence ''The Wall,'' depicts other forms of violence.

Clearly the rating systems are not working when

young children can go to films rated PG and be

exposed to horrible examples of killings and even

immoral sex acts. Not to mention the newspapers

which tend to cover only the most awful and

violent things that happen worldwide. Nothing good

is ever reported any more. Only the terrible

things that people do to one another.

> Anyone who
> reads a newspaper conscientiously must live in a
> terribly depressed state of mind because the only   ← *Topic*
> news reported is the news of terrorists blowing up   *sentence*
> airplanes, murderers let free by the court system,   *possibility*
> and other such atrocities too numerous to mention.

Obviously, we'd better be more willing to control

these acts of glorifying violence, or America will

be in a bad way.

POSSIBLE SKETCH OUTLINE BASED ON SAMPLE
FREEWRITING EXERCISE

Thesis possibility: Steps must clearly be taken to reduce the amount of violence depicted, or America is doomed.

Topic-sentence possibilities and evidence:

1. Violence in television cartoons
   a. *Tom and Jerry*
   b. *Bugs Bunny*
2. Violence on other television shows
   a. *Dynasty*
   b. *Dallas*
   c. *All My Children*
3. Violence on the evening news
4. Murder and torture in movies
   a. *Taxi Driver*
   b. *The Wall*
5. Newspaper coverage of violent events worldwide
   a. Terrorist activities
   b. Murderers freed by the legal system

Although later it may be advantageous to write a more formal outline, this is a perfectly appropriate sketch outline. Indeed, it reflects a most productive freewriting exercise, one that has generated the necessary information to provide focus, direction, and evidence for this essay topic.

6. Try Brainstorming

Brainstorming is a prewriting activity in which two or more people get together to exchange ideas and conversation on a particular essay topic. Unless the instructor specifically forbids such activities, students should seek out these exchanges for the same reason that scientists seek out those who are involved in similar areas of research. Such conversations can often be more stimulating and thought-provoking than several hours of silently pondering the essay topic in the privacy of one's room.

Brainstorming is, in many respects, very similar to freewriting—or at least they accomplish the same thing—because both put writers in touch with what they truly feel about an essay topic. Confronted with an audience that is willing to play the role of devil's advocate, writers are forced to develop stronger thesis positions while, at the same time, they learn to understand the arguments that can be made against their positions. Ultimately, writers who learn to use brainstorming to their advantage write with more force and conviction.

Many writers believe brainstorming activities are most beneficial when conducted within a limited period of time. For example, a group of writers might try to establish as many types of supporting evidence as they can in 15 minutes. The dynamic tension of trying to generate ideas within such a limited time frame can be most productive.

A word of caution: most of us, I am sure, have had the experience of engaging in some lively discussions that have left us feeling extremely enthusiastic about some activity in which we are involved. Yet when someone asks us, "What did you discuss that made you so excited about your project?", we can only respond, "I don't remember the details, but it sure was exciting!"

The same is true for many brainstorming activities. It is very easy to get caught up in the excitement of generating ideas, but unless we have some way of recording and using those ideas, brainstorming sessions serve only to create the *impression* that we are gathering material for the essay topic. But in the end, we have nothing of substance to show for our efforts.

At the same time, of course, successful brainstorming sessions depend on the spontaneous, rapid-fire exchange of ideas as writers test their observations and strategies on one another. However, since the best ideas tend to come in bunches, one after the other, it is almost impossible to take extensive notes during brainstorming activities without undermining these same group dynamics.

There are at least two ways to preserve the group dynamics of brainstorming sessions while, at the same time, recording the necessary information to be used in the essay assignment:

- If at all possible, use a tape recorder to tape the entire brainstorming session. If so, notes need not be taken during the session itself. Instead, the entire group can take extensive notes while they listen to the playback of their discussion. After listening to the tape, they can also further clarify and discuss any issues that still seem to be vague and/or confusing.

- If no tape recorder is available, take very sketchy notes during the session itself (two or three words to remind you of key issues that were discussed). Then, *immediately after* the brainstorming session, record these ideas in more extensive detail, asking your colleagues for assistance if you cannot remember some important issue or strategy that was discussed.

Above all else, do not wait until the next day to write down your notes on the ideas raised during the brainstorming session. If you are like the rest of us, by that time all you will have left is the rather vague impression that something truly profound happened. But you will remember few, if any, of the specific strategies, issues, and ideas that created your initial sense of enthusiasm for the writing project.

7. Talk, Then Write

Productive prewriting activities involve talking as much as writing. When the writer is engaged in discovering and clarifying meaning, there is no more valuable experience than the opportunity to talk about the subject for a period of time. In fact, during the prewriting stage it is a good strategy to set aside some time for talking about the essay topic with friends or colleagues.

All of us, I am sure, have had the experience of trying to explain something to our friends, only to find that our explanation confused both ourselves and them. Yet later, when we privately pondered the same idea and/or jotted it down on paper, we suddenly discovered the precise words needed to make the idea perfectly clear. Conversely, I am sure we have also had the experience of struggling with something in written form, only to find that the expression and meaning became clearer to us at the very moment that we tried to explain it to a friend.

What this proves is simply that the process of discovering and clarifying meaning is enhanced by both talking *and* writing about the subject. If you are confused about an oral explanation of something, try writing it down on paper. Conversely, if you are confused about a *written* explanation of something, try talking about it for a time. If you learn to both talk *and* write about the essay topic during the prewriting stage, chances are you will develop a much stronger rough draft.

Never pass up an opportunity to talk about the essay topic with some audience. Not only is talking easier than writing at this stage, but it can be every bit as productive.

8. Loosen Controls and Inhibitions

The problem with most writers is that they have too many controls and inhibitions. The purpose of prewriting is, thus, not to erect more barriers but to loosen the ones that are already there. It is for this reason, more than any other, that a knowledge of grammar can work against the writer if it is introduced too early into the writing and editing process. It is simply impossible to generate ideas if one is constantly distracted by the details of spelling, placement of commas, and so on. The prewriting stage is the place to loosen up and make mistakes; there is plenty of time later to apply the principles of English grammar and rhetoric.

At the same time, the process of learning how to loosen controls and inhibitions involves more than just learning how and when to apply the principles of English grammar. The process also involves abandoning some misconceptions we may have about how writers live and work. For example, the Hollywood stereotype of the writer—someone who locks himself or herself in a room and does not come out until the manuscript is completed—is not consistent with the way most writers conduct their daily affairs. Indeed, such work habits would probably guarantee a fairly mechanical, perhaps even neurotic writing style. On the contrary, most successful writers establish a certain time of the day when they will write, but they also set aside a certain time of the day when they will engage in various forms of physical activities and other diversions.

Why are most writers avid joggers, swimmers, hikers, and so on? Of course, they undoubtedly want to achieve some balance in their lives. But the purpose of these physical activities is also to loosen the controls and inhibitions that result from laboring neurotically, and without interruption, over a writing project.

Similarly, students should learn to engage periodically in some form of physical activity or other diversion, perhaps even prior to the prewriting exercises, so as to loosen controls and inhibitions. The end result will normally be a draft that is less mechanical and lifeless than the one produced by the writer who is a slave to the craft of writing.

9. Enjoy It

It might seem perverse, and perhaps even sadistic, to suggest that prewriting is enjoyable, but that is indeed the case. Whereas editing the final draft can, at times, be hard work, this is seldom the case when writers are actively engaged in discovering and clarifying how they actually feel about an issue.

We should remember that many writers have never been published, and yet they conscientiously keep diaries and journals of their daily activities throughout much of their adult lives. Why do they do this? Probably because nothing else they do makes them feel more alive!

Discovering new meanings and challenging old ones through the writing process—this is what life and learning are all about. Enjoy it. There are few things in this world that make one feel more alive.

10. Trust Your Instincts and Intuition

We often think of writing as a product of the intellect, but it is really much more than that. Effective writing involves instinct and intuition as well as intellect. In fact, writing that is created exclusively by the intellect tends to have a stagnant, mechanical style and tone. Writing that combines instinct, intuition, and intellect, on the other hand, normally has a much stronger ring of authenticity. After all, instinct and intuition are merely products of the intellect that have, over a period of time, informed the deepest levels of our personalities and values.

At the same time, of course, it is important to note that we must sharpen our writing instincts the same way we would sharpen our instincts in any skill—namely, through many hours of practice. For example, the baseball player who has sharpened his skills through many years of playing in the major leagues does not *think* about swinging the bat anymore. By the time he is through conceptualizing the idea of swinging the bat, it would be too late; the ball would be past him. Instead, his instincts take over and tell his body precisely when and how to swing the bat.

So it is with writing. There is no substitute for the learning experience that comes from the act of writing itself. The more we write, revise, and rewrite, the more sensitive our instincts will become to making the right choices when we are constructing sentences or searching for the right word combinations. After many years of experience, the writer becomes very much like the baseball player. Instinct takes over and tells the writer when it is time to eliminate a word, add a paragraph, or rearrange the sequence of words in a sentence.

Trust your instincts and your intuition during all stages of the writing process, and learn to sharpen them through constant practice, perhaps by keeping a daily diary or journal. In most cases, our instincts and intuition are more adept at discovering, clarifying, and expressing meaning than is our intellect.

11. Read

Reading is an indispensable part of the prewriting process, primarily because it, too, informs the intellect and sharpens the intuition and instincts. For all of these reasons, reading should be a natural, daily activity for anyone who hopes to become an effective writer. It is simply impossible to become sensitive to the flow and rhythms of effective English sentences unless we train the ear to hear the way these sentences sound. As E. B. White, the author of *The Elements of Style* and one of the most accomplished prose stylists of this century, has suggested, "Writers must learn to listen to what they write." And they can accomplish this only by becoming avid readers.

What precisely should you read to sharpen your instincts so you will begin to hear and feel the rhythms of effective sentences? Undoubtedly, your teacher or professor will have many writers to recommend to you. My own personal favorites are several of the contemporary newspaper columnists, especially Bob Greene, Mike Royko, and Carl Rowan. Each of these writers strives for a style that is precise, clear, and immediately accessible, not one that tries to impress the reader with pretentious words and hopelessly complex sentences. Their style is, in other words, the very style that is taught in most high school and college classrooms. And it is also the style that is most applicable to the kind of writing that is encouraged in both the business and professional communities.

Cheryl Reimold, who wrote a text on business writing entitled *How to Write a Million Dollar Memo,* also argues that reading is an essential activity for men and women who hope to become accomplished business writers. However, her recommended list of readings is not, as we would expect, examples of memorandums and business letters from the most successful corporate leaders in America. It is, rather, a list of creative works, especially poetry.

Although my experience has been that only a handful of students will heed the advice to read poetry so as to sharpen the ear to the flow and rhythms of English sentences, it is nonetheless important to recognize that this is precisely what many professional writers do. For example, Joseph Wambaugh, the highly successful best-selling novelist, has been quoted as saying he often reads poetry and other creative works for several minutes "prior to sitting down at the typewriter." He is convinced that this trains his ear to listen to what he himself writes.

Try it! Read poems such as Dylan Thomas's "Do Not Go Gentle into That Good Night" or Robert Browning's "Prospice," and try to imitate the power and force of their respective styles in your own writing. Or read poems such as Robert Frost's "Stopping By Woods on a Snowy Evening" and Alfred Lord Tennyson's "Crossing the Bar," and then try to imitate the serenity and graceful flow of their respective styles. Or perhaps ask your teachers and professors if they have any poems they would recommend to improve your ear for the flow and rhythms of English sentences.

At the same time, do not overlook contemporary newspapers, magazines, and books. In a very practical sense, reading a variety of prose forms is an effective way of generating ideas and producing lists of supporting evidence for essay topics. For this reason, make it a habit to read at least one newspaper a day and one magazine a week. Nothing can make so valuable a contribution to prewriting activities as the ideas and words that are generated in the daily newspapers and weekly magazines.

Also, actively seek out newspaper and magazine articles that discuss the essay topic you have been assigned. (Of course, if you use them, you must footnote.) Remember, we discover and clarify meaning by testing our own ideas against the ideas of other people who have taken positions on the same issues.

12. Do Not Try to Get Everything in Order Right Away

Although the sequence and arrangement of ideas and paragraphs is an important concern in the later stages of the writing process, *it is not one of the priorities of prewriting.* Prewriting is, by its very nature, chaotic and unorganized. But it is creative chaos through which writers eventually come to understand what they are attempting to argue and how best to present that argument.

If writers are too concerned about getting everything in order right away, it will generally work against the goals of the prewriting activities, goals that are to generate ideas as quickly and efficiently as possible. Only toward the end of prewriting activities should writers attempt to organize their ideas into thesis statements and outlines.

(See also "Group and Arrange Ideas," pages 20–24, and "Clarify Your Thesis Statement and Preliminary Outline," pages 25–27.)

13. Keep a Notebook Handy

The writing you do during prewriting activities will seldom be systematic. That is, it will not involve a thesis and an outline. Those are two of the *goals* of the various prewriting activities; they are not *the means to achieving those goals.*

The writing you do during prewriting activities is more a form of note taking. For this reason, it is wise to carry a pocket-sized notebook with you at all times. Should an idea suddenly occur to you while you are engaged in some other activity, you can quickly jot it down and perhaps use it later in a writing project.

The myth that writing takes place only in small rooms with typewriters or computers and crumpled paper scattered across the floor has to go. Good writers are always writing, even when they are jogging, walking to class, or simply gazing at the sunset. To be a writer means simply to be more sensitive to the internal dialogue all of us carry on with ourselves every minute of our lives—and to have some way of recording that dialogue.

Obviously, these ideas do not have to be recorded in a notebook in flawless prose or complete sentences. There is plenty of time for that later (unless, of course, the phrasing seems so precise that you want to preserve it in its entirety).

EXAMPLES OF TYPICAL PREWRITING NOTATIONS

Essay assignment: Write an essay in which you discuss the effects of media violence on American life.

Student notes during prewriting activities:

1. Even cartoons are violent. Young children are exposed to such things daily.
2. The nightly news devotes too much time to murders, hijackings, etc. Little coverage is given to the good things that happen around the world.
3. Wasn't John Hinckley influenced by some movie? (Check spelling of Hinckley's name.)
4. Bugs Bunny and Tom and Jerry are often very violent. They are always getting their heads bashed in or tongues bitten off.
5. "Adult television" is equally violent.
6. Commercials also resort to violence to sell products. Play into American love for potentially violent activities.
7. Check recent *TV Guide* descriptions of plots for *Dallas* and *Dynasty* and shows like that. Seems like plot always involves murder or suicide or rape.
8. Movie *The Wall* is a good example.
9. Yes, Hinckley was influenced by a movie called *Taxi Driver*. It was a movie about a young prostitute and a crazy taxi driver who sets out to kill the murderers and thugs on the streets of New York.
10. Thesis possibility: America is doomed unless something is done about violence.
11. Check to see if anyone, maybe a psychiatrist, has made a direct connection between viewing violence on film and committing violent acts.
12. Eliminate commercials maybe. (Might be too much for this paper.)
13. Another good example of television violence is *The Roadrunner* cartoons.

Granted, these are fragmented responses to the essay topic. Some of them are false starts, and others can only be understood by the student who jotted down these observations. *But there is nothing wrong with any of this during the prewriting stage.* In fact, it is a perfectly valid way to gather ideas and information for the essay topic.

14. Group and Arrange Ideas

Somewhat later in the prewriting stage, as the larger outlines of the essay begin to take shape in the writer's mind, it is generally wise to start grouping and arranging ideas into some logical sequence. In time, these groupings will provide the foundation for both the outline and the various paragraphs in the essay itself.

As always, these groupings are not necessarily permanent. Some of them might be eliminated, others might be added, and still others could be modified with new examples. The important thing is to start using these groupings to create an overview of how the essay might be developed in its entirety.

The following example was taken from the section of this text entitled "Examples of Typical Prewriting Notations." Notice how the grouping and arranging of these ideas enable the potential subdivisions of the essay to emerge out of the notes that were taken during prewriting activities.

[Note: The respective entries are numbered according to the original sequence established by this writer during prewriting activities.]

a. Grouping Ideas

Violence in television cartoons:

1. Even cartoons are violent. Young children are exposed to such things daily.
4. Bugs Bunny and Tom and Jerry are often very violent. They are always getting their heads bashed in or tongues bitten off.
13. Another good example of television violence is *The Roadrunner* cartoons.

Violence on other television shows:

5. "Adult television" is equally violent.
7. Check recent *TV Guide* descriptions of plots for *Dallas* and *Dynasty* and shows like that. Seems like plot always involves murder or suicide or rape.

Violence on television news:

2. The nightly news devotes too much time to murders, hijackings, etc. Little coverage is given to the good things that happen around the world.

Violence in movies:

3. Wasn't John Hinckley influenced by some movie? (Check spelling of Hinckley's name.)
9. Yes, Hinckley was influenced by a movie called *Taxi Driver.* It was a movie about a young prostitute and a crazy taxi driver who sets out to kill the murderers and thugs on the streets of New York.
8. Movie *The Wall* is a good example.

Probably eliminate:

6. Commercials also resort to violence to sell products. Play into American love for potentially violent activities.
12. Eliminate commercials maybe. (Might be too much for this paper.)

Thesis possibilities:

10. Thesis possibility: America is doomed unless something is done about violence.
11. Check to see if anyone, maybe a psychiatrist, has made a direct connection between viewing violence on film and committing violent acts.

b. Arranging Groupings

Once ideas are grouped into logical categories, it is often advantageous to rearrange them further into potential sequences for developing the essay as a whole. The examples below make several changes in the earlier groupings:

- The grouping entitled "Thesis Possibilities" is moved to the top of the list, because the thesis statement will eventually appear in the first paragraph of the essay.
- The grouping entitled "Probably Eliminate" will be temporarily set aside, because it appears it will probably not be used in this essay.
- The remaining groupings offer several enticing possibilities for organizing the essay as a whole, depending upon how the writer wants to limit the focus of this specific paper.

The writer might want to focus on the issue of *violence in both films and television,* in which case we could have the following sequence:

EXAMPLE 1

Thesis possibilities:

10. America is doomed unless something is done about violence.
11. Check to see if anyone, maybe a psychiatrist, has made a direct connection between viewing violence on film and committing violent acts.

Violence in television cartoons:

1. Even cartoons are violent. Young children are exposed to such things daily.
4. Bugs Bunny and Tom and Jerry are often very violent. They are always getting their heads bashed in or tongues bitten off.
13. Another good example of television violence is *The Roadrunner* cartoons.

Violence on other television shows:

5. "Adult television" is equally violent.
7. Check recent *TV Guide* descriptions of plots for *Dallas* and *Dynasty* and shows like that. Seems like plot always involves murder or suicide or rape.

Violence on television news:

2. The nightly news devotes too much time to murders, hijackings, etc. Little coverage is given to the good things that happen around the world.

Violence in movies:

3. Wasn't John Hinckley influenced by some movie? (Check spelling of Hinckley's name.)
9. Yes, Hinckley was influenced by a movie called *Taxi Driver*. It was a movie about a young prostitute and a crazy taxi driver who sets out to kill the murderers and thugs on the streets of New York.
8. Movie *The Wall* is a good example.

The writer might want to limit the focus to the issue of *television violence*, in which case the grouping entitled "Movie Violence" would have to be eliminated. (If the writer makes this decision, it is also conceivable that the grouping that addresses the issue of violence in commercials might be retained.)

EXAMPLE 2

Thesis possibilities:

10. America is doomed unless something is done about violence.
11. Check to see if anyone, maybe a psychiatrist, has made a direct connection between viewing violence on film and committing violent acts.

Violence in television cartoons:

1. Even cartoons are violent. Young children are exposed to such things daily.
4. Bugs Bunny and Tom and Jerry are often very violent. They are always getting their heads bashed in or tongues bitten off.
13. Another good example of television violence is *The Roadrunner* cartoons.

Violence on other television shows:

5. "Adult television" is equally violent.
7. Check recent *TV Guide* descriptions of plots for *Dallas* and *Dynasty* and shows like that. Seems like plot always involves murder or suicide or rape.

Violence on television news:

2. The nightly news devotes too much time to murders, hijackings, etc. Little coverage is given to the good things that happen around the world.

Violence on commercials:

6. Commercials also resort to violence to sell products. Play into American love for potentially violent activities.

The writer might want to limit the focus to the issue of *fictional violence* (as opposed to violence in *real life*), in which case the grouping entitled "Violence on Television News" would have to be eliminated. Also, the grouping entitled "Violence in Commercials" would probably be set aside again, because it does not logically fit into this sequence.

EXAMPLE 3

Thesis possibilities:

10. America is doomed unless something is done about violence.

11. Check to see if anyone, maybe a psychiatrist, has made a direct connection between viewing violence on film and committing violent acts.

Violence in television cartoons:

1. Even cartoons are violent. Young children are exposed to such things daily.
4. Bugs Bunny and Tom and Jerry are often very violent. They are always getting their heads bashed in or tongues bitten off.
13. Another good example of television violence is *The Roadrunner* cartoons.

Violence on other television shows:

5. "Adult television" is equally violent.
7. Check recent *TV Guide* descriptions of plots for *Dallas* and *Dynasty* and shows like that. Seems like plot always involves murder or suicide or rape.

Violence in movies:

3. Wasn't John Hinckley influenced by some movie? (Check spelling of Hinckley's name.)
9. Yes, Hinckley was influenced by a movie called *Taxi Driver*. It was a movie about a young prostitute and a crazy taxi driver who sets out to kill the murderers and thugs on the streets of New York.
8. Movie *The Wall* is a good example.

The point to these examples is simply that there are many ways to group and arrange notes and observations that are jotted down during the various prewriting activities. For this reason, do not be afraid to experiment. Shuffle the deck until you are convinced you have evaluated all of the possibilities.

Of course, the final decision on how to group and arrange these ideas will be determined by the specific thesis statement you establish. For example, the thesis, "Violence on television must be controlled or our society is doomed," would be compatible with *Example 2* above, but not with either of the other groupings. Similarly, the thesis, "Fictional violence on television and in films must be controlled or our society is doomed," would be compatible with *Example 3* above, but not with either of the other groupings.

15. Set Realistic Prewriting Goals

Be realistic about the goals you set for your prewriting activities. Many students have convinced themselves that prewriting activities are successful only if they produce flawless final drafts. Some students even believe that all they should have to do after a successful prewriting session is walk over to the typewriter or computer and pound the essay into the keyboard, word for word, from beginning to end.

This is not only unrealistic, but self-defeating, primarily because it raises expectations that even the most productive prewriting activities cannot satisfy. The myth of the flawless writer, who produces final drafts effortlessly and instantaneously after pondering the topic for only a few minutes, must go. That person is an exceedingly rare individual; in fact, that person probably does not exist.

Never expect to produce a flawless final draft immediately after engaging in prewriting activities. The following should be the more realistic goals of the prewriting experience:

- A working or preliminary thesis statement
- A working or preliminary outline (also known as a "sketch outline")

16. Clarify Your Thesis Statement and Preliminary Outline

Throughout the prewriting stage, you should concentrate on discovering the meaning of what you plan to write. Little attention should be devoted to clarifying and/or expressing that meaning. Toward the end of the prewriting stage, however, it is frequently advantageous to concentrate somewhat more on clarifying both the thesis statement and the preliminary outline.

This is not to suggest, however, that you should slave for hours to establish the precise thesis and detailed outline you will then use throughout the essay. It is, rather, to suggest that a few minutes of time devoted to clarifying word choices in the thesis and establishing some of the major subdivisions in the outline will probably make the writing of the rough drafts much easier.

EXAMPLE 1: PRELIMINARY SENTENCE OUTLINE

Thesis: Steps must be taken to reduce the types of violence depicted on television and in films or America will soon see a severe loss of values.

1. Violence on television is probably the larger problem, because it reaches a wider range of audiences, especially children.
2. As people grow older, they usually switch from cartoons to soap operas and nighttime television, but these shows are equally violent.
3. Television news also presents much violence.
4. Movies do not reach as large an audience as does television; nonetheless, they present even *more* violent forms of behavior.
5. Violence as shown in both television and movies must be greatly reduced.

EXAMPLE 2: PRELIMINARY TOPIC OUTLINE

Thesis: Steps must be taken to reduce the types of violence depicted on television and in films or America will soon see a severe loss of values.

I. Violence on television cartoons
  A. Effects on children
  B. Cartoons like *Tom and Jerry* and *The Roadrunner*
II. Violence on soap operas and nighttime television
  A. Effects on adults
  B. Shows like *Dallas, All My Children,* etc.
III. Television news
  A. Murders
  B. Terrorist activities
  C. Wars
IV. Movie violence
  A. Smaller audience but more violence
  B. *Taxi Driver*
  C. *The Wall*
V. Steps to reduce violence
  A. Movie rating systems

Either of the above preliminary outlines, or perhaps a modified version that combines the respective advantages of both approaches, will help to clarify both the focus and the major subdivisions in your paper. Certainly, in time, the thesis statement and the various subdivisions of the essay may be modified, revised, or perhaps even eliminated. But for now, the preliminary thesis and outline will provide a much stronger sense of focus and direction for the writing of the rough drafts.

(See the rough draft that evolved out of these outlines in the section of this text entitled "Set Realistic Writing Goals," pages 37–41. See also the final draft of the essay in the section entitled "Editing and Rewriting the Expository Essay," pages 234–246.)

B

Writing Strategies

Writing, at least for the purpose of this text, begins at the point where the writer makes the first attempt to systematically express the argument on paper from beginning to end. The writing that takes place during prewriting activities is seldom this systematic. Nonetheless, the spirit of the prewriting strategies should continue to prevail. Loosen up, trust your instincts, be willing to make mistakes, and do not worry about the principles of English grammar.

In this stage of the writing process, you should continue to concentrate on discovering the meaning of your argument. There should be somewhat more emphasis on clarifying the meaning, but you should not yet be too concerned with the details of sentence structure and punctuation. The clarity that comes into this stage of the writing process is normally a natural part of the evolution from idea to written word.

1. Bring Your Audience Back into Focus

An intelligent appraisal of one's audience is necessary if the writer is to adopt appropriate strategies for his or her writing project. None-theless, as the writing project develops into a coherent argument, it is perfectly natural for the writer to lose touch with that same audience. Often, the argument starts to take on a life of its own, one that dissociates itself almost spontaneously from the audience for whom it is intended. For this reason, it is wise to bring the audience back into focus prior to writing the first complete draft of the essay.

The strategies for bringing the audience back into focus are precisely the same as those discussed in the "Prewriting" section of this text. (See also "Identify Your Audience Immediately," pages 5–6.)

- If at all possible, meet with a member of your audience periodically.

- If it is impossible to meet with your audience (and this is probably the case for most writers), periodically imagine that you are in the same room with this person. Then talk your way through the argument, trying to visualize what that person's response might be to the language, evidence, and other strategies you are using in your writing project.

- Seek an ongoing exchange with those of your classmates who can serve as convenient substitutes for your real audience. In some respects, this kind of feedback is more valuable than feedback from an authority who is an expert in writing. The person who is *not* the expert will probably focus more on *what is being said* and less on the *manner in which it is being expressed.* And it is the former that is the more valuable feedback during the writing of rough drafts.

The important thing to remember is that choices regarding strategies will have to be made at every stage in the writing process. Choices that might be appropriate for one audience might very well be inappropriate for another audience. But those choices can be greatly simplified if you learn to bring your audience back into focus periodically.

2. Continue to Write to Discover and Clarify Meaning

Most of us begin to write when we think we understand our intended meaning. But writing being the dynamic process that it is, we all, at one time or another, discover that the meaning changes subtly (and sometimes dramatically) from draft to draft. Sometimes this can be a frightening experience, especially if we come to realize that our original position on the issue was indefensible. More often than not, however, these changes in meaning are healthy signs. They merely demonstrate that the writing process is working and that our ideas are evolving and clarifying themselves naturally.

The reason the meaning to any writing project is seldom permanent is that writing involves so many different facets of our personalities and our total life experiences. As we live with the writing project for a time, more and more of these facets of ourselves come into play. In time, they teach us meanings about the writing project we did not know existed. For this reason, effective writers seldom merely *record* words on paper; they are almost always *discovering* new meanings, even in the later stages of the writing (and editing) process.

Writers should be concerned only when the meaning does *not* change from draft to draft. This is often a guarantee that the writer is "going through the motions," while nothing of real interest is being generated by the writing process.

3. Learn to Use an Outline to Your Advantage

Since change, not permanency, is the nature of the writing process, many writers do not know how to use an outline to their advantage. Some writers abandon outlines almost as soon as they have written them. Others become slaves to every detail of the outline, refusing to depart from the outline even to introduce the most promising ideas into the essay.

Clearly, there is some middle ground here. *Never abandon your preliminary thesis statements and outlines without good cause.* But, at the same time, *do not be afraid to depart from the outline occasionally* as the meaning of the writing project becomes clearer to you. After all, you can always eliminate the new ideas and sentences if they turn out, in the end, to be unrelated to your specific thesis position.

It is important to remember that the best outlines *guide and direct,* but do not *stifle and restrict,* the process of discovery that is such an essential part of good writing. For this reason, if an outline does not work, get rid of it and write a new one. (It only takes a few minutes.) If parts of the outline prove to be unworkable, throw them away and try something new. Remember, outlines are like tourist maps. They will guide the writer safely through all the conventional points of interest, but they will also conceal some truly exciting and unconventional possibilities unless the writer has the courage to strike out occasionally into unexplored territory.

4. Do Not Try to Get It Right the First Time

Sometimes students have a tendency to write a sentence and then devote the rest of their writing time to correcting it. Not only is this a waste of energy and creativity, but it also impedes the flow of thoughts and ideas so essential at this point in the writing process.

Do not edit prematurely. Once a sentence is on paper, ignore its grammatical structure and move immediately to the next sentence. There is plenty of time later to go back and make the necessary changes and corrections.

For example, even a quick glance at the italicized words and sentences in the following paragraph will tell us that there are many grammatical problems and misspelled words that will eventually have to be corrected. For now, forget about those grammatical problems and misspelled words, and move on to the next paragraph.

EXAMPLE

News is another *violence impressionated* show. On every news station there is always information about murders, kidnappings, or wars. The news media is also famous for making celebrities out of *crimnals. Take for example the John Hinckley case.* He was just an *everyday* person until he decided to try to assassinate President Reagan. From the moment he *shot his gun* and injured three people, John Hinckley's name was known around the nation. If a person really had an identity *cricis* and *a lack of norms,* what is going to stop him from doing the same thing? *Because of the fact that television has a wide audience range.* The violence needs to be *screened out* to protect the general public from the dangers of the negative approach of today's television violence.

5. Do Not Worry about Appearances

Sometimes when students are required to turn in rough drafts with their final drafts, they very neatly retype everything to eliminate the messiness of their earlier efforts. In essence, they are trying to create the impression that everything they do in written form is neat and orderly.

Nonsense! The early stages of the writing process are messy and chaotic for everyone, even very gifted writers. If it is not, it generally means that the writer has not been actively engaged in the pursuit of truth.

Do not worry about appearances until you reach the end of the writing and editing process and are actually involved in the preparation of the final manuscript. Then, of course, appearances are very important, because we live in a world that often judges things by how they look. A neatly typed final draft can make the same kind of positive impression in the classroom that it will make later in the business world or professional communities.

For now, rest assured that a little messiness in the early stages of the writing process is both natural and inevitable.

6. If You Think It Is Stupid, Write It Down

One of the major causes of writer's block is the fear that what one writes down on paper will sound stupid. Paradoxically, the only cure for writer's block is to write it down—no matter how stupid it sounds.

All of us have, at one time or another, agonized for hours over a word or sentence that we are afraid will make us sound ignorant and uninformed. And when we finally work up the courage to touch the typewriter keys, we do so tentatively and with the conviction that this particular word or sentence is going to reveal to the world just how incredibly stupid we really are. The fear of being unmasked as a buffoon makes us stare for hours at the typewriter with the same wide-eyed expression of terror as the man who was trapped for an entire afternoon in a small outhouse with a rattlesnake.

What *is* stupid in all of this is spending hours working up the courage to put something down on paper. Everything else is forgivable, but that is truly stupid!

If it sounds stupid, write it down on paper immediately rather than allow it to intimidate you for hours. Once you have recorded it on paper, there are at least two possibilities:

- The idea might very well *be* stupid, but at least you are now in a position to cross it out and eliminate it from your life once and for all. You will be a better person for it, and the idea will no longer be in a position to contaminate all of the other truly remarkable ideas you have stored in your subconscious mind.

- Some ideas that appear stupid in the abstract turn out to be real gems once they are recorded on paper. (This is not to suggest that writers should try to pass off "stupid ideas" as "real gems"; it is, rather, to suggest that writers should avoid prejudging the relative merits of their ideas at this stage in the writing process.)

As Peter Elbow points out in his book *Writing Without Teachers,* "A person's best writing is oftentimes all mixed up together with his worst." In other words, if we do not allow the truly stupid ideas to be recorded on paper, the best ones are never going to get out in the open where they can be appreciated.

7. Do Not Worry about First- and Second-Person Pronoun References

Although many writers of the expository essay try to remove first-person ("I") and second-person ("you") pronoun references from the final drafts, there is nothing wrong with using them in the rough drafts. In fact, many writers find it easier to keep their audiences in perspective, and to write with purpose and conviction in the rough drafts, if they use first- and second-person pronoun references. Later, if necessary, these pronouns can be converted into more formal third-person references ("he," "she," "they," "one," and so on).

In the final draft, the audience will determine whether or not you use such pronoun references. If your teacher or professor encourages you to use first- and second-person pronouns, by all means do so. If, on the other hand, your teacher or professor prefers that you do not use them, make the necessary conversions just prior to writing the final draft of the essay. (There are, of course, reasons for either strategy, depending upon what kind of writing is being stressed and what, precisely, an instructor is trying to accomplish in a specific writing assignment.)

8. Write Too Much Rather Than Too Little

At this stage of the writing process, it is better to write too much than too little. Although wordiness is inappropriate in the final draft, it has a place in the rough drafts. Wordiness is a healthy sign that sufficient ideas have been generated—so many, in fact, that they cannot be contained within the perimeters established by individual sentences and paragraphs. There is always time later to eliminate unnecessary words and phrases.

There is another reason why it is important to produce a volume of prose in the rough drafts. The best strategies keep editing and writing responsibilities as distinct as possible. If there is a volume of prose to edit, this is very easy to do. If one must add a paragraph or two during the editing stage, this is more difficult. By their very nature, such additions combine the simultaneous skills and perplexities of editing and writing.

For all of these reasons, it is better to generate *too much* prose than *too little* in the rough drafts.

(See also "Eliminate Wordiness," pages 95–97.)

9. Make Mistakes and Learn from Them

Mistakes and false starts will be as much a part of the writing experience as they were of the prewriting experience. They cannot be avoided. Indeed, they are an essential part of the writing process, because they provide us with a means of evaluating our better efforts. In writing, as in prewriting, our mistakes eventually show us the way to more effective meanings and expressions.

10. Learn to Use Criticism to Your Advantage

If all the teachers and professors who teach writing courses were completely honest about it, they would have to admit that they have, at one time or another, felt "brutalized" by a reader's comments on something they wrote in college or graduate school. Many of these same teachers and professors probably also keep these essays and research papers somewhere in the darkest recesses of their closets, where they will not inadvertently stumble across them and once again feel humiliated by the marginal comments.

For example, a colleague of mine once showed me one of his graduate school essays on which a professor had written, "Please leave wider margins next time. I need more room to comment on your oversights!" Did my colleague feel humiliated? Yes, he certainly did. Did he feel angry? Absolutely. But over the years, he admitted that he had learned to rechannel his feelings of anger and humiliation so as to use criticism to his advantage.

Try to look at criticism in two ways:

- If it is *valid* criticism, it can only strengthen the final draft of your essay, primarily by providing you with lists of opposing views. Once these opposing views are out in the open, you can develop strategies for responding to them.

- If it is *invalid* or *totally unwarranted* criticism, it can, nonetheless, force you to rethink your original strategies and arguments, thus also strengthening your paper. The end result will be an essay that is argued with more purpose and conviction.

Criticism is a necessary part of all stages of the writing and editing process, and yet none of us likes to be told that something we have written needs to be strengthened. And the harder we have worked on the writing project, the less likely we are to accept further demands on our time and energies.

Whenever you receive criticism during a brainstorming session, or immediately after you receive a paper back from your instructor, be prepared to feel some anger. It is a perfectly normal human reaction. But work to rechannel that anger into a more productive way of looking at criticism; criticism provides the best opportunity you will have to sharpen and improve your writing strategies.

Also, writers who are unable to accept criticism will seldom be able to improve on their writing skills. They will inevitably be limited to one level of competency (or incompetency).

11. Run, Don't Walk, to the Nearest Word Processing Class

As soon as possible, enroll in the nearest school that teaches word processing. In the years ahead, it will be absolutely essential for all serious writers (and business people) to have some familiarity with this new technology.

Word processing has many advantages for students who are interested in learning how to write effectively:

- It cuts writing and editing time in half for most writers.

- There is no duplication of effort. If a word or phrase needs to be added or deleted, even at the very end, it can be done with very little effort.

- Since word processing makes editing and revising so much easier, the writer does not have to worry about making mistakes in the earlier stages of the writing process. And when writers do not have to worry about making mistakes, they generally adopt a more natural and effective style.

- Since one of the advantages of word processing is its ability to reposition complete paragraphs or even several pages of manuscript, it enables writers to focus on the larger concerns of organization and development during the writing stage. At the same time, it also encourages writers *not* to become overly concerned with the details of sentence structures and word choices too early in the writing process.

- It makes proofreading much easier, because most word processing systems come equipped with programs that can check the spelling of some 20,000 or more of the most common words in the English language.

- Similarly, since word processing makes editing so much simpler, it motivates the writer to aim for perfection—without sacrificing anything in the way of time.

- Most important, at least insofar as the writing stage is concerned, word processing enables writers to generate words quickly, easily, and in healthy abundance.

In sum, word processing greatly simplifies every stage of the writing and editing process. For this reason, word processing is compatible with—indeed, reinforces—all of the advice and principles discussed in this text.

12. Set Realistic Writing Goals

The primary goal of the writing stage should be to create a reasonably coherent rough draft. No writer should expect that the early stages of writing will create a polished final draft that is ready to be submitted to the instructor. Again, such expectations are both unproductive and self-defeating.

The following rough draft is by no means flawless (and it should not be), but it reflects a successful prewriting and writing session. Many ideas are generated, there is a healthy verbosity in sentences and paragraphs, and there is an underlying structure and focus to the essay.

EXAMPLE

Jane Morgan
English 10

Violence in America

Going to movies and staying home to watch television are two of America's favorite past times. They are common ways for many people to escape from their everyday problems and move in and out of their fantasies. After a busy day of work, there is nothing easier than relaxing on a couch, eating popcorn, and watching an entertaining movie on television. This may seem innocent enough, but what happens when one sees violent movies and is affected like John Hinckley? He saw a movie about a character trying to impress a girl by assassinating the President and in turn tried to make that fantasy come true for himself. Granted, movies and television can be great relaxing entertainers, but after the case of John Hinckley, one is required to believe that violent shows do effect the people who watch them often enough adversely. Does the public need to fear the affects of television on the minds of their viewers? Steps must be taken to reduce the types of violence depicted on television and in films or else America is doomed.

Violence on television is probably the larger problem because it reaches a wider range of audience. An average American views approximately 3½ hours of television a day. This is perhaps best exemplified by children. Since most of them have been old enough to watch television, children have been placed in front of it by their parents who use this machine as a baby-sitter. As they grow older, and come home from school, what is usually the first thing they do? They turn on the television set usually to watch their favorite cartoons. Cartoons can be enjoyable for most anyone, but often enough, the violence of them is ignored. For example, in viewing the cartoon Tom and Jerry, it is not uncommon to watch a tongue being bitten off or someone's head being bashed in by a club. Elmer Fudd of Bugs Bunny trying to gun down a rabbit every spare minute of his time. Also, Bamm Bamm from The Flintstones takes a person and knocks him around on rock floors. The Roadrunner is perhaps the most violent of all cartoons. In this cartoon, a coyote is depicted by trying to catch and kill a roadrunner by different methods, ranging from boulders to dynamite. Obviously, todays youngersters are spending too much time watching these types of programs. Children are very impressionable at such a young age and often mimic what they see. Since children are especially susceptible to influences from society, something must be done to limit the violence depicted on today's television shows.

As people grow older, they usually switch from watching television cartoons to watching soap operas and nighttime television. The violence on soap operas is astonishing. On All My Children, a daytime soap, one episode showed a woman hiding from her mother who was trying to kill her. Nighttime soap operas are no better and tend to focus on the benefits of achieving power. Dynasty, Dallas, and Falcon Crest are three of the nation's top-rated television shows, and they all focus on the deviant lifestyles of the main characters. For example, J. R. from Dallas is constantly scheming to increase his power and wealth regardless of whom he hurts, and, in one episode, he was shot down by his mistress. This one episode drew much attention from the public because the media overpublicized ''Who shot J. R.?'' No matter how old one is, he can never escape from the impact that television has had, and again the question is, does television really affect the public?

News is another violence impressionated show. On every news station there is always information about murders, kidnappings, or wars. The news media is also famous for making celebrities out of criminals. Take for example the John Hinckley case. He was just an everyday person until he decided to try to assassinate President Reagan. From the moment he shot his gun and injured three people, John Hinckley's name was now known around the nation. If a person really had an identity crisis, and had a lack of norms, what is going to stop him from doing the same thing? Because of the fact that television has a wide audience range. The violence needs to be screened out to protect the general public from the dangers of the negative approach of today's television violence.

Movies, on the other hand, do not reach as large an audience as television, and they also show more sex and violent situations. President Nixon, during his term of office, asked sociologists to perform a series of tests explaining the overall effect of pornographic movies on the public. The results were not significant enough to report, but this also concluded that people were being influenced, and somebody was in fact trying to initiate action against them. As was stated before, and need not be overstated, was the case of John Hinckley. He enacted his fantasy after seeing the movie Taxi Driver which involved a young prostitute. Another movie, The Wall, depicts violence, and its theme is violence in a violent world. This movie is geared on affecting the human senses, but what will happen if someone cannot handle these reactions? Again the question arises, will the public have to fear its affects? Necessary steps must be taken to reduce these types of movies, and critics should try to discourage the public from viewing them.

Violence as shows in both television and movies must be heavily reduced. The screening and rating of such shows must be made harder to pass. It is up to the reader to answer the previous questions and decide what should or should not be done about such shows. The last thing to be stated is, does the public really need to be afraid of the affects of violence on the minds of it's viewers that is depicted in movies and on television?

There is absolutely nothing wrong with the above essay as *a rough draft*. It is not, however, *a final draft*, and it should never be submitted as one. The writer is only halfway into the writing and editing process. Now she must move beyond writing as a way of discovering and clarifying meaning and into writing as a way of expressing that meaning.

Editing (also referred to by some instructors as ''revising'') and rewriting are the stages in the writing process where expressing the meaning is of paramount importance. Now the rules of English grammar and rhetoric must be applied rigorously to produce a final draft that will be impressive in both appearance and content.

[Note: See the revised drafts of the above essay in Part III of this text, "Editing and Rewriting the Expository Essay," pages 234–246.]

II

Editing
and Revising

A

Editing Strategies

When writers enter the editing stage, they must adopt a very different way of looking at the words and ideas they have generated. They must be precise, merciless, and systematic in seeking out the major problem areas in paragraphs, sentence structures, and punctuation. Most important, they must avoid the tendency to edit haphazardly—adding a comma here, a capital letter there, and so forth. All of this is purely cosmetic work; it might add something to the appearance of the essay, but it will do little to improve the essay's overall effectiveness. Instead, the writer should learn to *systematically* edit and revise the various drafts of the writing project.

An analogy might be helpful here. When contractors build homes, they first decide whether each one will be a one-story or a two-story structure, and where the various rooms will be located, before they worry about the types of paneling and the colors of the paint to be used on the walls. It is simply a matter of common sense for contractors to proceed in this way. Why should they worry about the color of paint to be used in the upstairs bedrooms if it is going to be a one-story house? Or why should they worry about the type of paneling to be used in the den until they are absolutely certain that there will *be* a den in the house?

Similarly, during the editing stage, writers should focus on the larger concerns of the writing project first (i.e., essay development, paragraphing, and so on) and only later on editing individual sentences and words. After all, why worry about editing individual sentences and word choices if they might be eliminated from the final draft of the essay?

1. Follow a List of Priorities

The editing process involves a list of priorities, each of which should be satisfied before the writer moves on to the next stage. In order of importance, this list of priorities (stated as questions the writer must ask of himself or herself) is as follows:

a. The Essay as a Whole

1. Does the thesis statement accurately reflect the position I am arguing in the body of my essay?
2. Does the essay have an effective introduction, body, and conclusion?
3. Should some paragraphs be divided and/or combined?
4. Is the body of the essay sufficiently developed, or should I add another paragraph or two for reinforcement?
5. Are there irrelevant paragraphs that should be eliminated from the body of the essay?
6. Similarly, are the paragraphs in the body of the essay arranged in the most logical sequence?
7. Does the formal outline reflect a solid framework for the essay?

b. Individual Paragraphs

1. Does each paragraph have a topic sentence, and do the topic sentences accurately reflect and reinforce the thesis position?
2. Are the individual paragraphs sufficiently developed?
3. Do the paragraphs have a balance of generalizations and supporting evidence?
4. Are the sentences in the paragraphs arranged in the most *logical* sequences?
5. Are there sentences that are irrelevant to the topic sentences?
6. Are there sentences that are repetitive?

c. Individual Sentences

1. Have I eliminated all clearly ineffective sentences and expressions

(i.e., wordy expressions, repetitive phrases and clauses, clichés, and so on)?
2. Are there sentences that should be combined or divided?
3. Are the sentences complete?
4. Have I corrected all inappropriate word sequences in the individual sentences (i.e., misplaced modifiers, dangling modifiers, passive constructions, and so on)?
5. Are the sentence structures consistent in terms of organization and expression (i.e., subject-verb agreement, pronoun-antecedent agreement, parallel structure, mixed constructions, and so on)?

d. Individual Words

1. Are all word choices appropriate?
2. Have I eliminated all problems with usage, awkward expressions, coinages, malapropisms, double negatives, and other such problems with word choices?

e. Punctuation

1. Have I supplied the appropriate end punctuation?
2. Have I supplied the appropriate internal punctuation?

f. Final Revisions and Proofreading

1. Is everything spelled correctly?
2. Are there adequate transitions between sentences?
3. Has everything been capitalized correctly?
4. Are there any missing letters or words?
5. Are there any other stylistic lapses?
6. Are there any problems with tone or sexist or other inappropriate language?

g. Manuscript Preparation

1. Does the title accurately reflect the subject of the paper?
2. Have all sources been accurately footnoted?

3. Has a bibliography been affixed to the end of the paper?
4. Have I complied with all other guidelines for manuscript preparation (i.e., type of paper, margins, color of typewriter ribbon, and so on)?

In essence, the writer should focus on the larger units first (the essay as a whole and the paragraphs) before moving on to the smaller units (sentences and words). This systematic way of editing will eliminate much wasted effort and, at the same time, enable the writer to avoid mere cosmetic work during the editing stage.

It is also important to emphasize that there will be some overlapping and some retracing of the steps outlined above, especially as sentences continue to be divided, blended, and merged throughout the editing and rewriting process. Also, some writers may feel more comfortable if they make slight adjustments in the above scale of priorities to suit their personal editorial preferences (for example, perhaps establishing sentence completeness somewhat later in the editing process).

2. Use These Editing Strategies

1. Do not try to do it all in one draft. If it seems clear that the rough drafts need major revisions in the areas listed under "The Essay as a Whole" and "Individual Paragraphs," solve those problems and write a new draft before attempting to deal with the problems of sentence structure, punctuation, word choice, and spelling.
2. If at all possible, edit for short periods of time over several days, rather than all at once for an extended period of time. Many editorial problems can be solved simply by getting away from the essay and coming back to it later with a more objective attitude toward what has been written.
3. Try to edit when you are fresh, preferably early in the morning. One can *write* occasionally when one is tired, but *editing* demands rigorous concentration and mental discipline. For this reason, most professional writers save their more productive hours for the editing process.
4. Pretend you are writing for a newspaper that has rigidly confined

you to the limited space available in the editorial column. Much unnecessary wordiness can be eliminated this way.

5. Always read everything out loud before you type the final draft. The eye has a tendency to pay more attention to the details of individual word choices, punctuation, and spelling when the voice forces it to slow down.

B

Editing the Essay as a Whole

Expository writing, the prose form practiced in most high school and college composition classes, is written in Standard English and is both explanatory and persuasive in nature. The value of expository writing is that it introduces students to the formal style of composition used in the professional and business communities most of them will enter after graduation. Obviously, there are some differences between expository-writing assignments and the written communications and transactions of the world beyond the classroom, but the principles of effective writing and editing are precisely the same.

When editing the essay as a whole—or, in later life, when editing the office memorandum, business letter, or company report—the important thing to remember is to avoid becoming bogged down too early in the details of sentence structure and punctuation. There is, of course, a natural tendency for all writers to try to correct everything in the early stages of the editing process. However, this practice is self-defeating, primarily because much time and effort may be wasted on correcting sentences and paragraphs that could very well be eliminated from the final draft.

Instead, concentrate on the following in the earliest stages of the editing process:

1. Clarifying and refining the thesis position (main idea)
2. Developing the essay sufficiently
3. Eliminating irrelevant paragraphs
4. Dividing and/or combining paragraphs when appropriate
5. Establishing the most logical paragraph sequences

6. Clarifying and refining the outline to monitor the structure of the essay

To return briefly to our analogy between the writing of an essay and the building of a house, the thesis position is comparable to the house's foundation because both support the weight of their respective structures. The length of the essay is comparable to the total square footage of the house. And the formal outline is comparable to the master plan or blueprint, which illustrates the overall design of the house.

In the early stages of the editing process, the writer must, like the contractor, make certain that these prerequisites have been satisfied before devoting too much time to other considerations.

1. Establish a Thesis Statement

"Why do I need a thesis? I usually don't know what I'm writing about anyway!"

One of the writer's major responsibilities at the end of the prewriting stage is to establish a preliminary thesis statement. The preliminary thesis statement is the central idea that organizes and controls the entire expository essay. Without a strong thesis, the essay loses its purpose—the reason for writing it in the first place. (See also "Clarify Your Thesis Statement and Preliminary Outline," pages 25–27.)

At the same time, it is important to note that thesis statements should change and become more refined and focused during the writing and editing stages. Although writers often feel insecure when this happens, they should rest assured that it is a healthy sign. It merely indicates that the writing and editing process is producing an argument that has a greater sense of clarity and precision.

1. Normally, the best thesis statements are short, preferably no longer than one sentence. A one-sentence thesis statement forces the writer to establish the paper's focus as precisely as possible.
2. Each word in a thesis statement should be selected with great care and with extreme sensitivity to what it might contribute to the essay as a whole. Individual word choices in the thesis often alert

the reader to the issues that will be developed in the body of the essay.

3. The thesis statement should appear in the introductory paragraph, usually in the first or the last sentence. (See "Introductory Paragraph," pages 73–76.)

4. Avoid thesis statements that are too broad and too general. The purpose of the thesis statement is to narrow the focus of the subject matter so that it can be covered adequately in a short essay.

5. Avoid thesis statements that are awkwardly stated. Awkward constructions are confusing enough in the body of the essay, but they undermine the entire argument if the writer uses them in a thesis statement. (See also "Revise Awkward Constructions," pages 158–160.)

SAMPLE THESIS STATEMENTS

Original

1. The book was really good, and I liked everything about it. *[This thesis is unworkable because it is much too broad.]*

2. The painter has, through the use of the situation, the head-on vantage point, and the color, expressed that amidst the evil forces of nature, man's aimless struggle alone for survival continues. *[This sentence is much too awkward to establish a clear focus.]*

3. Missionary zealousness and excessively fanatical motives continue to stir the pot in the Middle

Revision

1. Structure, characterization, and plot are the three elements that contribute the most to making Emily Bronte's *Wuthering Heights* a great work of art. *[Now there is a focus and a manageable format to the essay.]*

2. Through the use of color, dramatic situation, and point of view, the painter has expressed man's struggle for survival against the evil forces of nature.

3. Zealotry and fanaticism continue to exacerbate the situation in the Middle East.

East. *[The word choices here are too imprecise to provide a clear focus for the essay.]*

4. In *The Great Gatsby*, Nick Carraway goes through a wavering moral sense in that he has mixed feelings about Jay Gatsby and his world. *[This is a good thesis statement—but one that could be further strengthened by more precision in word choices and sentence structure.]*

4. In *The Great Gatsby,* Nick Carraway's vacillating moral sense makes him very confused about Jay Gatsby and the American Dream.

5. Space exploration is expensive, but the technology it has created has profoundly influenced communication systems, medical care, and even food production.

5. *[Nothing wrong here. This is an excellent thesis statement.]*

Most writers continue to refine their respective thesis statements throughout the writing and editing process. The reason for this is simply that the process of discovering the meaning of the writing assignment does not end after the prewriting stage. Rather, the dynamic process of writing continues to reveal implications about the thesis position throughout the editing and rewriting stages.

Continue to work on thesis statements until they narrow the subject matter and establish a precise focus for the argument. The end result will be a much more coherent and persuasive essay.

2. Develop and Unify Your Essay

"The expository essay is always written in Standard English. There just cain't be no other way."

In the early stages of the editing process, the writer should concentrate on placing paragraphs in the best possible sequence for the logical development of the essay as a whole. This will involve combining and/or dividing some paragraphs and rearranging, developing, or eliminating others.

The only *sentence* that should be clarified and refined at this time, if it seems appropriate to do so, is the thesis statement. The other details of sentence structure, punctuation, and spelling should be considered much later in the editing process.

[Note: The paragraphs in the essay below are numbered for quick reference. They should not, of course, be numbered in the final draft of the essay. Similarly, the thesis statement is underlined, although it need not be underlined or italicized in the final draft].

EXAMPLE 1: FIRST DRAFT

Clearly, this essay will need more development before the writer proceeds any further into the editing process. The thesis, "In *The Great Gatsby*, Nick Carraway goes through a wavering moral sense in that he has mixed feelings about Gatsby and his world," is only lightly touched upon in paragraphs 2 and 5 of the essay. The other paragraphs in the essay do little to develop this particular thesis. For this reason, the thesis position will definitely have to be developed through another paragraph or two in the body of the essay.

1) In F. Scott Fitzgerald's The Great Gatsby, the novel revolves around one central theme; that theme is the world-known American Dream. This dream was created by millions of immigrants in the past and is still thought of as being attainable, even in today's society. The titular hero of the story, Jay Gatsby, tries to live the rags-to-riches story but, along the way, meets up with one

important character who develops throughout the course of the novel. In *The Great Gatsby*, Nick Carraway goes through a wavering moral sense in that he has mixed feelings about Jay Gatsby and his world.

2) In the start of the novel, Nick tends to reserve his personal judgments about the other characters in the story and remains uninvolved in their lives in that he is not willing to act on his judgment. He realizes that Jordan Baker, a young woman golfer who eventually becomes involved with Nick, is an incurable liar and that it is a major defect in her personality, similar to the brutality and irresponsibility of Tom and Daisy, but at this point, he is willing to put up with her defects. As Nick himself realizes, he is never totally a part of the action around him yet acting as a link for that action by bringing Daisy and Gatsby together.

Develop through careful analysis of Nick's relationship to all of these characters (and to himself).

3) The novel, to a large extent and for many reasons, grew out of Fitzgerald's own experiences.

Fitzgerald always lived on the edge of the very wealthy Saint Paul, Minnesota, neighborhoods, which contributed much to his obsession with the very wealthy people in the world. And Daisy, in the eyes of some readers, is the symbol of Fitzgerald's own frustrations when he looked over the brick fences at the lifestyles of the very rich.

4) Willy Loman is another literary figure who is driven by the pursuit of a dream. Loman in Arthur Miller's play is much older than Jay Gatsby, and yet both men are afflicted with the same disease—— the disease of money. And both men are destroyed because they cannot control the disease.

5) Although Nick is not the hero of the novel, his importance as the narrator and as a functioning character makes him almost as much a central figure as Gatsby himself. The Great Gatsby opens and finishes with the life of Nick Carraway and, throughout the changes of the story, he develops and grows on the idea of the American experience.

EXAMPLE 1: SECOND DRAFT

1. The essay is now adequately developed, but the thesis in paragraph 1 will still have to be strengthened and clarified somewhat.
2. Paragraph 3 is improperly and illogically positioned in the essay, primarily because it separates two paragraphs that focus on the question of Nick Carraway's values.
3. Paragraph 4 contains far too much unrelated information. It should be divided in some meaningful way to improve the logical development of both the paragraph and the essay as a whole.
4. Paragraph 5 should be eliminated because it has nothing to do with this particular thesis position.

1) In F. Scott Fitzgerald's The Great Gatsby, the

novel revolves around one central theme; that

theme is the world-known American Dream. This

dream was created by millions of immigrants in the

past and is still thought of as being attainable,

even in today's society. The titular hero of the

story, Jay Gatsby, tries to live the rags-to-

riches story but, along the way, meets up with one

important character who develops throughout the

course of the novel. In The Great Gatsby, Nick

Carraway's vacillating moral sense makes him very confused
~~Carraway goes through a wavering moral sense in~~ ∮
about Jay Gatsby and the American Dream.
~~that he has mixed feelings about Gatsby and his~~ ∮

~~world.~~ ∮

Clarify word choices in your thesis.

Essay unity:
Move ¶ 2 to
¶ 3.

2.) In the start of the novel, Nick tends to reserve his personal judgments about the other characters in the story and remains uninvolved in their lives in that he is not willing to act on his judgment. He realizes that Jordan Baker, a young woman golfer who eventually becomes involved with Nick, is an incurable liar and that it is a major defect in her personality, similar to the brutality and irresponsibility of Tom and Daisy, but at this point, he is willing to put up with her defects. As Nick himself realizes, he is never totally a part of the action around him yet acting as a link for that action by bringing Daisy and Gatsby together.

Essay unity:
interchange
paragraphs
2 and 3.

3) The novel, to a large extent and for many reasons, grew out of Fitzgerald's own experiences. Fitzgerald always lived on the edge of the very wealthy Saint Paul, Minnesota, neighborhoods, which contributed much to his obsession with the very wealthy people in the world. And Daisy, in the eyes of some readers, is the symbol of

Fitzgerald's own frustrations when he looked over the brick fences at the lifestyles of the very rich.

4) When Nick reaches the age of 30, he quickly develops a full moral responsibility. He realizes he can no longer tolerate the moral emptiness that lies beneath the wealth and sophistication of eastern society, and so he returns to the middle west after carefully fulfilling his personal responsibilities. Nick's preoccupation with the fact that he is now 30 is actually a very relevant detail. The age is symbolic of the passing of youth, and so the turning point in Nick's life occurs simultaneously with the turning point in Gatsby's life, the death of his youthful dream.

New paragraph → ¶ Also, the death of Myrtle Wilson forces Nick to become more aware of his morals. Myrtle's violent departure is the ultimate piece of carelessness of the Buchanans, and it causes Nick to abandon them as well as Jordan. The coldness of her personality has been evident all through the novel, but here it is finally enough to drive Nick away. Nick's new sense of responsibility is evident in his desire to warn Gatsby, for in this act he definitely takes sides, committing himself to his friend. Nick's statement that Gatsby is "worth the whole damn bunch put together" indicates that Nick has developed to where he can no longer reserve judgment. Despite his total disapproval of Gatsby's vulgarity and self-delusion, Nick respects him for the strength and unselfish nature of his idealism. In the end, Nick expresses a desire to leave things in order rather than just hoping they take care of themselves.

Eliminate this ¶. It is unrelated to your thesis.

5) Willy Loman is another literary figure who is driven by the pursuit of a dream. Loman in Arthur Miller's play is much older than Jay Gatsby, and yet both men are afflicted with the same disease—the disease of money. And both men are destroyed because they cannot control the disease.

6) Although Nick is not the hero of the novel, his importance as the narrator and as a functioning

character makes him almost as much a central

figure as Gatsby himself. The Great Gatsby opens

and finishes with the life of Nick Carraway and,

throughout the changes of the story, he develops

and grows on the idea of the American experience.

EXAMPLE 1: THIRD DRAFT

The essay will still need some careful editing, revising, and proofreading, but these tasks have been made much easier by the fact that the essay is now adequately developed and the paragraphs arranged in a more logical sequence.

1) In F. Scott Fitzgerald's The Great Gatsby, the

novel revolves around one central theme; that

theme is the world-known American Dream. This

dream was created by millions of immigrants in the

past and is still thought of as being attainable,

even in today's society. The titular hero of the

story, Jay Gatsby, tries to live the rags-to-

riches story but, along the way, meets up with one

important character who develops throughout the

course of the novel. In *The Great Gatsby*, Nick

Carraway's vacillating moral sense makes him very

confused about Jay Gatsby and the American Dream.

2) The novel, to a large extent and for many
reasons, grew out of Fitzgerald's own experiences.
Fitzgerald always lived on the edge of the very
wealthy Saint Paul, Minnesota, neighborhoods,
which contributed much to his obsession with the
very wealthy people in the world. And Daisy, in
the eyes of some readers, is the symbol of
Fitzgerald's own frustrations when he looked over
the brick fences at the lifestyles of the very
rich.

3) In the start of the novel, Nick tends to reserve
his personal judgments about the other characters
in the story and remains uninvolved in their lives
in that he is not willing to act on his judgment.
He realizes that Jordan Baker, a young woman
golfer who eventually becomes involved with Nick,
is an incurable liar and that it is a major defect
in her personality, similar to the brutality and
irresponsibility of Tom and Daisy, but at this
point, he is willing to put up with her defects.
As Nick himself realizes, he is never totally a

part of the action around him yet acting as a link
for that action by bringing Daisy and Gatsby
together.

4) When Nick reaches the age of 30, he quickly
develops a full moral responsibility. He realizes
he can no longer tolerate the moral emptiness that
lies beneath the wealth and sophistication of
eastern society, and so he returns to the middle
west after carefully\fulfilling his personal
responsibilities. Nick's preoccupation with the
fact that he is now 30 is actually a very relevant
detail. The age is symbolic of the passing of
youth, and so the turning point in Nick's life
occurs simultaneously with the turning point in
Gatsby's life, the death of his youthful dream.

5) Also, the death of Myrtle Wilson forces Nick to
become more aware of his morals. Myrtle's violent
departure is the ultimate piece of carelessness of
the Buchanans, and it causes Nick to abandon them
as well as Jordan. The coldness of her personality

has been evident all through the novel, but here it is finally enough to drive Nick away.

6) Nick's new sense of responsibility is evident in his desire to warn Gatsby, for in this act he definitely takes sides, committing himself to his friend. Nick's statement that Gatsby is "worth the whole damn bunch put together" indicates that Nick has developed to where he can no longer reserve judgment. Despite his total disapproval of Gatsby's vulgarity and self-delusion, Nick respects him for the strength and unselfish nature of his idealism. In the end, Nick expresses a desire to leave things in order rather than just hoping they take care of themselves.

7) Although Nick is not the hero of the novel, his importance as the narrator and as a functioning character makes him almost as much a central figure as Gatsby himself. The Great Gatsby opens and finishes with the life of Nick Carraway and, throughout the changes of the story, he develops and grows on the idea of the American experience.

3. Formal Outlines and Organization

"I. Outline every essay
  A. with great care
    1. so you will know where
      you are going
    2.
    3. every step of the way."

Although formal outlines are a matter of personal choice, it is important to remember that most professional writers use them conscientiously. William Faulkner's friends, for example, described how the famous author virtually covered the walls of his study from floor to ceiling with detailed outlines of his various novels. The reason for such conscientious attention to detail is that Faulkner understood the value of meticulous organization in the writing process.

Since most professional writers use formal outlines, it seems wise to encourage students to do the same. Still, even though professional writers recognize the value of formal outlines, they all have their idiosyncrasies when it comes to the ways in which they organize their respective writing projects. In fact, there is perhaps more diversity of opinion in the area of outlining than there is in any other area of the writing and editing process. About the only thing professional writers agree on is that the best formal outline is the outline that works for the writer who is using it. For this reason, the following discussion of formal outlining procedures is meant to serve as a guideline; it is not meant, in any way, to be dogma.

The primary function of formal outlines is not so much to provide focus and direction for the writing project—that has already been established by the preliminary outline—as it is to monitor the organization of the developing essay from draft to draft. If the organization is strong, it should be reflected in the formal outline. If the organization is weak, that too should be reflected in the formal outline, and the necessary adjustments should be made.

[Note: The "groupings" established during prewriting activities normally form the various subdivisions for the formal outline. The

items within each grouping generally have something in common *that enables them to be discussed in the same paragraph or paragraphs. (See "Group and Arrange Ideas," pages 20–24.]*

a. Formal Topic Outline

The following is an example of a formal topic outline of the type required in many expository-writing classes. The Roman numerals represent the various paragraphs in the essay, and the capital letters and Arabic numerals represent the various subdivisions within each paragraph. With the exception of the thesis and the conclusion, the entries are listed in an abbreviated form.

EXAMPLE

Nick Carraway and the American Dream

Thesis: In F. Scott Fitzgerald's *The Great Gatsby*, Nick Carraway's vacillating moral sense makes him very confused about Jay Gatsby and the American Dream.

I. Introduction
  A. A brief definition of the American Dream
  B. Nick and Gatsby's relationship to the American Dream
II. Fitzgerald's background
  A. His early life in Saint Paul, Minnesota
  B. Living on the edge of great wealth
  C. His frustrations
III. Nick Carraway as "point of view"
  A. His refusal to get "involved"
  B. His hypocrisy
    1. His relationship to Jordan Baker
    2. His role in bringing Gatsby and Daisy together
IV. Nick's crises
  A. His age
  B. The "emptiness" of his world
  C. His fatal attraction to the American Dream

   V. Myrtle Wilson's death
     A. The impact on Nick's values
     B. Nick's emergence as the central character
  VI. Nick's renewed commitment to Gatsby
     A. What he deplores in Gatsby
     B. What he respects in Gatsby
 VII. Conclusion: Nick Carraway becomes the central character in *The Great Gatsby* as he discovers the true significance of the American Dream.

b. Formal Sentence Outline

Some teachers and professors prefer a more detailed formal sentence outline. The sentence outline lists the thesis, the first sentence for each paragraph, and the types of evidence that will be used to support each of the paragraphs. Unlike the topic outline, in which the subdivisions appear in an abbreviated form, everything in the sentence outline is listed as a complete sentence.

EXAMPLE

Nick Carraway and the American Dream

Thesis: In F. Scott Fitzgerald's *The Great Gatsby*, Nick Carraway's vacillating moral sense makes him very confused about Jay Gatsby and the American Dream.

   I. The American Dream involves certain cultural attitudes toward money, power, and eternal love.
     A. Gatsby is obsessed with the American Dream.
     B. Nick has ambivalent feelings about it.
  II. Fitzgerald's background involved an early obsesssion with the American Dream.
     A. He grew up in an upper-middle-class home in Saint Paul, Minnesota.
     B. Living on the edge of some extremely wealthy neighborhoods, he became frustrated by his inability to share in the dream.
  III. Nick Carraway, who shares Fitzgerald's frustrations, provides a complex "point of view" in the novel.

Editing the Essay as a Whole   **67**

    A. Nick claims that he does not like to get involved with other people.
    B. He is, however, a hypocrite, for he becomes deeply involved with others in the story.
      1. He has a love affair with Jordan Baker.
      2. He is instrumental in bringing Gatsby and Daisy together.
 IV. Nick is experiencing several crises in his life.
    A. He is bothered by his age.
    B. He is bothered by the "emptiness" of his world.
    C. He is attracted to the American Dream even though he realizes it could destroy him.
  V. The death of Myrtle Wilson is central to Nick's development.
    A. Nick's values begin to change.
    B. Nick starts to emerge as the central character in the story.
 VI. Nick spends much time analyzing Jay Gatsby's values.
    A. There is much about Gatsby that Nick deplores.
    B. There is much about Gatsby that Nick respects.
VII. Conclusion: Nick Carraway becomes the central character in *The Great Gatsby* as he discovers the true significance of the American Dream.

c. Comparison and Contrast

Many expository writing assignments require students to compare and contrast two or more things. There are several ways to organize such a paper, two of which are illustrated below. Example 1 allows for the comparison to be a continuing, ongoing concern in each of the paragraphs in the essay. Example 2, on the other hand, discusses the two stories separately and then makes the comparison much later in the body of the essay.

EXAMPLE 1

Jay Gatsby and Willy Loman: Two Views of
the American Dream

Thesis: In F. Scott Fitzgerald's *The Great Gatsby* and Arthur Miller's *Death of a Salesman*, the two main characters—Jay Gatsby and Willy Loman—

are eventually destroyed by their respective versions of the American Dream.

I. Introduction
   A. A brief definition of "the American Dream"—its attitude toward wealth, time, and the meaning of success
   B. Fitzgerald's and Miller's personal involvement in that dream

II. Wealth and the American Dream
   A. Jay Gatsby has "made it"; Willy has not
   B. Gatsby's relationship to Wolfsheim; Willy's to Ben
   C. Gatsby's wealth necessary to give him access to Daisy; for Willy, wealth necessary to be respected
      1. Significance of the two characters' names
      2. Comparison of their respective homes

III. Time and the American Dream
   A. The attempts of both Gatsby and Willy to live in the past
   B. Gatsby's death; Willy's death
   C. Images of time and mortality in both stories

IV. Success and the American Dream
   A. Gatsby one step removed from "having it all"; Willy has never been successful
   B. Gatsby's need to be a "legend"; Willy's need to be "well liked"
   C. Characters who give a different view of the meaning of success:
      1. Biff
      2. Jordan Baker
      3. Charley

V. Conclusion: Both *The Great Gatsby* and *Death of a Salesman* present central characters who are obsessed with, and eventually destroyed by, the American Dream.

EXAMPLE 2

Jay Gatsby and Willy Loman: Two Views of the American Dream

Thesis: In F. Scott Fitzgerald's *The Great Gatsby* and Arthur Miller's *Death of a Salesman*, the two main characters—Jay Gatsby and Willy Loman—

are eventually destroyed by their respective versions of the American Dream.

I. Introduction
   A. A brief definition of "the American Dream"—its attitude toward wealth, time, and the meaning of success
   B. Fitzgerald's and Miller's personal involvement in that dream
II. Jay Gatsby and the American Dream—the meaning of wealth and success
   A. Gatsby has "made it" and is enormously wealthy
   B. His relationship to Wolfsheim
   C. Wealth as a means to an end
      1. Significance of his name
      2. His home
   D. His need for Daisy to complete his success
   E. His attempts to become a "legend"
III. Jay Gatsby, time, and the American dream
   A. His attempts to repeat the past
   B. His attitude toward Daisy's daughter
   C. Nick Carraway on "the orgiastic future"
   D. Jordan Baker: a more realistic view of time
IV. Willy Loman and the American Dream—the meaning of wealth and success
   A. Willy has not "made it"
   B. Ben's "success"
   C. Willy's definition of success: to be "well liked"
      1. Significance of his name
      2. Description of his home
V. Willy Loman, time, and the American Dream
   A. His need to escape into the past
   B. Ben as a symbol of time and mortality
   C. Willy's death
   D. Biff: learning to accept time
VI. A Comparison of Jay Gatsby and Willy Loman in the context of the American Dream
   A. The significance of wealth to Jay Gatsby and Willy Loman
   B. The meaning of success to Jay Gatsby and Willy Loman
   C. Time, Jay Gatsby, and Willy Loman

VII. Conclusion: Both *The Great Gatsby* and *Death of a Salesman* present central characters who are obsessed with, and eventually destroyed by, the American Dream.

d. The Formal Outline as a Monitoring Device

All of the above outlines reflect essays that have structures, or "master plans," capable of supporting the essay as a whole. Some formal outlines, however, reveal problems in the logical organization and arrangement of ideas. Note, for example, the placement of the italicized section III in the following outline. It reveals a serious problem in essay unity and coherence.

EXAMPLE

Nick Carraway and the American Dream

Thesis: In F. Scott Fitzgerald's *The Great Gatsby*, Nick Carraway's vacillating moral sense makes him very confused about Jay Gatsby and the American Dream.

I. Introduction
  A. A brief definition of the American Dream
  B. Nick's and Gatsby's relationship to the American Dream
II. Nick Carraway as "point of view"
  A. His refusal to get "involved"
  B. His hypocrisy
    1. His relationship to Jordan Baker
    2. His role in bringing Gatsby and Daisy together
III. Fitzgerald's background
  A. His early life in Saint Paul, Minnesota
  B. Living on the edge of great wealth
  C. His frustrations
IV. Nick's crises
  A. His age
  B. The "emptiness" of his world
  C. His fatal attraction to the American Dream

    V. Myrtle Wilson's death
       A. The impact on Nick's values
       B. Nick's emergence as central character
   VI. Nick's renewed commitment to Gatsby
       A. What he deplores in Gatsby
       B. What he respects in Gatsby
  VII. Conclusion: Nick Carraway becomes the central character in *The Great Gatsby* as he discovers the true significance of the American Dream.

Even a quick glance at this outline will reveal that there is something wrong with the placement of the italicized section III. The information about Fitzgerald's background illogically separates two paragraphs that focus specifically on a central character in the novel. For this reason, section II and section III should be interchanged to establish a more logical organization to the essay. (See also "Develop and Unify Your Essay," pages 53–64, for the essay that evolved out of this outline.)

Remember, effective writing is always organized writing, and a formal outline can very quickly reveal the strengths and weaknesses of the essay's overall organization. For this reason, learn to use formal outlines as monitoring devices during the editing stage.

C

Editing Paragraphs

Once the larger concerns of developing the essay as a whole and establishing logical paragraph sequences are satisfied, most writers next address themselves to the question of effective paragraphing. Paragraphs provide the major subdivisions for the expository essay. They are as important to the essay as the various rooms are to a house.

Effective paragraphing is based to a large extent on the writer's awareness of the differences between introductory paragraphs, paragraphs in the body of the essay, and concluding paragraphs.

1. Introductory Paragraph

"Here I go!"

The first sentence of most introductory paragraphs starts the narrowing process whereby the subject of the essay is organized into a manageable framework, and the perimeters of the argument are established. Each subsequent sentence is more specific and more precise as the perimeter and scope of the subject are limited and more clearly defined. Normally, the last or the first sentence in the introductory paragraph states the thesis and takes a position on the subject.

Sometimes it is helpful to think of the introductory paragraph as an *inverted triangle,* leading from a general introduction of the subject to a specific statement of thesis in the last sentence.

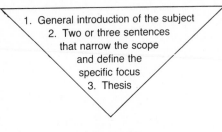

1. General introduction of the subject
2. Two or three sentences that narrow the scope and define the specific focus
3. Thesis

EXAMPLE

(1) The issue of vigilante justice is one that is currently being debated at every level of our society. (2a) Those who support the concept of vigilante justice insist that it is a natural reaction to a system of law and order that has broken down completely. (2b) Those who criticize the idea of vigilante justice are equally adamant that it would eventually destroy our civilization. (3) *Although both views are understandable, society would be better served by the strengthening of existing laws than by the sanctioning of vigilante justice.*

Some writers and professors prefer to make the thesis statement the first sentence in the introductory paragraph. Although this *pyramid-shaped* model can be a fairly abrupt introduction to the thesis position, it has the advantage of immediately focusing the reader's attention on the main idea that will be discussed throughout the essay. (Either method is, of course, valid, depending upon what an instructor is attempting to accomplish in a specific essay assignment.)

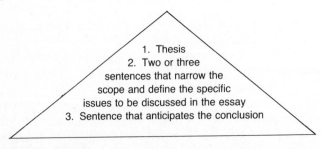

1. Thesis
2. Two or three sentences that narrow the scope and define the specific issues to be discussed in the essay
3. Sentence that anticipates the conclusion

EXAMPLE

(1) *Society would be better served by the strengthening of existing laws than by the sanctioning of vigilante justice.* (2a) Those who support the concept of vigilante justice insist that our current laws are ineffective and unenforceable. (2b) Conversely, those who criticize the idea of vigilante justice are convinced that it would eventually create a form of violence that would destroy our civilization. (3) Advocates and critics both agree, however, that the debate will influence legislative and judicial decisions for years to come.

1. Some introductory paragraphs are weak because the perimeters of the argument are undefined and the narrowing process never takes place. Instead, the first sentence of the introductory paragraph is repeated over and over again with slight variations.

   Due to the alarming increase in the number of violent crimes committed in this country, the issue of vigilante justice is one that is currently being debated at every level of our society. Upper-, lower-, and middle-class people are all concerned about the issue of vigilante justice and the rights of individuals to protect themselves against violent crime. Except for the criminal element among us, everyone seems to be debating the issue of vigilante justice. No segment of our society is safe from violent crime—a fact that perhaps explains why the issue of vigilante justice is on everyone's mind and why it is being debated so much.

2. Some introductory paragraphs are weak because specific examples are introduced too early and/or the movement from generalizations to specifics is haphazard and illogical.

   Vigilante justice is a controversial issue. Look what happened to Bernhard Goetz when he had to protect himself on the subway! Common criminals receive far more protection in our society than do the victims of violent crime. Last week, in Chicago, another person had to protect himself from a possible mugging—only to be arrested by the Chicago police. No wonder people resort to vigilante justice. People have a right to ride on the subways without the fear of being attacked. Examples of such incidents are reported every day in newspapers throughout this country.

3. Some introductory paragraphs are ineffective because the writer becomes too emotional and/or resorts to name-calling. (See also

"Eliminate Logical Fallacies," pages 105–106, and "Check for Tone," pages 225–226.)

Why do we even have to debate the issue of vigilante justice in this country? The bastards who roam our city streets looking for innocent victims deserve to be locked up for life! Who the hell do they think they are, anyway? And the courts? My God, only a madman would let some of those people loose! No wonder vigilante justice is making a comeback. Shoot criminals on sight, I say. Make the streets safe once again for those of us who want to follow the laws of this land.

4. Some introductory paragraphs are ineffective because the writer strikes a pretentious pose of intellectual superiority. More often than not, such introductions serve only to alienate the reader at the same time that they produce a very wordy and unfocused thesis. (See also "Eliminate Wordiness," pages 95–97, and "Eliminate Euphemisms," pages 97–99.)

The much debated, almost inflammatory issue of vigilante justice is one that deserves serious consideration by reasonable men and women concerned about inequities in our contemporary system of legal jurisprudence. Much debated, even in the most ancient of human civilizations, the issue of vigilante justice is a controversial one. It would serve us well, however, to remember that unprovoked and unwarranted violent attacks have touched the same nerve in modern men as they did in their predecessors—the Neanderthals and the Cro-Magnon men, for example. Indeed, the most instinctive, the most fundamental, the most immutable and undeniable right of *Homo sapiens* from the dawn of civilization to these unsettling moments in human history is—check me if I'm wrong—the right to protect one's physical self from extreme bodily injury or a debilitating death.

Select every word and every sentence in the introductory paragraph with great care. The success or failure of the entire essay depends on the writer's ability to narrow the topic and establish a specific focus in the introductory paragraph.

2. Paragraphs in the Body of the Essay

"Never, never, under any circumstances should a paragraph have only one sentence!
   Shape up!"

The body of the essay consists of a series of paragraphs, each of which develops a specific aspect of the thesis statement. Each paragraph in the body of the essay should contribute significantly to the thesis position and to the essay as a whole. In a 500- to 750-word expository essay, there should normally be no more than three to six paragraphs between the introduction and the conclusion.

Never develop the body of the expository essay with a series of one- and two-sentence paragraphs. Such paragraphs seldom develop a convincing argument. To the contrary, they generally create the impression that insufficient thought and research have gone into the essay topic.

Also, the paragraph in the body of the essay is a miniature essay to the extent that it takes a position and demonstrates the validity of that position through a balance of generalizations and specific supporting evidence. As miniature essays, most effective paragraphs in the body of the essay have several things in common.

1. Effective paragraphs have strong topic sentences that provide focus and direction. The topic sentence is to the paragraph what the thesis position is to the essay as a whole. Both determine what is or is not relevant to the argument. The topic sentence can appear at the end or in the middle of the paragraph, but normally it is the first sentence in the paragraph.

   Within the past decade, environmentalists and conservationists have turned their attention to the problems created by unregulated billboard advertising. Both of these groups argue that the reason it is so difficult to regulate these activities is that several billions of dollars are generated each year by this form of advertising. One of these concerned citizens, Robert Walker of Omaha, Nebraska, has said that "our rural areas are becoming uglier and uglier as everything from soda pop to toilet paper is advertised on huge billboards propped up alongside our nation's highways."

Citing example after example, he goes on to point out how the courts and most state legislatures have consistently ignored the public's rights in this area. Clearly, he reasons, there are other ways for legitimate businesses to advertise; they do not need "to destroy the scenic beauty of our rural areas."

2. Effective paragraphs have a beginning, a middle, and an end. The last sentence in a paragraph does not necessarily have to conclude or summarize the argument that has been presented, but it should give the reader some sense that the issue raised by the topic sentence has been adequately discussed.

   a. Beginning
   Within the past decade, environmentalists and conservationists have turned their attention to the problems created by unregulated billboard advertising.

   b. Middle
   Both of these groups argue that the reason it is so difficult to regulate these activities is that several billions of dollars are generated each year by this form of advertising. One of these concerned citizens, Robert Walker of Omaha, Nebraska, has said that "our rural areas are becoming uglier and uglier as everything from soda pop to toilet paper is advertised on huge billboards propped up alongside our nation's highways." Citing example after example, he goes on to point out how the courts and most state legislatures have consistently ignored the public's rights in this area.

   c. End
   Clearly, he reasons, there are other ways for legitimate businesses to advertise; they do not need "to destroy the scenic beauty of our rural areas."

3. Effective paragraphs strive for a balance between generalizations and specific supporting evidence. In the above paragraph, the quotations are the primary means of substantiation. Statistics, facts, analogies, examples, definitions, and other forms of evidence can also be used as evidence. For example, the paragraph could have been rewritten as follows:

   Within the past decade, environmentalists and conservationists have turned their attention to the problems created by unregulated billboard advertising. Both of these groups argue that the reason it is so difficult to regulate these activities is that several billions of dollars are generated each year by this form of advertising. One of these concerned citizens, Robert Walker of Omaha, Nebraska, has said that "our rural areas are becoming uglier and uglier as everything from soda pop to toilet paper is advertised on huge billboards propped up alongside our nation's highways." Through the efforts of Mr. Walker and other such environmentalists, the courts and various state legislatures have been pressured to do something about the problem. *In Idaho, for example, stricter regulatory procedures for billboard advertising went into effect last year. As was reported in several Idaho newspapers, the argument that "excessive billboard advertising is a form of environmental pollution, as damaging in its own way as air and water pollution" convinced enough of the Idaho state senators to vote for the new regulatory measures.*

Now the paragraph is substantiated through quotations, examples, and analogies.

4. Effective paragraphs develop topic sentences at some length. Note what happens if the paragraph ends after the first two sentences. In this case, the reader has a right to feel that the issue raised in the topic sentence was insufficiently developed.

   Within the past decade, environmentalists and conservationists have turned their attention to the problems created by unregulated billboard advertising. Both of these groups argue that the reason it is so difficult to regulate these activities is that several billions of dollars are generated each year by this form of advertising.

5. Effective paragraphs do not contain any information or supporting evidence that is irrelevant to the topic sentence. Note what happens to paragraph unity and coherence when the writer suddenly goes off on a tangent.

   Within the past decade, environmentalists and conservationists have turned their attention to the problems created by unregulated billboard advertising. Both of these groups argue that the reason it is so difficult to regulate these activities is that several billions of dollars are generated each year by this form of advertising. One of these concerned citizens,

Robert Walker of Omaha, Nebraska, has said that "our rural areas are becoming uglier and uglier as everything from soda pop to toilet paper is advertised on huge billboards propped up alongside our nation's highways." *And look at all the trash that people dump along our highways and freeways. Every traveler has had the experience of seeing rusty beer cans, broken bottles, and old newspapers lying in ditches.* Clearly, as Mr. Walker argues, there are other ways for legitimate businesses to advertise; they do not need "to destroy the scenic beauty of our rural areas."

6. Effective paragraphs avoid repetition. Note what happens to the flow of the argument when the writer repeats the topic sentence over and over again with slight variations. (See also "Avoid Repetition," pages 99–101.)

   Within the past decade, environmentalists and conservationists have turned their attention to the problems created by unregulated billboard advertising. Both of these groups have become more and more concerned about the absence of meaningful controls on those who use billboards to advertise their products. These unregulated activities have, for years, caused environmentalists and conservationists extreme anxiety and consternation. Meaningful controls on unregulated billboard advertising is a must in the minds of those groups that have seen fit to address themselves to the problem over the past decade.

7. Effective paragraphs have an inherent logic that is due to all of the above, but also because the writer has used transitional terms to assist the reader in moving from one sentence to the next. These "bridges" help to establish flow and movement from sentence to sentence throughout the paragraph. (See also "Provide Clear Transitions," pages 216–220, for a complete list of transitional devices.)

   Within the past decade, *environmentalists and conservationists* have turned their attention to the problems created by unregulated billboard advertising. *Both of these groups* argue that the reason it is so difficult to regulate these activities is that several billions of dollars are generated each year by this form of advertising. *One of these concerned citizens,* Robert Walker of Omaha, Nebraska, has said that "our rural areas are becoming uglier and uglier as everything from soda pop to toilet paper is advertised on huge billboards propped up alongside our nation's highways." Citing example after example, *he* goes on to point out how the courts and most state legislatures have consistently ignored the public's rights in this area. Clearly, *he* reasons, there are other ways for legitimate businesses to advertise; they do not need "to destroy the scenic beauty of our rural areas."

8. Transitions *between* paragraphs are as important as transitions *within* paragraphs. Always connect two paragraphs within the body of the essay with a word or phrase in the second that briefly refers back to a central idea discussed in the first.

Within the past decade, *environmentalists and conservationists* have turned their attention to the problems created by unregulated billboard advertising. Both of these groups argue that the reason it is so difficult to regulate these activities is that several billions of dollars are generated each year by this form of advertising. One of these concerned citizens, Robert Walker of Omaha, Nebraska, has said that "our rural areas are becoming uglier and uglier as everything from soda pop to toilet paper is advertised on huge billboards that are propped up alongside our nation's highways."

Other environmentalists and conservationists are equally adamant that something has to be done to control unregulated billboard advertising. In Iowa, for example, several small towns have started a grass-roots movement to monitor the type of billboard advertising that takes place just beyond their respective city limits. . . .

During the editing stage of the writing process, carefully reshape paragraphs in the body of the essay according to the principles described above. The end result will be a much more forceful and logically coherent essay.

3. Concluding Paragraph

"Thank God I'm finished!"

Conclusions summarize and complete the expository essay, but they do not merely repeat the introductory paragraph or thesis. Also, the conclusion is normally the shortest paragraph in the expository essay (no longer than three or four sentences) because it is a general, summarizing statement that requires no substantiating evidence. The argument has already been made in the body of the paper, or at least it should have been.

1. There are many things the writer should avoid when concluding the expository essay:

   a. Avoid introducing the conclusion with mechanical terms and phrases such as "in conclusion" or "to summarize the argument." If a transitional term is necessary, use words such as "also," "thus," or "finally." Better yet, find more innovative ways of making the transition from the body of the paper to the conclusion.

   b. Avoid introducing a new idea or argument into the conclusion. There is no time to develop it.

   c. Avoid adopting the informal "I" or "you" relationship in the conclusion unless it has been established earlier in the essay. (See also "Do Not Worry About First- and Second-Person Pronoun References," pages 33–34.)

   Now that you have read what I have written, I am sure you will agree with me that nuclear war must be avoided at all costs. Your life, my life—indeed, the lives of all people—are imperiled by this threat. I hope you will agree with me that total nuclear disarmament is the only answer.

   d. Avoid concluding the essay with an emotional outburst or a preachy, sermonizing tone. (See also "Eliminate Logical Fallacies," page 106.)

   I could weep for those poor unfortunate wretches who must sleep in cardboard boxes on cold winter nights! Why? Why? Why? Is there no compassion left among us? Is everyone so caught up in greedy, materialistic concerns that they no longer feel pity? Everybody in this country who ignores the plight of these people should be ashamed of themselves!

   e. Avoid concluding the essay with platitudes and clichés. Generally, they serve only to insult the reader's intelligence at the very point that the writer is engaged in a final attempt to enlist the reader's support for the position that is being advocated in the essay. (See also "Eliminate Clichés," pages 101–104, and "Eliminate Logical Fallacies," page 105.)

It has been said that "the pen is mightier than the sword," and that is certainly the case here. Without tooting my horn too loudly, it can safely be said that the above argument should touch the hearts of all men, no matter their race, religion, or the color of their skin. Anyone who might think otherwise just can't be playing with a full deck.

2. Good conclusions are such an intrinsic part of the essays they summarize that it is somewhat artificial to wrench them out of context and present them as examples of effective summarizing statements. Nonetheless, most good conclusions have several things in common:

   a. They create a sense of unity and coherence by subtly returning the reader's attention to the thesis statement and introductory paragraph.

   b. They summarize the major points in the body of the essay and emphasize the importance of these ideas.

   c. They emphasize the magnitude of the problem and predict the consequences if no solution is forthcoming.

   d. They adopt a tone that is compatible with the body of the essay. (See also "Check for Tone," pages 225–226.)

EXAMPLES OF EFFECTIVE CONCLUSIONS

1. The abuse of language in today's society is not only annoying but potentially dangerous. Hitler and other dictators clearly rose to power by utilizing language and manipulating it as an instrument for concealing and preventing thought. As the illiteracy rate continues to rise dramatically in America, everyone should keep this in mind. The very real possibility exists that language could also be used in this country as an instrument of political suppression.
2. Today's young people obviously do not trust in the appearance of things. They have experienced enough charades, deceptions, and political scenarios, staged for the benefit of the media, to make them cynical of much

that they see and hear. Yet they clearly yearn for, and would support, political leaders who are honest with them—leaders who are more concerned with the issues than with the way they comb their hair.

Recognizing that conclusions are difficult to write, some writers solve the problem, at least in their own minds, by refusing to write them. *Always have a conclusion.* Your reader was kind enough to go sailing with you; do not throw him overboard and sail home alone.

Think about your conclusions. Go out in style, like a ship fading gracefully into the sunset, not like one with broken masts and limp sails sinking on the horizon.

4. Editing Paragraphs: All Forms

One of the perplexities of the editing process is that, although it is possible to isolate and discuss *individual* problems in sentences and paragraphs, those same problems seldom come to us so clearly defined. Rather, they tend to come in bunches, often hopelessly entangled in one another. Nonetheless, at this stage in the editing process, it is important to train the eye to see the major subdivisions in the paragraph, while, at the same time, temporarily ignoring details such as word choices and spelling.

When editing and revising individual paragraphs, try to concentrate on the larger word groupings (i.e., complete sentences or significant parts of sentences). Focus all of your attention on eliminating sentences and expressions that disturb paragraph unity and coherence, and adding sentences that are necessary to develop the paragraph adequately. Specific word choices, with the possible exception of some refinements of the thesis position and some clearly inappropriate expressions, can be edited *after* you decide which sentences are to remain in the paragraph.

For example, note how the writer of the following paragraphs concentrates on the larger word groupings before moving on to the more detailed editorial work:

C 4

EXAMPLE: EDITING THE INTRODUCTORY PARAGRAPH

Going to the movies and staying home to watch television are two of America's favorite past times. They are common ways for many people to escape from their everyday problems and move in and out of their fantasies. After a busy day of work, there is nothing easier than relaxing on a couch, eating popcorn, and watching an entertaining movie on television. This may seem innocent enough, but

and is affected adversely by them?

what happens when one sees violent movies and is 😐

affected like John Hinckley. He saw a movie about a character trying to impress a girl by assassinating the President and in turn tried to make that fantasy come true for himself. Granted, movies and television can be great relaxing entertainers, but after the case of John Hinckley, one is required to believe that violent shows do adversely effect the people who watch them often enough.

Specific examples introduced too early. Eliminate or move to the body of the essay.

Does the public need to fear the affects of television on the minds of their viewers? Steps must be taken to reduce the types of violence of violence depicted on television and in films or else America is doomed.

EXAMPLE: EDITING PARAGRAPHS IN THE BODY OF THE ESSAY

Movies, on the other hand, do not reach as large an audience as television, and they also show more sex and violent situations. President Nixon, during his term of office, asked sociologists to perform a series of tests explaining the overall effect of pornographic movies on the public. The results were not significant enough to report, but this also concluded that people were being influenced, and somebody was in fact trying to initiate action against them. As was stated before, and need not be overstated, was the case of John Hinckley. He enacted his fantasy after seeing the movie Taxi Driver which involved a young prostitute. Another movie, The Wall, depicts violence, and its theme is violence in a violent world. This movie is geared on affecting the human senses, but what will happen if someone cannot handle these reactions? And the recent television

Unity. Eliminate, develop as a separate ¶, or move to a ¶ that focuses on this specific issue.

movies are even worse, bringing violence right
into our living rooms as they do. Again the
question arises, will the public have to fear its
affects? Necessary steps must be taken to reduce
these types of movies, and critics should try to
discourage the public from viewing them.

EXAMPLE: EDITING THE CONCLUDING PARAGRAPH

Violence as shows in both television and movies
must be heavily reduced. The screening and rating
of such shows must be made harder to pass. Take,
for example, the recent horror films that in spite
of all the violence, received PG ratings. It is up
to the reader to answer the previous questions and
decide what should or should not be done about
such shows. The last thing to be stated is, does
the public really need to be afraid of the affects
of the violence depicted in movies and on
television on the minds of it's viewers? Is it true
that we really have that much to fear from
violence on television and films? The evidence is
overwhelming. Yes, we do!

*Conclusion.
Should
not
introduce
new issues
and
examples.
Eliminate or
move to the
body of the
essay.*

D

Editing Sentences: A Brief

Review of English Grammar

"Grammar is a form of medieval torture that survived into the twentieth century. Those who were 'sentenced to death by grammar' didn't die—they just sounded that way for the rest of their lives."

Few students object to the idea that organization, paragraphing, and the other larger concerns of the writing and editing process are important considerations. Some, however, think that detailed attention to the grammatical principles that govern word choices, sentence structure, and punctuation are busywork more than anything else—something of concern to teachers and professors but certainly not to anyone outside of the academic community.

Are sentence structure, punctuation, word choices, and the other principles of English grammar so important in everything we write? Rather than answering that question directly, let us look at how the following grammatical lapses distorted the ideas certain writers were trying to express in their respective essays, business letters, and other forms of written communication:

1. Proofreading lapses

My Aunt Margaret would never dream of moving away from her small town, but when she comes to the city she loves to *hop* at the downtown malls.

[Unless "s" is added to create the word "shop," the reader is going to assume that Aunt Margaret is a rabbit.]

2. Dangling modifier

   Before sending the mourners scurrying back to their cars, Frank Simpson was eulogized at a graveside ceremony as a violent storm suddenly swept across the area.

   [Frank Simpson, the deceased, sent the mourners back to their cars?]

3. Inappropriate cliché

   We must continue to learn what we can from the past. History is, and always will be, the greatest of teachers. However, since *you can only squeeze so much blood out of a turnip,* we must never trust that a knowledge of history will always guide us safely into the future.

   [History is a turnip?]

4. Inappropriate repetition and vague pronoun reference

   The Civil War, *which* started in 1861 and *which* ended in 1865, was fought while Abraham Lincoln was president, *which* was a very troublesome thing for him to deal with.

5. Run-on sentence

   We have adjusted your brakes as per factory specifications, and we can guarantee that your car will now *stop occasionally,* these problems are more complicated than first anticipated.

   [A good brake job—the car now stops occasionally!]

Certainly, I think we can all agree that a knowledge of English grammar would have helped most of these writers express their ideas more effectively. Quite simply, there are some basic grammatical principles that writers cannot afford to overlook without hopelessly confusing their readers.

Still, I am sure most of us have opened a handbook on grammar only to encounter a sentence much like the following:

   When the nominative predicate is joined to the subjunctive predicate nominative by a coordinating conjunctive adverb, the result is clearly a compound sentence of dubious grammatical origins.

Granted, this is a deliberate exaggeration of grammatical terminology, but it is not that far removed from the language used in many grammar books.

Clearly, students do not need to know this kind of technical jargon to become effective writers and editors. But a brief familiarity with the following grammatical terms can help to define and explain most problems in sentence structure and punctuation:

1. Words

1. *Subject:* The most important word or words in every sentence. The subject is the person, place, or thing involved in the action.

   Example: **John** walked slowly across the narrow street.

2. *Verb:* The action word in the sentence

   Example: John **walked** slowly across the narrow street.

3. *Adverb:* A word that gives us some specific detail about a verb, adjective, or another adverb

   Example: John walked **slowly** across the narrow street.

4. *Adjective:* A word that gives us some specific detail about a person, place, or thing in the sentence

   Example: John walked slowly across the **narrow** street.

5. *Noun:* A person, place, or thing in the sentence

   Example: John walked slowly across the narrow **street.** *[The subject, "John" is also a noun.]*

6. *Object:* The noun or pronoun the verb acts upon in some sentences

   Example: John kicked a **can** as he walked slowly across the narrow street.

7. *Pronoun:* The word that is substituted occasionally for a noun.

   Example: John kicked a can as **he** walked slowly across the narrow street.

8. *Antecedent:* The word the pronoun replaces. Normally, the antecedent is also the subject of the sentence.

Example: **John** kicked a can as he walked slowly across the narrow street.

9. *Preposition:* The word that generally establishes the location of a noun or pronoun in space and/or time

   Example: John kicked a can as he walked slowly **across** the narrow street.

10. *Object of the preposition:* The noun or pronoun that follows the preposition

    Example: John kicked a can as he walked slowly across the narrow **street.**

11. *Coordinating conjunction:* The word that links other words or word groupings together

    Example: John kicked a can **and** hummed softly to himself as he walked slowly across the narrow street to meet Barbara.

12. *Modifier:* The word, phrase, or clause that gives us more detailed information about other words and expressions. All of the following words in bold print are modifiers.

    Example: John kicked a can and hummed **softly** to himself as he walked **slowly** across the **narrow** street to meet Barbara.

13. *Parenthetical expression:* The expression that interrupts the normal flow of a sentence to provide a transition, interjection, explanation, or cause-effect relationship

    Example: Not paying any attention to what was going on around him, John was, **thus,** run over by an extremely old man on a ten-speed bike.

2. Word Groupings

1. *Independent clause:* Another term for a complete sentence. An independent clause can stand alone.

   Example: John walked slowly across the narrow street. *[This is a sentence, but it is also an independent clause.]*

2. *Dependent clause:* An incomplete thought introduced by words such as "when," "who," "what," "which," and "that." A dependent clause must be connected to an independent clause to form a complete sentence.

Example: When John walked slowly across the narrow street. . . . *[The word* "when" *makes this a dependent clause—it cannot stand alone.]*

3. *Phrase:* Similar to a dependent clause except that a phrase does not have a subject and verb. The following are the four most common phrases:

   a. A prepositional phrase is a word grouping introduced by a word that normally determines a noun's location in time and space (*over the mountain, under the car, around the corner,* and so on).

   b. An infinitive phrase is a word grouping introduced by the word "to" plus a verb (*to walk downtown, to sing poorly,* and so on).

   c. A participial phrase is a word grouping introduced by a verb with an *"-ing"* or *"-ed"* ending (*running the race, walking the dog, parked on the corner,* and so on).

   d. An appositive is a phrase that renames or relabels a noun.

   Example: (John, *my very best friend,* is now in the hospital recuperating from his injuries).

   [Note: A phrase must be connected to an independent clause to form a complete sentence.]

   Example: Humming softly to himself, John walked slowly across the narrow street to meet Barbara, his very best friend.

4. *Simple sentence:* A sentence containing one independent clause

   Example: John walked slowly across the narrow street.

5. *Complex sentence:* A sentence containing one independent clause and one or more dependent clauses

   Example: As John walked slowly across the narrow street, he kicked a can and hummed softly to himself.

6. *Compound sentence:* A sentence containing two independent clauses that are joined together by a coordinating conjunction

Example: John failed to watch the oncoming traffic, and he was run over by an extremely old man on a ten-speed bike.

Other grammatical terms will be introduced throughout the course of this text, but the above definitions provide sufficient background for a meaningful discussion of most problems in sentence structure and punctuation.

E

Eliminating Ineffective

Sentences and Expressions

Once the essay has been adequately developed and organized and individual paragraphs have been edited and revised, most writers devote some time to eliminating clearly ineffective sentences and expressions. Excessively wordy sentences, repetitive phrases and clauses, clichés, and other such expressions should be edited out of the essay before any attempt is made to establish sentence completeness and organize sentence structures.

It is important to remember that just about everything we do in life involves a stage during which we must devote some time to simply "cleaning up our work areas." Indeed, if we fail to remove the "clutter" that surrounds us, our various projections can become hopelessly confusing and perhaps even impossible to complete.

For example, once we have marked off the boundaries of a garden and have established the rows in which the individual seeds are to be planted, we might devote some time to removing the remaining rocks and other debris from the area. Similarly, once a house has been constructed, contractors will devote some time to pounding in the exposed nails, scraping off the spilled plaster, and sanding down the rough surfaces on the walls before proceeding to paint and wallpaper the individual rooms. The reason gardeners, contractors, and other skilled workers devote some time to "cleaning up their respective work areas" is very simple. In the long run, it not only saves much time and energy, but it also guarantees that their efforts will produce quality products.

The same can be said for writers. If writers learn to clean the "clutter" out of their sentences at this point in the editing process, they will generally find that it takes much less time and energy to write quality drafts. Conversely, if their sentences remain cluttered with excessively wordy statements, repetitive phrases and clauses, and other ineffective expressions, they will often find that they have to retrace their steps and do much of the editorial work over again. (One obvious reason is that it is almost impossible to establish the logical word sequences in sentences until the unnecessary words have been eliminated.)

At the same time, it is important for writers to remember that they should not pay too much attention to individual word choices at this point—unless, of course, these word choices are clearly inappropriate.

Go for the big stuff—phrases, clauses, and other word groupings that clutter up sentences and paragraphs!

1. Eliminate Wordiness

"After giving the next question considerable thought, I have con-cluded—since over the years as a teacher I have become somewhat of a minor authority on this subject and can speak with some degree of certainty about it, having made it one of my life's interests—that excessive wordiness is confusing."

Wordiness is epidemic in the twentieth century. Politicians, lawyers, teachers, businessmen—everyone occasionally resorts to a writing style that is both pretentious and excessively wordy. And generally we do so because wordiness makes us sound impressive, conceals our true intentions, and camouflages our muddled thinking.

There *is* a place for wordiness in the writing process, but that place is in the early drafts, when the writer is trying to generate ideas. At that point, wordiness is actually a good sign because it indicates that the writer has too many ideas—so many, in fact, that they cannot be contained within the perimeters established by the individual sentences.

Such a wealth of ideas, once properly organized and edited, should lead to a much stronger essay. Wordiness becomes a problem only when the writer fails to remove unnecessary sentences and expressions from the later drafts. (See also "Write Too Much Rather Than Too Little," page 34.)

The part of our society most responsible for such prose is the academic community, so let us take our examples this time from an administrative memorandum, two scholarly essays, and a student essay.

An Administrative Memorandum

The growth factors in a multifaceted institution demand that contingency preparations be made in those areas that involve the least practical serviceability to the organization as a whole. Furthermore, we must consider the market feasibility of expanding our existing operations into more profit-oriented areas.

Revision

Since your enrollments are down, we are going to close your department to make room for the new School of Business.

A Scholarly Essay

The situational ethics that evolved out of the post-Watergate morality has its philosophical roots in the Kantian theory of Truth, which perceives reality as a continuous state of flux wherein subject and object are no longer intrinsically related through what we know as the "act of cognition" but, rather, are nebulously postulated in congruity with, or in juxtaposition to, one another.

Revision

The situational ethics that evolved out of the post-Watergate morality has its philosophical roots in the Kantian theory of Truth. This idea suggests that ethical values are not permanent but, rather, change from experience to experience.

Another Scholarly Essay

The personification of human discourse, predicated as it has been upon the insatiable desire to communicate symbolically, transcends ordinary terrestrial existence, elevating *Homo sapiens* closer to Plato's "Realm of the Universals."

Revision

The symbolic use of language enables humans to rise above earthly concerns and experience universal truths.

A Student Essay

The primary function of language is to humanize the human race. It was when people first put pen to paper—or, rather, when they first scratched messages to posterity on the walls of a cave—that these apelike creatures became human. That was the dawn of humanity.

Revision

This excerpt speaks for itself. It is clear, direct, and immediately accessible. It is the only example that tries to communicate an idea in plain English.

Eliminate excessive wordiness from all sentences. Strive for a style that is direct and immediately accessible to the reader.

2. Eliminate Euphemisms

"Avoid euphemisms. These strategic verbal manipulators only serve to clutter up your sentences."

Euphemisms are verbose, sometimes deliberately deceptive phrases and statements that are frequently associated with the language of bureaucrats. Euphemisms are generally used by these people to conceal and prevent thought and communication—often for personal gain.

Euphemisms tend to create two very serious problems for most writers. Like all wordy expressions, they make the editing process more complicated than it need be, primarily because their very purpose is to create ambiguity and confusion. Second, euphemisms distort the very function of language because they enable the writer to avoid real communication at the same time that they deliberately mislead the reader.

Euphemisms	**Plain English**
1. A debilitating vehicular confrontation	1. A minor traffic accident
2. A transparent-wall maintenance engineer	2. A window cleaner
3. Preowned cars	3. Used cars
4. Low nutrient-per-calorie-density foods	4. Junk foods
5. Relocation of population	5. Forced death marches

Some euphemisms are inoffensive enough, although they are nonetheless annoying. For example, an apology for "the inconvenience" seems hardly appropriate when one has been waiting for several hours for an airplane to depart. Other euphemisms even serve a necessary social function. We would not rush up to someone and blurt out, "Sorry to hear your grandfather's dead." At a time when people are grieving over the loss of a loved one, it serves no purpose to be so callously blunt and direct. Instead we might say, "I'm sorry to hear your grandfather passed away." The euphemism "passed away" softens the remark and enables the mourners to establish a necessary emotional distance between themselves and their loss.

Other euphemisms are unintentionally humorous because of the writer's pretentious attempts to make something unimportant sound terribly important. For example, "rejected biodegradable food by-products" (garbage) is a term used to further enhance the stature of "sanitary engineers" (garbage collectors). And the military can be charged more for an "upper-level, decorative waste-removal feature" and a "manually operated, suction-inducing apparatus" than it can for a common "toilet seat" and "plunger."

Most writers of euphemisms, however, have far more duplicitous and insidious motives. For example, Soviet dissidents are sent to "political reeducation centers," not to psychiatric hospitals where they will be administered painful, mind-altering drugs. Similarly, "reinforcers for behavior modification" are more acceptable than the common instruments of torture utilized by some governments to subjugate their political opposition.

Unfortunately, when euphemisms are used this way, they deaden the sensibilities and justify morally and ethically reprehensible actions. The immoral becomes moral, the unacceptable becomes acceptable, and the intolerable becomes tolerable. It is for all of these reasons that George Orwell argued so fervently against the euphemistic use of language in his classic essay, "Politics and the English Language."

Similarly, students should avoid euphemisms in the expository essay. Euphemisms, by their very nature, undermine the objectives of expository writing (i.e., to explain and persuade through logic, clear prose, and solid evidence). Instead, euphemisms seek to mislead the reader through language that is deliberately imprecise and deceptive.

For all of these reasons, eliminate euphemisms from your sentences and paragraphs, and rewrite them in plain English.

3. Avoid Repetition

"Repetition is annoying, you know, because the argument can't possibly develop, you know, if the repetition makes the reader feel like he's inside an empty oil drum, you know, and someone is beating on it with a two-by-four—if you know what I mean?"

Avoid unnecessary repetition of words, phrases, sounds, ideas, sentence structures, or synonyms. Unnecessary repetition (also known as "redundancy") sets up an annoying and monotonous rhythm that tends to work against, rather than with, the meaning of the sentence.

Unnecessary Repetition	Revision
1. My *friend* Julia is the *friendliest* person I have ever known, and her *friendship* is most dear to me.	1. Julia is one of the *kindest* people I have ever known, and her *friendship* is most dear to me.
2. *Torn and worn* after 3 days of *mourning* over her low LSAT scores, my sister *warned* me never to aspire to be a lawyer.	2. *Tired and exhausted* after 3 days of *mourning* over her low LSAT scores, my sister *urged* me never to aspire to be a lawyer.

Unnecessary Repetition	Revision
3. The *person drowning* struggled in the arms of the *person trying to save him,* but the riptides tore the *person drowning* from the *person trying to save him,* and the *person drowning drowned.*	3. The *drowning man* struggled in the arms of the *lifeguard* who was trying to save him, but the riptides tore the *victim* from the *lifeguard's* grasp and pulled *him* back out to sea.
4. In *this country of ours, this great nation known as America,* everything has become *so immense and large in size,* the individual feels *alienated* and *unable to relate to other people.*	4. In *America,* everything has become so *large and overwhelming* that the individual often feels *alienated* from other people.
5. *Human persons* must all learn to act with a sense of moral and ethical responsibility.	5. *People* must all learn to act with a sense of moral and ethical responsibility.
6. *There are ways* to study for exams. *There are ways* to make good grades. *There are ways* to excel in extracurricular activities.	6. *There are ways* to study for exams, make good grades, and excel in extracurricular activities.

Occasionally, skillful repetition can be used to emphasize a major point. In *The Fire Next Time,* for example, James Baldwin has one sentence in which he repeats the pronoun ''we'' five times:

> What it comes to is that if we, who can scarcely be considered a white nation, persist in thinking of ourselves as one, we condemn ourselves, with the truly white nations, to sterility and decay, whereas if we could accept ourselves as we are, we might bring new life to the Western achievements, and transform them.

The repetition in this sentence sets up a haunting refrain that reinforces the point Baldwin is trying to make, namely, that America cannot afford to be a divided nation of blacks and whites. It must learn to act and speak with one voice—the ''we'' that echoes throughout the sentence.

Somewhat later in *The Fire Next Time,* Baldwin creates a powerful, accelerating rhythm by using six uninterrupted participial phrases in the same sentence:

> It is very hard to believe that those men and women [the early black slaves], raising their children, eating their greens, crying their curses, weeping their tears, singing their songs, making their love as the sun rose, as the sun set, were in any way inferior to the white men and women who crept over to share these splendors after the sun went down.

In the hands of a lesser writer, this sentence might have sounded both monotonous and redundant. However, once again the repetition is appropriate to the point Baldwin is trying to make, namely, that the black slaves who were engaged in "eating," "crying," "weeping," "singing," "raising their children," and "making their love" were infinitely more human than those who had enslaved them.

Remember that repetition should normally be avoided. If it seems necessary to repeat a word, phrase, or clause, make certain the strategy reinforces, rather than undermines, the meaning of the sentence.

(See also "Paragraphs in the Body of the Essay," page 80, and "Check for Style and Variety in Sentence Structures," pages 223–225.)

4. Eliminate Clichés

"Avoid clichés. You can only squeeze so much blood out of a turnip, and they've been squeezed enough."

Clichés are worn-out or obsolete figures of speech that are no longer effective because most readers have heard them so often the meanings they express seem commonplace, trite, and boring.

EXAMPLES

1. Get something off your chest
2. A bolt out of the blue
3. A picture is worth a thousand words.

4. You can only squeeze so much blood out of a turnip.
5. Snatching victory from the jaws of defeat
6. The grass is always greener.
7. Cool as a cucumber
8. The road to hell is paved with good intentions.
9. A penny saved is a penny earned.
10. We must tighten our belts.
11. Blind as a bat
12. The early bird catches the worm.

Years ago, when I was teaching one of my first writing courses, I learned how dangerous an inappropriate cliché could be in certain situations. I had just assigned an essay on the theme of women's liberation, and I was explaining to the class that "although it is an emotional issue, I nonetheless want you to use clear prose, logic, and evidence to support whatever position you choose to take on the subject." Glancing around the room, I sensed that many of the students had not understood my instructions, and so I added, "What I'm trying to say is that I want you to be objective. I don't want you to use the essay assignment as just another excuse for *getting something off your chest.*" As the room filled with laughter, I suddenly realized that I had selected the most inappropriate (and embarrassing) cliché imaginable to summarize this specific essay topic.

Inappropriate clichés, especially when they are used to summarize profound ideas, can destroy an argument.

EXAMPLES

1. People have always searched for the ultimate meaning to human existence, and nowhere is this reflected more clearly than in Scripture. Jonah, Moses, Job, and countless other biblical figures spent much of their time searching for the Almighty. And *like the early bird that catches the worm,* they all found him.
2. Death is the great, dark void that separates this world from the next. It is the impenetrable veil, the shroud of darkness, the unfathomable mystery . . . . So, *blind as bats,* we continue to search for the answers.

Normally, the best thing to do with most clichés is to rewrite them in plain English.

Original	Revision
1. After Ann tried for many years to sell her watercolors, success finally came to her *like a bolt out of the blue.*	1. After Ann tried for many years to sell her watercolors, success finally came to her *suddenly and unexpectedly.*
2. They *tightened their belts* in every conceivable way in order to pay off their creditors.	2. They *budgeted and economized* in every conceivable way in order to pay off their creditors.
3. Hoping that the *grass might be greener* in California, the Joad family in Steinbeck's *The Grapes of Wrath* loaded all of their belongings into the back of a pickup truck and drove west.	3. Hoping that *they might find a better life in California,* the Joad family in Steinbeck's *The Grapes of Wrath* loaded all of their belongings into the back of a pickup truck and drove west.

Sometimes clichés can be effective if the writer gives them a clever twist for rhetorical effect.

EXAMPLES

1. A penny saved is a penny lost to inflation.
2. Continuing its losing ways, Carson College once again snatched defeat from the jaws of victory when it committed a crucial turnover on the last play of the game.
3. Many of us live today from hand to mouth—our hands, the government's mouth.
4. If the road to hell is paved with good intentions, hopefully it will make the traveling easier for the people who invented the federal income tax forms.
5. Where there is a will there is a way. But often as we grow older, we come to realize that even when there is a way, there is not always the will to pursue it.

Clichés tend to create two very serious problems in the writer-reader relationship. They often undermine perfectly serious expressions and reduce them to the level of the ludicrous. And they send a signal to the reader that the writer's mind is no longer actively engaged in his or her efforts. A cliché is, thus, like a straight line streaking across an encephalogram. It creates the impression that all mental activity has ceased in the mind of the writer.

Eliminate all clichés unless they can be used imaginatively. Find new, livelier, and more direct ways to express these ideas.

(See also "Concluding Paragraph," pages 82–83, and "Eliminate Logical Fallacies," page 105.)

5. Eliminate Logical Fallacies

"All writers are neurotic. I am somewhat neurotic myself. Therefore, I must be a writer."

Even though some sentences and paragraphs are grammatically correct, they may be weak or confusing because they contain illogical statements. There are sophisticated Latin terms for these logical fallacies, but the important thing is to learn to recognize and eliminate absurd or misleading statements when we see them. Otherwise, these logical fallacies will tend to "clutter up" our sentences and paragraphs, thus making our jobs as writers and editors much more difficult.

Common sense and careful editing procedures can help us to identify and eliminate most logical fallacies. For example, when asked to demonstrate their knowledge of the various logical fallacies by deliberately writing some sentences that contained faulty logic, the students in one of my writing classes responded as follows:

1. Avoid faulty cause-effect relationships.

   Since medical-malpractice lawsuits have increased dramatically over the past decade, it seems obvious that doctors are not as careful as they used to be.

   [There are many other possible explanations: there are more operations, people are more aware of their legal rights, lawyers are encouraging people to file such lawsuits, we live in a society that is obsessed with litigation, and so on.]

2. Avoid statements that have hidden meanings and implications.

One way to end the problem of overcrowded prisons is to execute everyone who breaks the law.

[A parking ticket could get you the electric chair.]

3. Avoid leaping to hasty or overly simplified solutions, conclusions, and generalizations.

Since many scientists are predicting that we will run out of our major sources of energy by the end of this century, it seems clear that something drastic must be done. One way to conserve energy would be to pass a law requiring everyone to turn off their lights and go to bed by 7 o'clock. But, of course, that might add to the problem of overpopulation.

4. Avoid misleading or inappropriate analogies.

The arms race has to stop, or one day we will all wake up to find the planet earth blowing smoke rings at the moon.

5. Avoid mixing metaphors, analogies, and clichés. (See also "Eliminate Clichés," pages 101–104, and "Concluding Paragraph," pages 82–83.)

We are far too sensitive in this country to the problem of racial prejudice. If the newspapers and television networks would just stop focusing so much attention on it, the problem would eventually go away. Remember, America is "the great melting pot of nations," but "a watched pot never boils."

6. Avoid hopelessly jumbled syntax and logic.

God made Eve out of Adam's rib. He didn't make her out of his head; then she'd be superior because Adam would have no brain. He didn't make her out of his foot because then Adam wouldn't be able to walk, and she'd have to carry him. So God made Eve out of Adam's rib, which means she's equal.

7. Avoid statements that do not logically follow one another.

She was an extremely virtuous woman. All three of her lovers made statements to that effect in court.

8. Avoid name calling. (See also "Check for Tone," pages 225–226, and "Introductory Paragraph," pages 75–76.)

In order to motivate students, a firm grading standard must be established in every high school and college in this country. The theory that one can "grade by objectives" is *assinine.*

[The sharp break in tone here would serve only to undermine a serious argument.]

9. Avoid arguments to authority.

Everyone knows that her editorial on deficit spending appeared in almost all the major newspapers in this country, so her position on the issue must be valid.

[Many things that are printed are not valid.]

10. Avoid appeals to emotion. (See also "Introductory Paragraph," pages 75–76, and "Concluding Paragraph," page 82.)

We must sympathize with the central character in Stephen King's latest novel. Never mind that he bores holes through people's bodies just by closing one eye and looking at them with the other eye. He came from a very poor home. He never had enough to eat. His life was wretched—wretched, I tell you! And, oh, the loss of his mother when she tried to wipe a bug out of one of his eyes with a handkerchief! Small wonder that we should sympathize with his psychopathic tendencies later in life!

11. Avoid begging the question with terms that are inappropriate and/or not adequately defined. (See also "Check for Tone," pages 225–226.)

His support of the United States government's policies in the Middle East proves that he is a *chauvinistic warmonger.* Those policies are *jingoistic,* reminiscent of the terribly destructive *fascist mentality* of another era.

[To be fair to the person and the position being described here, the italicized terms need to be clarified.]

12. Avoid placing false limitations on choices.

Noah probably only had two choices as he finished loading the ark. He could have taken the unicorns, but that would have meant leaving his wife and children behind. Fortunately, he decided to take his wife and family instead. Otherwise, today there would be no human race, and the world would be populated by unicorns.

[There were many other animals—skunks, rats, noisy dogs, and so on—that might have gone overboard to make room for the unicorns. It was simply a <u>bad choice</u> on Noah's part, but it was not the <u>only choice</u> open to him.]

13. Avoid trying to pass off falsehoods and distortions of the truth as facts.

No one should ever invest money in the stock market. It is much too risky. Besides, no one has made any money in the stock market since the 1920s.

[This is clearly untrue. Playing the stock market is, indeed, "risky," but many people have made money at it in the decades following the 1920s.]

14. Avoid avoiding the issue.

Senator Fitzpatrick is certainly not the one to advocate drastic revisions in the federal tax code. His wife left him two years ago, he was a barber before he ran for the Senate, and last year he was picked up for drunken driving after a party in a Washington suburb.

[None of these details about Senator Fitzpatrick's personal life is relevant to his position on tax reform.]

OR

Senator Fitzpatrick is advocating that "the federal income tax forms be greatly simplified." How can any responsible public official argue for a complete abolition of the income tax structure? No civilization could survive without some meaningful form of taxation.

[This is a distortion of Senator Fitzpatrick's position; he is arguing that the tax forms be <u>simplified</u>, not that taxes be <u>abolished</u> altogether.]

Carefully scrutinize individual sentences and paragraphs to eliminate all logical fallacies. Logical fallacies not only clutter up sentences and paragraphs, but they can also destroy an argument a writer may have labored long and hard to put together.

6. Eliminating Ineffective Expressions: All Forms

The following paragraph illustrates a variety of problems with wordiness, euphemisms, repetition, clichés, and faulty logic. Note how the revised version is tightened up considerably when these expressions are eliminated. Notice also how much easier it is for the writer to identify the remaining editorial problems (inappropriate word sequences, word choices, and so on) once the clutter is removed from this paragraph.

ORIGINAL

All people who go to the movies act out their
fantasies later one way or another. But ~~film~~

Euph   *people*
~~aficionados~~ with psychological problems ~~or who~~

    ~~suffer from schizophrenic or psychopathic~~   *Rep*

    ~~tendencies~~ seem to be more vulnerable to harmful

movies. These types of movies ~~and films~~ are   *Rep*

thriller, violent crime, and hard-core

pornography. Mostly these unstable, ~~excessively~~

    ~~and psychologically imbalanced~~ types are prone to   *Wdy/rep*

violence anyway, but what movies tell them is that

"it is okay to act out these bizarre fantasies."

Unstable
  People ~~who aren't playing with a full deck~~ cannot   *Clic*
 ∧

always tell the difference between what is real

and what is not. Take, for example, the case of

John Hinckley, the man who tried to assassinate

President Reagan. All of the newspapers that

reported on the incident indicated that he was

motivated to do this horrible thing when he became

obsessed with the film Taxi Driver. *Although* ~~so there must~~ *Log*

this is only one case, it does prove that violent movies can

~~be something to the idea that films can cause~~

motivate some people to

~~people to~~ commit violent acts. But still, in spite

of the overwhelming evidence that violence-prone

personalities

Rep ~~personality and character types~~ are influenced

negatively by whatever it is they see ~~on the~~ | *Euph*

in America's movie theaters,

~~silver screen across this great country of~~ | *Wdy*

oblivious

~~America~~ our society still remains ~~blind as bats~~ | *Clic*

to what must be done to solve this problem.

REVISION

Many people who go to the movies act out their
fantasies later one way or another. But people with
psychological problems seem to be more vulnerable to
harmful movies. These types of movies are thrillers,
violent crime, and hard-core pornography. Mostly these
unstable types are prone to violence anyway, but what
movies tell them is that ''it is okay to act out these
bizarre fantasies.'' Unstable people cannot always tell
the difference between what is real and what is not.
Take, for example, the case of John Hinckley, the man who
tried to assassinate President Reagan. All of the

newspapers that reported on the incident indicated that
he was motivated to do this horrible thing when he became
obsessed with the film <u>Taxi Driver</u>. Although this is only
one case, it does prove that violent movies can motivate
some people to commit violent acts. But still, in spite
of the overwhelming evidence that violence–prone
personalities are influenced negatively by whatever it is
they see in America's movie theaters, our society still
remains oblivious to what must be done to solve this
problem.

F

Establishing Sentence

Completeness

Once wordiness, repetitive phrases and clauses, clichés, and other clearly ineffective expressions have been eliminated, writers will often discover that what is left is a series of incomplete and/or run-on sentences. For this reason, most writers make it a point to reestablish some preliminary sentence boundaries at this stage in the editing process. That is, they concentrate on blending, merging, and dividing the remaining words and word groupings into complete units. The reason for employing such a strategy is again very simple. Before deciding on the most appropriate word sequences for their respective sentences, writers need to have some sense of precisely which words will or will not be included in those same sentences.

The writer, in this respect, is proceeding in much the same manner as many other skilled workers. The house painter, for example, will use masking tape to separate the windows and the fireplace from the walls of a room that are about to be painted. Without such clearly defined boundaries, the painter would find it almost impossible to complete the project. Similarly, before planting seeds, the gardener determines precisely where the various rows of the garden will begin and end. Otherwise, it would be impossible for the gardener to complete the work in an orderly fashion.

Writers are confronted with much the same problem. They, too, must establish some preliminary boundaries for their sentences if they are to be at all successful in shaping them into coherent units. Many grammatical lapses, we must remember, can be concealed from even the most experienced editors unless they are working with complete sentences.

At the same time, it is important to remember that the process of blending, merging, and dividing sentences into complete units does not end here. Indeed, it continues throughout the editing process as the meaning of the essay is discovered and clarified.

1. Avoid Sentence Fragments

"Concerning these long phrases and clauses that turn out in the end to be nothing more than sentence fragments."

A fragmentary sentence, one that lacks either a subject or a verb, is normally created when the writer mistakenly assumes that a phrase or a dependent clause is an independent clause. Fragmentary sentences can be corrected by attaching them to, or rewriting them as, independent clauses. (See also "Editing Sentences: A Brief Review of English Grammar," pages 91–93, and "Periods," page 168.)

1. Infinitive, participial, and prepositional phrases are not complete sentences.

Fragment

1. *To make the most of a difficult situation.* [This is an infinitive phrase.]
2. *Wanting more out of life.* [This is a participial phrase.]
3. *On the other side of the horizon.* [These are prepositional phrases.]

Complete Sentence

1. *To make the most of a difficult situation,* one must start with a positive attitude.
2. *Wanting more out of life,* Martha quit her job as a banker and booked a flight to Europe.
3. There must be something more exciting *on the other side of the horizon.*

2. Dependent clauses are not complete sentences.

Fragment	**Complete Sentence**
1. *Who writes books for a living.*	1. Anyone *who writes books for a living* knows that it involves much hard work and very little security.
2. *While the baby screamed and the pot roast burned in the oven.*	2. *While the baby screamed and the pot roast burned in the oven,* the young mother wondered why she had turned down that job as a sales representative.

3. Appositives are not complete sentences.

Fragment	**Complete Sentence**
A man of high ethical and moral principles.	Reverend Meyers, *a man of high ethical and moral principles,* resigned from his parish to assist with missionary work in the remote jungles of Africa.

4. Occasionally, sentence fragments can be used to emphasize major points, but, more often than not, they are the result of sloppy editing.

An Acceptable Sentence Fragment

It has been estimated that one American dollar could feed the average Ethiopian for as much as a month. *A small price to pay for a human life, certainly!*

An Unacceptable Sentence Fragment

It has been estimated that one American dollar could feed the average Ethiopian for as much as a month. This is certainly a small price to pay for a human life. *Which is about the price of a loaf of bread.*

Avoid sentence fragments unless they are absolutely essential to emphasize major points. In rough drafts, sentence fragments tend to obscure major problems in sentence structure and punctuation. In the final draft, sentence fragments cause serious problems in communication, while, at the same time, creating all the wrong impressions—impressions that undermine the writer's credibility.

2. Learn How to Use Subordination and Coordination

"Subordination is a good technique. So is coordination. They eliminate choppy sentences. Like these."

The techniques of subordination and coordination enable the writer to eliminate the choppiness that results from having too many short sentences and/or sentence fragments in the same paragraph. They also enable the writer to vary sentence structures and clarify the degree of importance of ideas in the same sentence. (See also "Check for Style and Variety in Sentence Structures," pages 223–225, and "Avoid Repetition," pages 99–101.)

1. The principle of subordination places ideas of greater importance in independent clauses and ideas of lesser importance in dependent clauses or phrases.

Without Subordination

The sea was choppy. The waves were unpredictable. The boat suddenly capsized. The people in the water fought for their lives.

With Subordination

Because the sea was choppy and the waves unpredictable, the boat suddenly capsized, and the people in the water fought for their lives.

[*Note: Subordinating conjunctions such as* since, because, if, unless, when, after, before, *and so on always introduce information that is of lesser importance than the information contained in independent clauses.*]

2. The principle of coordination places ideas of equal value in similar constructions.

Without Coordination

1. The sea was choppy. The waves were unpredictable.

With Coordination

1. The sea was choppy, and the waves were unpredictable.

Without Coordination	With Coordination
	OR
	The sea was choppy and unpredictable.
2. The boat suddenly capsized. The people in the water fought for their lives.	2. The boat suddenly capsized, and the people in the water fought for their lives.

3. Avoid faulty subordination and faulty coordination. Faulty subordination occurs when the writer places information of greater value in dependent rather than independent clauses. Faulty coordination occurs when the writer balances information of unequal value.

Faulty Subordination	Correct
Because the boat had capsized and the people in the water were fighting for their lives, it was obvious that the sea was choppy and the waves were unpredictable. *[The most important information has been placed in the dependent clause, not in the independent clause where it belongs.]*	Because the sea was choppy and the waves were unpredictable, the boat capsized, and the people in the water fought for their lives.

Faulty Coordination	Correct
The sea was choppy, and the boat capsized. *[The information in the second part of the sentence is of greater importance than is the information in the first part.]* OR The waves were unpredictable, and the people in the water fought for their lives. *[Same here.]*	The sea was choppy, and the waves were unpredictable. OR The boat capsized, and the people in the water fought for their lives.

Knowing how to use the techniques of subordination and coordination to vary sentence structures and eliminate short, choppy sentences is one of the marks of an experienced writer. Learn how to use these principles to establish sentence completeness and to simplify the editing process.

3. Correct Run-on Sentences

"Good writers avoid run-on sentences they know when it is time to punctuate."

A run-on, or fused, sentence occurs when two or more sentences (independent clauses) are joined together without the appropriate punctuation. (See also "Correct Comma Splices," pages 184–186.)

Example: There should never be a third world war another war would destroy the human race.

Run-on sentences cause problems during the editing stage because they often make it impossible for the writer to make intelligent decisions regarding word sequences, internal punctuation, and so on. And in the final draft, run-on sentences are confusing because they make it impossible for the reader to understand the major subdivisions in a paragraph. Without the appropriate punctuation, the reader is also led to believe that the sentence contains one thought, when, in actuality, it contains two closely related thoughts.

Run-on sentences can be corrected in one of several ways:

1. With a period:

    There should never be a third world war. Another war would destroy the human race.

2. With a semicolon:

    There should never be a third world war; another war would destroy the human race.

3. With a comma and coordinating conjunction:

    There should never be a third world war, for another war would destroy the human race.

4. With a dependent clause:

There should never be a third world war because another war would destroy the human race.

There is no one way that is best for correcting all run-on sentences. The decision must be made in the context of the sentences that precede and immediately follow the run-on sentence. For example, the period is grammatically correct, but it can also create a very choppy flow and rhythm to the paragraph. The semicolon, or the comma and coordinating conjunction, on the other hand, would eliminate the choppiness, but they might also be less forceful than the shorter, more emphatic sentences.

As a general rule of thumb, the following guidelines can be helpful when one is attempting to correct a run-on sentence:

- A period tends to preserve the distinctive features of the two thoughts.
- A semicolon tends to emphasize what the two thoughts have in common.
- The comma and coordinating conjunction tend to create a stronger flow and rhythm to the sentence and, at the same time, emphasize what the two thoughts have in common.
- The dependent clause emphasizes the fact that one of the thoughts is of greater importance than the other one.

Remember to correct all run-on sentences so that the editing process will be simplified and the reader will not be confused or misled in the final draft.

4. Establishing Sentence Completeness: All Forms

The following paragraph illustrates a variety of problems with incomplete, choppy, and/or run-on sentences. Notice how the revised version helps to clarify the remaining problems in word sequences, word choices, punctuation, and so on. Notice, also, how the flow and movement of the paragraph are greatly enhanced, and the major subdivisions in the paragraph are clarified, once sentence completeness is established.

ORIGINAL

Frag Movies and television shows can affect the public as a whole. Some containing psychotic themes that are destructive to society. Halloween

Run-on II is one such example this movie contains several scenes that make people think about what could happen to them. It is definitely not a film for

Frag young people, ~~Nor~~ old people either. The Streets

Sub/coor of San Francisco is another example. ~~It~~ which was on the air for several years, It taught people how to break into buildings, elude police officers, and deal drugs. Chips is a better show for everyone to

Frag watch. Especially young people. In Chips, there is

Run-on very little violence the writers try, instead, to create nonviolent solutions to the many problems the two highway patrolmen encounter.

REVISION

Movies and television shows, some containing psychotic themes that are destructive to society, can affect the public as a whole. Halloween II is one such example; this movie contains several scenes that make people think about what could happen to them. It is definitely not a film for young people or old people. The Streets of San Francisco, which was on the air for several years, is another example. It taught people how to break into buildings, elude police officers, and deal drugs. Chips is a better show for everyone, especially young people, to watch. In Chips, there is very little violence because the writers try, instead, to create nonviolent solutions to the many problems the two highway patrolmen encounter.

G

Establishing Appropriate

Word Sequences

Once all ineffective expressions have been eliminated, and the preliminary sentence boundaries have been established, it may be necessary to backtrack a bit in the editing process. All of which is to say that the writing and editing process does not always progress in a straightforward and linear fashion. There are times when it is necessary for writers to move backward in the scale of editorial priorities as they address themselves once again to questions such as paragraph development and completeness.

Normally, at this stage in the editing process, most writers will discover that they have tightened up their sentences and paragraphs considerably. However, once much of the clutter is edited out of existing sentence structures, and sentence completeness is established, many writers will also discover that there is insufficient supporting evidence for topic sentences and thesis positions. Now is a good time to work the necessary supporting evidence into the remaining paragraphs and sentence structures.

For example, the italicized sentences were added to the following paragraph *after* ineffective expressions were eliminated and sentence completeness was established. Notice how these sentences help to achieve a necessary balance between generalizations and specific supporting evidence.

EXAMPLE

Satellites are artificial bodies that orbit the earth to gather as much scientific information as possible or else to provide effective communication systems. Through satellites, our government has recorded an abundance of information on the sun and the stars, information which tells us a great deal about our own planet. *For example, Explorer 1 was designed to study both our own sun and the stars in the more remote reaches of space. Gathering this information, new predictions about the age of the universe were made by the scientists who were working with Explorer 1.* Similarly, satellites have been used effectively to make significant advances in methods of communication. *For example, the U.S.S.R.'s Mohniya, America's Intelstat system, and Canada's Anik have tied nations together in a way never known before.*

Now this writer is prepared to devote some time to establishing the appropriate word sequences in the sentences throughout this paragraph. (For example, the fourth sentence contains a problem with an inappropriate word sequence—one that is known as a "dangling modifier.")

It is important to remember that effective sentences create the impression that every word has been placed precisely where it should be to maximize both the rhythm and the meaning the writer is trying to express. In the very best sentences, the reader also has the impression that if even one word was moved out of sequence, it would destroy the meaning. Note, for example, what happens to both the rhythm and the meaning in the following sentences when the italicized words and phrases are moved out of sequence.

Appropriate Word Sequence

1. The *peaceful* river flowed *quietly and serenely* toward the sea.

Inappropriate Word Sequences

1. The river *flowed peaceful* toward the sea *quietly and serenely.*
2. The river *flowed peaceful quietly and serenely* toward the sea.
3. The *peaceful* river *quietly and serenely* toward the sea *flowed.*

Writers who learn to "listen" to what they have written will seldom allow sentences such as those in the right-hand column to go unedited. Instead, they will "hear" that the rhythm of the sentences is inappropriate and will make the necessary adjustments in word sequences.

1. Correct Misplaced Modifiers

"Misplaced modifiers lurk in the shadows of our imaginations, ready to spring on even the most conscientious writers. Get those vampires out of your hideous, bloodthirsty prose."

Word order in English sentences is extremely important. When a word, phrase, or clause is out of sequence, it can drastically alter the meaning of a sentence. Often, when this happens, the writer has created a misplaced modifier.

In the broadest sense, a modifier is any word, phrase, or clause that gives the reader additional information about another word, usually a noun. With the exception of the subject and the verb, almost every other element in the English sentence can function as a modifier.

Misplaced modifiers are troublesome because they frequently attach themselves to the wrong word or words in the sentence, thus creating much confusion and ambiguity.

EXAMPLES

1. The girl threw a temper tantrum in front of her mother *when she was 6 years old.*
   [The mother was 6 years old?]
2. The student annoyed the professor *snoring in the front of the classroom.*
   [The professor was snoring in front of the class?]

The remedy for misplaced modifiers is to change the sequence of words in the sentence so that the modifier is placed as close as possible to the word or words it modifies.

EXAMPLES

1. *When she was 6 years old,* the girl threw a temper tantrum in front of her mother.
2. The student *snoring in the front of the classroom* annoyed his professor.

[Now it is clear that the girl *is 6 years old and the* student *is snoring in front of the classroom.]*

Word order can distance the modifier from the word it modifies, thus causing much confusion and ambiguity.

Misplaced Modifier	Correct
1. The automobile skidded across the ice-covered road *with bald tires. [The road had bald tires?]*	1. The automobile *with bald tires* skidded across the ice-covered road.
2. The walls of the room in which the elderly couple was to be honored, *once stripped and replastered,* were painted a beautiful pale blue. *[The elderly couple was stripped and replastered?]*	2. *Once stripped and replastered,* the walls were painted a beautiful pale blue to prepare the room for the elderly couple's honorary dinner.

The modifier can be positioned so that it could conceivably modify either of two words.

Misplaced Modifier	Correct
1. Butch Cassidy and the Sundance Kid fled from the relentless Pinkerton men *in the movie version of their lives. [Whose lives? Butch and Sundance or the Pinkerton men?]*	1. *In the movie version of their lives,* Butch Cassidy and the Sundance Kid fled from the relentless Pinkerton men.

Misplaced Modifier	Correct
2. He approached her cautiously and, *with the best of intentions,* she slapped him. *[Who had the best of intentions?]*	2. *With the best of intentions,* he approached her cautiously, and yet she slapped him.

Inaccurate and inappropriate punctuation can attach the modifier to the wrong part of the sentence. (See also "Commas," pages 175–181.)

Misplaced Modifier	Correct
He kissed her *passionately while belching* gray smoke poured into the sky from the nearby nuclear-power plant. *[A passionate kiss is followed by a belch?]*	He kissed her *passionately, while belching* gray smoke poured into the sky from the nearby nuclear-power plant.

Adverbs ending in -ly are easily misplaced. Note, for example, how the word "lively" can be positioned to create sentences with several very different meanings:

1. The *lively* images in this poem create a contrast between the waves slamming into the shore and the sea gulls frolicking in the blue sky overhead.

2. The images in this *lively* poem create a contrast between the waves slamming into the shore and the sea gulls frolicking in the blue sky overhead.

3. The images in this poem create a *lively* contrast between the waves slamming into the shore and the sea gulls frolicking in the blue sky overhead.

4. The images in this poem create a contrast between the *lively* waves slamming into the shore and the sea gulls frolicking in the blue sky overhead.

5. The images in this poem create a contrast between the waves slamming into the shore and the *lively* sea gulls frolicking in the blue sky overhead.

Any of these sentences could be correct (or incorrect). It all depends on the *precise* meaning the writer is trying to convey.

Usually, misplaced modifiers dramatically alter the rhythms of the sentences in which they appear. For this reason, they can often be detected by writers who take the time to read their essays out loud.

EXAMPLE

Nonetheless, even skilled writers have to be

wary of these silent thieves in the night who

plunder and pillage the English language with the

best of intentions.

2. Correct Dangling Modifiers

"Being that they confuse the reader and are grammatically incorrect, the writer should avoid dangling modifiers."

One of the more common English constructions is to introduce a sentence with a modifying phrase that tells the reader something about the subject of the independent clause that follows. Most modifying phrases are introduced by participles (verbs with -*ing* or -*ed* endings) or infinitives (the word "to" plus a verb).

Modifying Phrase

1. Wanting nothing more to do with John,
2. To raise enough money for summer camp,
3. Parked at the end of the street,

Independent Clause

1. *Sarah* refused to speak to him on the telephone.
2. *Janet* sold cookies to her neighbors.
3. The newly waxed automobile glistened in the sunlight.

A modifier dangles when the word it modifies is either unclear or omitted from the sentence. The following sentences create an understandable confusion in the reader's mind as to who or what is being referred to in the modifying phrase.

Unclear	Omitted
1. *Walking through the forest,* the trees that surrounded *me* were in their autumn splendor. *[The modifying phrase is attempting to modify the pronoun "me," but the sentence structure makes it appear that the trees are walking through the forest.]*	1. *Walking through the forest,* the trees were in their autumn splendor. *[There is no word in the independent clause that the modifying phrase can logically modify.]*
2. *After sinning with reckless abandon,* the Reverend Peterson challenged *certain members* of his congregation to improve their standing with the Lord. *[This sentence structure makes it appear that the Reverend Peterson has sinned with reckess abandon.]*	2. *After sinning with reckless abandon,* the sermon described how the Lord would deal with such problems on Judgment Day. *[Now it is either the sermon or the Lord that has sinned with reckless abandon.]*
3. *Having no clearly defined sexuality,* I could not identify the sea life in the tide pool. *[In this sentence, the writer has indicated that he or she has no clearly defined sexuality.]*	3. *Having no clearly defined sexuality,* the tide pool was a puzzle to me. *[Again, there is no word in the independent clause that the modifying phrase can logically modify—unless the tide pool can have sexuality.]*
4. *Gathering this information,* new predictions about the age of the universe were made by the scientists who worked with *Explorer 1.* *[New predictions gathered the information?]*	4. *Gathering this information,* the age of the universe was predicted to be different than thought previously. *[There is no noun in this sentence that could gather information.]*

Dangling modifiers can be corrected by placing the word modified *in,* or immediately *after,* the introductory modifying phrase.

In the Phrase

1. While *Kristen* was walking through the forest, the trees were in their autumn splendor. *[Placing the noun "Kristen" in the modifying phrase eliminates the dangling modifier. It also, of course, creates a dependent clause.]*

2. After *certain members* of his congregation had sinned with reckless abandon, the Reverend Peterson challenged them to improve their standing with the Lord.

3. Since *the sea life* in the tide pool had no clearly defined sexuality, I could not identify it.

4. After *the scientists* who were working with *Explorer 1* had gathered the necessary information, they made new predictions about the age of the universe.

After the Phrase

1. Walking through the forest, *Kristen* noticed that the trees were in their autumn splendor. *[Again, it is clear who is walking through the forest.]*

2. After sinning with reckess abandon, *certain members* of the Reverend Peterson's congregation were challenged by their minister to improve their standing with the Lord.

3. Having no clearly defined sexuality, *the sea life* in the tide pool was unidentifiable.

4. Gathering this information, *the scientists* who were working with *Explorer 1* made new predictions about the age of the universe.

Whenever a sentence is introduced by a modifying phrase, ask yourself the question, "Is the noun it modifies perfectly clear to the reader?"

If not, the phrase is probably a dangling modifier, and it should be corrected as illustrated in the examples above.

3. Passive and Active Constructions

"An annoying problem are these passive constructions."

In sentences written in the active voice, the subject that is performing the action appears *before* the verb. In sentences that are written in the passive voice, the subject-agent that is performing the action appears *after* the verb.

Active Voice:	Subject	Verb	Direct Object
	The pope	blessed	the crowd.
Passive Voice:	Direct Object	Verb	Subject-Agent
	The crowd	was blessed	by the pope.

In the technical sense, "crowd" is now the new subject of this sentence, and "the pope" is the object of the preposition "by."

However, to make the meaning clearer to the reader, the agent that performs the action should almost always be placed in the role of the subject of the sentence. Conversely, whatever responds to, or is the recipient of, that action should be placed in the role of the direct object.

To avoid ambiguity, writers should try to rewrite passive constructions in the active voice.

Passive Voice	**Active Voice**
1. The latest rock concert was attended by all of my best friends.	1. All of my best friends attended the latest rock concert.
2. The essay assignment was turned in by all but two of the students in the writing class.	2. All but two of the students in the writing class turned in the essay assignment.
3. An annoying problem are these passive constructions.	3. These passive constructions are an annoying problem.

[Note: Whenever the word "by" follows shortly after the verb, there is a strong possibility that the sentence is a passive construction.]

In some passive constructions, the agent that performs the action is either unclear or omitted from the sentence. For greater clarity and precision, these sentences should also be rewritten in the active voice.

Passive Voice

The landscaping around the back patio was completed by the time the Watson family returned from its brief vacation.

Active Voice

The *professional landscapers* had completed their work around the back patio by the time the Watson family returned from its brief vacation.

Passive constructions are not grammatically incorrect, but they tend to create many of the problems one associates with weak and/or ineffective sentence structures. Sentences written in the passive voice are often ambiguous, wordy, confusing, and imprecise.

Whenever possible, use the active voice in English sentences. Active-voice constructions make for a much clearer and more persuasive writing style.

4. Try Not to Split Infinitives

"The worst sin in writing is to callously split infinitives."

The traditional wisdom regarding infinitives (the word "to" plus a verb) is that they should never be split. In many respects, this is extremely good advice, especially if the word that splits the infinitive is unnecessary in the sentence, if several words split the infinitive, or if the word that splits the infinitive would be positioned more appropriately elsewhere in the sentence.

Split Infinitives

1. Sylvia decided *to really try* harder in this year's 12-mile marathon run.

2. Sylvia decided *to firmly and courageously try* harder in this year's 12-mile marathon run.

Correct

1. Sylvia decided *to try* harder in this year's 12-mile marathon run. *[The word "really" adds nothing to this sentence.]*

2. *Firmly and courageously,* Sylvia decided *to try* harder in this year's 12-mile marathon run. *[Too many words split this infinitive.]*

G 4

Split Infinitives

3. Sylvia decided *to only run* in one marathon this year.

Correct

3. Sylvia decided *to run* in *only* one marathon this year. *[The modifier "only" belongs in closer proximity to "one," the word it modifies.*

The rule regarding split infinitives is not, however, hard and fast. Indeed, there are times when the flow and rhythm of a sentence almost dictates that some infinitives be split. If we follow the traditional wisdom in these sentences, we can actually create some fairly awkard expressions.

Awkward:

Truly to appreciate the full range and depth of her voice, you should sit in the last row of the theater.

Acceptable split infinitive:

To truly appreciate the full range and depth of her voice, you should sit in the last row of the theater.

[The adverb "truly" justifiably intensifies the meaning of the verb "appreciate" in this split infinitive.]

Acceptable but less forceful:

To appreciate truly the full range and depth of her voice, you should sit in the last row of the theater.

[Coming after the verb "appreciate," the adverb "truly" is weakened as an intensifier.]

Whenever possible, try to keep infinitives intact. If it seems necessary occasionally to split an infinitive, be certain it is the best way to convey the intended meaning and rhythm of the sentence.

5. Establishing Appropriate Word Sequences: All Forms

The following paragraph contains a variety of sentences that have inappropriate and/or confusing word sequences:

ORIGINAL

Split

Young people seem to *O* ~~often,~~ and for all the wrong reasons, pay to see movies with adult themes. Why are these movies seen by so many young people? For one thing, movies of this type give them access to adult lifestyles and patterns of behavior. ~~Being~~ *Since young people* ~~that they themselves~~ want to act "grown-up," these movies encourage ~~young people~~ *them* to do likewise. But often these movies create *the wrong* impressions of what it

M mod

means to act grown-up, ~~in the wrong way~~ Foul language, sexual deviancy, and other such things in today's films are teaching young people that "once you get to be big, you can do anything you want." ~~Approaching one's later~~ *As young people approach their late* teenage years, *Dang*

these are definitely not the kind of messages *they* ~~young people~~ should be hearing. Instead, they should be introduced to good role models who try

to ~~definitely~~ act (all their lives) conscientiously ⌉ *Split/m mod*

All young people should learn

and responsibly ∧ Such values and standards of ⌉

Pass

behavior ~~should be learned by all young people~~ ⌋

before they leave their teenage years.

Notice how both the rhythm and the meaning of the paragraph are clarified once the proper word sequences are established.

REVISION

Often, and for all the wrong reasons, young people pay to see movies with adult themes. Why do so many young people see these movies? For one thing, movies of this type give them access to adult lifestyles and patterns of behavior. Since young people want to act "grown-up," these movies encourage them to do likewise. But often these movies create the wrong impressions of what it means to act grown-up. Foul language, sexual deviancy, and other such things in today's films are teaching young people that "once you get to be big, you can do anything you want." As young people approach their late teenage years, these are definitely not the kind of messages they should be hearing. Instead, they should be introduced to good role models who try to act conscientiously and responsibly all their lives. All young people should learn such values and standards of behavior before they leave their teenage years.

Establishing Sentence Consistency

Consistency is one of the keys to writing effective paragraphs and effective essays. If writers begin with one style, they should continue to use that same style. If they begin by addressing one audience, they should continue to address that same audience. And if they begin by discussing one thesis, they should continue to discuss that same thesis—with occasional modifications, of course—throughout their essays and paragraphs. The reason consistency is so important is that paragraphs and essays are coherent only when their parts are clearly related, and they have a well-defined organization and focus.

Similarly, sentences need to have a consistent organization and focus if the reader is to follow the development of the thought. There must be agreement between subject and verb and between pronoun and antecedent. Furthermore, verbs need to be consistent in tense, and sentence structures need to have consistent organizations. Without such consistency, our sentences will inevitably confuse both ourselves and our readers.

For all of these reasons, it is important at this point in the editing process to begin to establish consistent patterns in sentence structures.

1. Establish Subject-Verb Agreement

"The subject of a sentence, especially when it is separated from the predicate by several words and phrases, nonetheless have to agree with the verb."

In one respect, the question of subject-verb agreement is a simple one. Singular subjects require singular verbs, and plural subjects require plural verbs. When the writer combines a singular subject with a plural verb, or a plural subject with a singular verb, the result is a grammatical inconsistency and much confusion as to who or what is doing the action.

Why, then, do so many writers have problems with subject-verb agreement? In part, the answer to this question involves one of the idiosyncrasies of the English language—namely, that adding "s" to most nouns will create plural nouns, but adding "s" to most verbs will create singular verbs.

It would be much simpler, of course, if the language were more consistent; we could then add an "s" to both the subject and the verb to create plurals, and we could eliminate the "s" from both subject and verb to create singulars. But since we cannot do this, we must develop other strategies for identifying and correcting basic problems with subject-verb agreement.

Remember that the subject and verb of a sentence normally share one "s" ending. If both the subject *and* the verb end in "s," there is a strong likelihood that they do not agree in number.

Incorrect

1. The football *players runs* out of the locker room and onto the playing field.

Correct

1. The football *players run* out of the locker room and onto the playing field.

OR

The football *player runs* out of the locker room and onto the playing field.

[Note: Singular nouns that already end in "s," and plural nouns that end in "s" but are singular in meaning, are the exceptions to this rule.]

2. The forward *pass have revolutionized* the game of football.

2. The forward *pass has revolutionized* the game of football.

Incorrect

3. *News* of the big game *were spread* across the sports pages of just about every newspaper in the city.

Correct

3. *News* of the big game *was spread* across the sports pages of just about every newspaper in the city.

Problems in agreement frequently occur when the subject and verb are separated by phrases and clauses. Remember, intervening clauses and phrases *do not* affect the way the subject and verb agree in number.

Incorrect

1. The *quarterback,* followed by his teammates, *were introduced* to the cheering crowd.
2. The *quarterback,* who was surrounded by his teammates, *were dressed* in one of the school's new uniforms.
3. *One* of the screaming fans *were* suddenly *seen* throwing a roll of toilet paper onto the playing field.

Correct

1. The *quarterback,* followed by his teammates, *was introduced* to the cheering crowd.
2. The *quarterback,* who was surrounded by his teammates, *was dressed* in one of the school's new uniforms.
3. *One* of the screaming fans *was* suddenly *seen* throwing a roll of toilet paper onto the playing field.

[Note: The subject of the sentence <u>can never</u> be part of a prepositional phrase, a verbal phrase, or a dependent clause.]

Compound subjects always take plural verbs.

Incorrect

Margaret and her *brothers* and *sisters was* glad to be at the football game even though it was a very cold evening.

Correct

Margaret and her *brothers* and *sisters were* glad to be at the football game even though it was a very cold evening.

If the subject follows the verb, it must still agree with the verb in number.

Incorrect

Standing near the very center of the field *was* two slightly overweight *officials.*

Correct

Standing near the very center of the field *were* two slightly overweight *officials.*

Plural nouns working as one unit take singular verbs.

Incorrect

Twenty-five dollars were all the officials would be paid to work the game.

Correct

Twenty-five dollars was all the officials would be paid to work the game.

Collective nouns, when considered as a single unit, take singular verbs.

Incorrect

1. The home *team have* one of the best records in the school's history.
2. The student *body were* out in force for the most important game of the year.

Correct

1. The home *team has* one of the best records in the school's history.
2. The student *body was* out in force for the most important game of the year.

In neither/nor and either/or constructions, the verb takes the number of the subject nearer to it. Put another way, in such constructions the verb is always singular unless the subject nearer to it is plural. (See also "Avoid Double Negatives," page 163.)

Incorrect

1. Neither the home team's mascot nor its head *cheerleader were* able to make it to the game.
2. Neither the coach of the home team nor the *sportswriters was expecting* it to be a close game.

Correct

1. Neither the home team's mascot nor its head *cheerleader was* able to make it to the game.
2. Neither the coach of the home team nor the *sportswriters were expecting* it to be a close game.

Incorrect

3. Either the sportswriters or *one* of the coaches *were quoted* as predicting that the weather would be a major factor in the game.

Correct

3. Either the sportswriters or *one* of the coaches *was quoted* as predicting that the weather would be a major factor in the game.

[Note: Do <u>not</u> intermingle neither/nor and either/or constructions.]

4. *Neither* the home team's mascot *or* its head cheerleader was able to make it to the game.

4. *Neither* the home team's mascot *nor* its head cheerleader was able to make it to the game.

Indefinite pronouns (words such as "someone," "somebody," "nobody," "each," "everyone," "everybody," "every," "anyone," and "either," take singular verbs. (See also "Establish Pronoun-Antecedent Agreement," page 142.)

Incorrect

1. *Each* of the band members *were* covered by thick woolen blankets when the rain began to fall out of the dark sky.

2. *Somebody* in the back row of screaming fans *were* wise enough to sit next to a woman with an umbrella.

Correct

1. *Each* of the band members *was* covered by a thick woolen blanket when the rain began to fall out of the dark sky.

2. *Somebody* in the back row of screaming fans *was* wise enough to sit next to a woman with an umbrella.

The relative pronouns—"that," "which," and "who"—take singular verbs if the antecedent is singular and plural verbs if the antecedent is plural.

Incorrect

1. Unfortunately, the *player* who *have* the most experience with running on a wet field is hobbling along the sidelines on crutches.

Correct

1. Unfortunately, the *player* who *has* the most experience with running on a wet field is hobbling along the sidelines on crutches.

Incorrect

2. The *flags* that *keeps flapping* on top of the scoreboard attest to the force of the wind.

Correct

2. The *flags* that *keep flapping* on top of the scoreboard attest to the force of the wind.

Verbs in sentences beginning with "there" and "here" take the number of the noun that follows the verb.

Incorrect

1. Here *are* the opening *kick-off*.
2. There *goes* the two *teams* racing toward each other on the muddy playing field.

Correct

1. Here *is* the opening *kick-off*.
2. There *go* the two *teams* racing toward each other on the muddy playing field.

Problems in subject-verb agreement often escape the attention of even the most skilled writers and editors. For this reason, it is sound editorial practice to establish agreement between subjects and verbs at this stage in the editing process, and then to check it again just prior to typing the final draft.

2. Establish Pronoun-Antecedent Agreement

"Pronouns should clearly refer back to antecedents that are stated earlier in the sentence or paragraph, which is just fine with me."

Pronouns ("he," "she," "we," "they," "him," and so on) are words that are used occasionally as convenient substitutes for nouns. The purpose of pronouns is to eliminate the tedious and awkward repetition of a word, phrase, or clause in the same sentence or paragraph. Note, for example, what happens in the following paragraph when the writer fails to use pronouns effectively:

The car that Margaret bought was the car that Margaret had first seen when Margaret first drove past the Buick dealership several days earlier. Margaret's car has a beautiful sunroof, and Margaret's car has a five-year, unconditional warranty.

The style and flow are improved considerably when the writer substitutes pronouns for some of the nouns:

The car that Margaret bought was the one she had first seen when she drove past the Buick dealership several days earlier. That car has a beautiful sunroof, and it has a five-year, unconditional warranty.

However, the word, phrase, or clause to which the pronoun refers must immediately be made clear to the reader. Otherwise, pronouns only create inconsistent patterns of expression that make communication more dificult. When this happens, the problem is known as "faulty pronoun-antecedent agreement." (The antecedent is the word, phrase, or clause to which the pronoun refers.)

Faulty Pronoun Agreement	Correct
B. F. Skinner is most famous for his experiments with rats. The rat learns that, by pressing down on a lever or a button, *he* will be primarily reinforced by food. Skinner became quite proficient at *this. [The pronouns, in this case, make it sound like Skinner is in the cage, and he is the one being rewarded with food.]*	B. F. Skinner is most famous for his experiments with rats. The rat learns that, by pressing down on a lever or a button, *it* will be primarily reinforced by food. Skinner became quite proficient at *conducting these rat-testing experiments. [Now it is clear that the rats are the ones being tested and rewarded with food.]*

Some pronoun references are ambiguous because they have two or more possible antecedents.

Faulty Pronoun Agreement	Correct
The *manager* told a *coach* that it was not *her* duty to choose the starting lineup. *[In this sentence, the pronoun "her" could refer back to either the manager or the coach.]*	The *manager* told a *coach,* "It is not your duty to choose the starting lineup." *[Now it is immediately clear that the pronoun "your" refers back to the coach and not the manager.]*

Some pronouns refer to nonexistent antecedents.

Faulty Pronoun Agreement

1. Margaret studied piano all her life with the sole intention of becoming *one*. *[The pronoun "one" has no antecedent to which it can logically refer.]*

2. If the city's recreation program is abolished, *they* will have to find new ways to keep our young people involved in productive activities. *[Again, the pronoun "they" has no antecendent.]*

Correct

1. Margaret studied piano all her life with the sole intention of becoming a *concert pianist.*
   OR
   Wanting all her life to be a *concert pianist,* Margaret studied diligently to become *one.*

2. If the city's recreation program is abolished, the *city councilmembers* will have to find new ways to keep our young people involved in productive activities.

Some pronouns are too far removed from their antecedents to be effective.

Faulty Pronoun Agreement

1. The *executive branch* of our government is, at times, almost rendered powerless by our system of checks and balances and the other constitutional restrictions provided for by law; for this reason, *it* has been reshaped by some presidents, who take their case directly to the public.

Correct

1. The *executive branch* of our government is, at times, almost rendered powerless by our system of checks and balances and the other constitutional restrictions provided for by law; for this reason, *the executive branch* has been reshaped by some presidents, who take their case directly to the public. *[In this long sentence, one has no choice but to repeat the noun.]*
   OR
2. Since our system of checks and balances and other constitutional restrictions have, at times, almost rendered the *executive branch* of

Faulty Pronoun Agreement	Correct
	our government powerless, some presidents have reshaped *it* by taking their case directly to the public. *[Now the pronoun and its antecedent are in closer proximity to one another.]*

Some antecedents are obscured by intervening phrases. Remember, the antecedent is almost always found *outside* of prepositional phrases and/or verbal phrases.

Faulty Pronoun Agreement	Correct
Not a single *member* of this year's class of graduating seniors voted to have *their* commencement activities indoors. *[The rhythm of this sentence lures the writer into assuming that "seniors" is the antecedent, but it is not. It is the object of the preposition "of".]*	Not a single *member* of this year's class of graduating seniors voted to have *his or her* commencement activities indoors.

Pronouns must agree with their antecedents in person and number. (See also "Avoid Shifts," pages 146–147.)

Faulty Pronoun Agreement	Correct
1. Whenever people start to get ahead in life, *you* can always expect that someone will resent their success. *["People" is third person—"you" is second person.]*	1. Whenever people start to get ahead in life, *they* can always expect that someone will resent their success. *[Now the pronoun and its antecedent are both third person.]*
2. Whenever *someone* starts to get ahead in life, *they* can expect to feel some resentment from those	2. Whenever *someone* starts to get ahead in life, *he or she* can expect to feel some resentment

Faulty Pronoun Agreement

who are less successful.
["Someone" is singular—
"they" is plural.]

Correct

from those who are less successful. *[Now the pronoun and its*
antecedent are both singular.]

[Note: When they function as antecedents, the indefinite pronouns ("someone," "somebody," "nobody," "each," "everybody," "anyone" and "either") usually have singular-pronoun references. (See also "Establish Subject-Verb Agreement," page 137.)]

Faulty Pronoun Agreement

3. Neither Clara nor *Jill* was convinced that *they* would be interviewed for the new position in the real estate office.
4. Neither Clara nor her two best *friends* were convinced that *they* would be interviewed for the new position in the real estate office.

Correct

3. Neither Clara nor *Jill* was convinced that *she* would be interviewed for the new position in the real estate office.
4. *[If all of them are interested in being interviewed, then this is correct.]*

[Note: In either/or and neither/nor constructions, the pronoun usually takes the number of the second antecedent.]

Pronouns such as "which," "that," "this," "they," "it," and "such" are sometimes used too loosely or ambiguously to refer effectively back to their antecedents.

Faulty Pronoun Agreement

1. Highway 10 is a freeway and Highway 294 is a county road, *which* makes the traveling much easier. *[Is the traveling easier because one highway is a freeway or because the other is a county road?]*
2. Highway 294 has several treacherous curves, and one must be constantly on the alert for cows

Correct

1. The traveling is much easier on Highway 10 because it is a freeway, whereas Highway 294 is a county road.

2. Driving on Highway 294 can be a most frustrating experience because there are several treacher-

Faulty Pronoun Agreement

that cross the road. *This* is most
frustrating.

Correct

ous curves, and drivers must be
constantly on the alert for cows
that cross the road. *[Sometimes
it is best not to use pronouns.]*

3. Case

"You and me know how to use pronouns, but I'm not too sure about
he and she."

Most problems with case involve an uncertainty as to whether a
pronoun is functioning as the subject (acting upon something else) or
the object (being acted upon). The pronouns "I," "he," "she," "we,"
"they," "who," and "whoever" always function as subjects. The
pronouns "me," "him," "her," "us," "them," "whom," and
"whomever" always function as objects. (See also "Avoid Sexist
Language," pages 226–228.)

Subjects

1. John and *I* both plan to apply for
   the job in the cafeteria.

2. My best friend is about to decide
   if *she* will accept an athletic
   scholarship at the University of
   Michigan.

3. *They* are going on a vacation in
   three days.

Objects

1. The job in the cafeteria will require someone as experienced as
   John or *me*.

2. The University of Michigan has
   just offered *her* an athletic scholarship.

3. Their vacation will take *them* to
   Colorado and Utah.

Problems in case occur when the above roles are reversed.

Incorrect	**Correct**
1. Bill and *me* plan to attend graduate school together.	1. Bill and *I* plan to attend graduate school together. *[The test is to remove the first part of the compound subject. You would not say "Me plan to attend graduate school." You would say "I plan to attend graduate school."]*
2. Sarah and *him* will marry in the fall.	2. Sarah and *he* will marry in the fall. *[You would not say "Him will marry in the fall." You would say "He will marry in the fall."]*

The pronouns "who," "whoever," "whom," and "whomever" are frequently used incorrectly. Remember, "who" and "whoever" are subjects, and "whom" and "whomever" are objects.

Subject	**Object**
1. *Who* will run in the race?	1. The race will be run by *whom?*
2. Here is a gentleman *who* can tell you how to get to Cedar Street.	2. You are going to Cedar Street to see *whom*?
3. *Whoever* takes a strong position on women's rights will get my vote in this next election.	3. The letter outlining our position on women's rights can be mailed to *whomever* you choose.

Problems in case occur when these roles are reversed.

Incorrect	**Correct**
1. *Whom* will take you to the prom?	1. *Who* will take you to the prom? *[The pronoun "who" is the subject of this senence.]*
2. They expect *who* to win the election this fall?	2. They expect *whom* to win the election this fall? *[The pronoun "whom" is the object of this sentence.]*

In more complicated sentence structures, it is frequently difficult to determine whether the pronouns "who" or "whoever," or the pronouns "whom" or "whomever," are appropriate. There is, however, a test writers apply when the distinction is not immediately clear.

EXAMPLE

The courts will undoubtedly impose an extremely harsh sentence on (whoever or whomever) *committed this horrible crime.*

1. Ignore the rest of the sentence and concentrate on the words that follow "whoever" or "whomever" (the italicized words in the above example).
2. Substitute the pronoun "he," "she," or "they" for "whoever" or "whomever" in the above example. (*He committed this horrible crime.*)
3. If a complete sentence is created, as is clearly the case in the example above, the pronoun "whoever" is the proper one. Otherwise, the pronoun "whomever" would be appropriate.

4. Avoid Shifts

"Unnecessary shifts are confusing, especially if it occurs in the thesis."

A shift occurs when the writer unnecessarily switches verb tenses or pronoun references in the middle of the sentence. The result is both a structural inconsistency and a confusion as to who or what is doing the action and when the action is taking place.

Avoid shifts in tense. A shift in tense occurs when the writer uses past, present, and future tenses interchangeably and inappropriately.

Shift in Tense	**Correct**
1. As Marsha *contemplates* a career in marine biology, she carefully *considered* all of the other op-	1. As Marsha *contemplated* a career in marine biology, she carefully *considered* all of the other

Shift in Tense

tions that *were available* to her.
[The first verb is present tense; the second and third verbs are past tense.]

2. As Marsha *contemplated* a career in marine biology, she carefully *considered* what she *would want* to be doing for the next ten or twenty years of her life. *[The first and second verbs are past tense; the third verb is future tense.]*

Correct

options that *were available* to her. *[Now all of the verbs are past tense.]*

OR

As Marsha *contemplates* a career in marine biology, she carefully *considers* all of the other options that *are available* to her. *[Now all of the verbs are present tense.]*

2. *[This is a justifiable shift in verb tense. When comparing past, present, and future actions, it is necessary to shift verb tenses.]*

Avoid shifts in person. A shift in person occurs when the writer uses first-, second-, and third-person pronouns interchangeably.

Shift in Person

As *Marsha* contemplated a career in marine biology, *she* wondered how *you* would apply for a job on the *Calypso*. *["Marsha" and "she" are both third-person pronouns; "you" is a second-person pronoun.]*

Correct

As *Marsha* contemplated a career in marine biology, *she* wondered how *one* would apply for a job on the *Calypso*. *[Now they are all third-person pronouns.]*

Avoid shifts in number. A shift in number occurs when the writer uses singular and plural pronouns interchangeably and unjustifiably. (See "Establish Pronoun-Antecedent Agreement," pages 141–142.)

Shift in Number

1. When *one* is contemplating a career, *they* should consider both financial and personal rewards. *["One" is singular; "they" is plural.]*

2. When *anyone* is contemplating a career, *they* should consider both financial and personal rewards.

Correct

1. When *one* is contemplating a career, *he or she* should consider both financial and personal rewards. *[Both pronouns are now singular.]*

   OR

   When *people* are contemplating careers, *they* should consider both financial and personal rewards. *[Pronoun and antecedent are now plural.]*

2. When *anyone* is contemplating a career, *he or she* should consider both financial and personal rewards.

[Note: Indefinite pronouns, such as "anyone," "each," "everyone," "somebody," "nobody," and "someone," always take singular pronoun references.]

Avoid all unnecessary shifts in tense, person, or number. The reader needs to have a much clearer sense of when the action is taking place and who or what is involved in that action.

5. Use Parallel Structure

"Parallel structure is important because it helps us to think logically, to organize our thoughts on paper, and just because it looks good."

Parallel structure is one of the most effective strategies writers can use to develop sentences into well-structured, consistent units.

The principle of parallel structure states that, when listing items in a series or when balancing and paralleling ideas in the same sentence, nouns should be matched with nouns, adjectives with adjectives, phrases with similar phrases, dependent clauses with dependent clauses, independent clauses with independent clauses, and so forth.

Faulty parallelism occurs when the writer uses these parts of speech indiscriminately and interchangeably when listing items in a series or when balancing and paralleling ideas in the same sentence.

Be consistent when listing items in a series. Continue to use the part of speech (noun, adjective, phrase, and so forth) that is used to express the first item in that series.

Faulty Parallelism

1. Sylvia Plath was a poet who could write with great *power, sensitivity,* and *whose poems displayed a rare passion. [Two nouns are matched with a dependent clause.]*

2. Before my roommate can go home this weekend, he has *to write two expository essays, study for a math quiz,* and *he also has to find a ride. [Two infinitive phrases are matched with an independent clause.]*

Parallel Structure

1. Sylvia Plath was a poet who could write with great *power, sensitivity,* and *rare passion.* *[Now we have three nouns.]*

2. Before my roommate can go home this weekend, he has *to write two expository essays, study for a math quiz,* and *find a ride. [Now we have three infinitive phrases.]*

Be consistent when balancing and paralleling two ideas that are meant to work as a pair. Continue to use the part of speech (noun, phrase, dependent clause, independent clause, and so forth) that is used to express the first item in the pair.

Faulty Parallelism

1. John F. Kennedy was a man *who aspired to the presidency* and *he had the financial resources to achieve his goals. [A dependent clause is paired with an independent clause.]*

Parallel Structure

1. John F. Kennedy was a man *who aspired to the presidency* and *who had the financial resources to achieve his goals. [Now we have two dependent clauses.]*

OR

Faulty Parallelism	Parallel Structure
	2. *John F. Kennedy aspired to the presidency,* and *he had the financial resources to achieve his goals.* [*Now we have two independent clauses.*]

Remember, parallel structure is one of the most effective strategies the writer can use to organize sentences into coherent units and to establish relationships between ideas in the same sentence. When used properly, parallel structure creates a far more consistent and forceful writing style.

6. Avoid Faulty Comparisons

"A sentence that creates an inappropriate or illogical comparison is lesser effective than one that doesn't."

Faulty parallelism often occurs in sentences in which two or more things are being compared. When this happens, it is known as a "faulty or illogical comparison." (See also "Eliminate Logical Fallacies," page 105.)

Be sure to compare only those things that can logically be compared. Also, be sure that no essential words are omitted and that the words and phrases are precise enough to direct the reader's attention immediately to the things being compared.

Faulty Comparison	Correct
1. The baseball team's *schedule* this year is much more difficult than any other *team* in the county. [*This sentence structure forces the reader to make an illogical comparison between a schedule and a team.*]	1. The baseball team's *schedule* this year is much more difficult than *the schedule* of any other team in the county. OR The baseball team's *schedule* this year is much more difficult than *that of* any other team in the

Faulty Comparison   **Correct**

                                         county. *[Either way, we now
                                         have a logical comparison.]*

2. My backyard is at least *as large,*   2. My backyard is at least *as large
   if not larger than, my neighbor's.   as*, if not larger than, my neigh-
                                            bor's. *[The word "as" is nec-
                                            essary to complete this com-
                                            parison.]*

Know when to use possessives to clarify precisely what is being compared. (See also "Apostrophes," pages 197–198.)

Faulty Comparison   **Correct**

My *backyard* is at least as large as,   My *backyard* is at least as large as,
if not larger than, my *neighbors*.   if not larger than, my *neighbor's*.
[Without the possessive, the sen-   *["Neighbor's backyard" is im-*
tence illogically compares a   *plied by the use of the posses-*
backyard to the neighbors who   *sive; it is now a logical compari-*
live next door.]   *son.]*

Adjectives ending in *-er* are normally used to compare any two things. Adjectives ending in *-st* or *-est* are normally used to compare three or more things and/or to compare something to everything else in its group or classification.

Faulty Comparison   **Correct**

1. With respect to Alaska and   1. With respect to Alaska and
   Texas, Alaska is the *largest* state   Texas, Alaska is the *larger* state
   in terms of total square miles.   in terms of total square miles.
                                                        OR
                                            Alaska is *larger* than Texas in
                                            terms of total square miles.

2. Alaska is *larger* than the other   2. Alaska is the *largest* state in the
   states in the union.   union.

7. Avoid Mixed Constructions

"The product of indecision and confusion makes these mixed constructions most difficult to understand."

Mixed constructions occur when the writer begins the sentence with one construction in mind and ends it with another. The problem is that the first part of the sentence raises expectations that are not fulfilled by the second part. The result is a troubling grammatical inconsistency, a mutation of sorts in which the words, phrases, and clauses seem to vanish into a black hole somewhere in the middle of the sentence.

Mixed constructions can be corrected in one of two ways. Writers can either continue to use the construction implied in the first part of the sentence, or they can rewrite the first part of the sentence so that it is brought into conformity with the second part.

Mixed Construction	Correct
1. The product of indecision and confusion makes these mixed constructions difficult to understand.	1. The product of indecision and confusion, these mixed constructions are difficult to understand. OR The writer's obvious indecision and confusion make mixed constructions difficult to understand.
2. By sailing on the ocean side of the reef will save us much time and needless anxiety.	2. By sailing on the ocean side of the reef, we will save much time and needless anxiety. OR Sailing on the ocean side of the reef will save us much time and needless anxiety.

Like many other grammatical inconsistencies, mixed constructions can usually be detected if the writer will take the time to read the essay out loud. The tone, rhythm, and flow of the sentence generally break down at the very point where the two constructions come into conflict with one another.

8. Establishing Sentence Consistency: All Forms

The following paragraph illustrates a variety of problems with inconsistent sentence structures. Note how both the flow and the meaning are considerably improved and clarified in the revised version.

ORIGINAL

The Star Wars saga ~~was~~ one film series that

Shft ~~teaches~~ *taught* all the right values. Luke Skywalker was   *Shft*

the hero of this series, and ~~they~~ *he* fought for a

mystical thing called "the Force." Darth Vader, on

Shft the other hand, ~~fights~~ *fought* for the dark side of the

Force. *Although* Luke Skywalker and Darth Vader are mortal

enemies, ~~but he~~ *Luke* learns to cope with tragedy and   *Pro*

becomes like his mentors, the Jedi warriors. Darth

¶ comp Vader is *as* strong as Luke Skywalker, but neither he

S-V agr nor his cronies ~~is~~ *are* truly good, just, ~~and they~~ *or*   *¶ par*

~~definitely are not~~ honorable. ~~Being that they~~ *Since Darth Vader* work

for the dark side of the Force, ~~makes~~ *is* it   *Mix*

impossible for ~~Darth Vader~~ *him* to do anything other

than commit evil acts. The viewer is, thus, led to

cheer for Luke Skywalker, ~~and you~~ learns to hate *at the same time that he or she*   *Shft*

Darth Vader, until the very end when it turns out

ca that ~~him and Luke Skywalker~~ *the two* are father and son.

REVISION

The <u>Star Wars</u> saga was one film series that taught all the right values. Luke Skywalker was the hero of this series, and he fought for a mystical thing called "the Force." Darth Vader, on the other hand, fought for the dark side of the Force. Although Luke Skywalker and Darth Vader are mortal enemies, Luke learns to cope with tragedy and becomes like his mentors, the Jedi warriors. Darth Vader is as strong as Luke Skywalker, but neither he nor his cronies are truly good, just, or honorable. Since Darth Vader works for the dark side of the Force, it is impossible for him to do anything other than commit evil acts. The viewer is, thus, led to cheer for Luke Skywalker, at the same time that he or she learns to hate Darth Vader, until the very end when it turns out that the two are father and son.

Editing Individual Word Choices

With the exception of missing letters and certain forms of punctuation, individual words are the smallest units writers must edit during this stage of the editing process. Although it might seem inconceivable that a single word choice could be so important, there is ample evidence to suggest that this is, indeed, the case. For example, a newspaper account of a reception at the United Nations was to have read as follows:

> When the representatives from the Soviet Union arrived at the United Nations building, they were greeted in unison by various representatives from the other participating nations who were lined up on both sides of the hallway. The various ambassadors greeted the Soviet delegation with a series of *obscure* gestures of questionable diplomatic significance.

Unfortunately, in the hands of a copy editor, one word was changed, and the newspaper account was printed as follows:

> When the representatives from the Soviet Union arrived at the United Nations building, they were greeted in unison by various representatives from the other participating nations who were lined up on both sides of the hallway. The various ambassadors greeted the Soviet delegation with a series of *obscene* gestures of questionable diplomatic significance.

Granted, this is an extreme case. Most of our individual word choices do not, of course, have such a devastating effect on what we write. Nonetheless, at this stage in the editing process, it is important to devote some time and attention to determining whether or not our individual word choices are the most appropriate ones for the precise meanings we are trying to convey.

1. Wrong Word

"Check word choices to make sure they are irrelevant."

Writing is a process of trial and error during which the writer is confronted with many choices, some of which simply will not work. In the typical 500- to 750-word expository essay, the writer will undoubtedly have at least one alternative choice for every word that appears in the final draft. For some words, there may be as many as five, or even ten, alternatives. Small wonder, then, that even professional writers occasionally make word choices that distort the meanings of their sentences and essays.

It is also important to remember that, although a thesaurus may create the impression that words are interchangeable, this is seldom the case. Words take on subtle shades of meaning in different contexts and circumstances; a word that is appropriate for one situation can be extremely inappropriate for another. For example, consider this long list of adjectives, each of which has roughly the same meaning: "distant," "remote," "aloof," "withdrawn," "secluded," "isolated," and "removed." Some of these adjectives, however, apply to persons, some to places, and still others to things. Clearly, they cannot be used interchangeably.

Wrong Word

1. My next-door neighbor is *removed.*
2. That tribe lives in a *withdrawn* part of Africa.
3. That house was built at the end of an *aloof* canyon.
4. That city in Alaska is certainly *distant* from the rest of the world.

Appropriate Word

1. My next-door neighbor is *aloof.*
2. That tribe lives in a *remote* part of Africa.
3. That house was built at the end of a *secluded canyon.*
4. That city in Alaska is certainly *isolated* from the rest of the world.

Occasionally, the writer can get by with an inappropriate word choice. (Indeed, if we eliminated everything from the library shelves that has an inappropriate word choice, the librarians would be sitting in empty rooms.) Some words, however, are so crucial that writers cannot afford to make the wrong choice without seriously undermining their arguments.

Be vigilant of all word choices. Ask yourself two questions: (1) "Is this word the best choice among the various options available to me?" and (2) "Will this word be appropriate in the context in which I plan to use it?" If the answer to either of these questions is no, try other alternatives until you have found the best possible word to express a certain idea.

The word you choose may not be perfect—language seldom is—but at least it will not undermine your argument.

2. Usage

"One guaranteed way to alienate your audience is to use slang, colloquialisms, and obscenities. So, air-brain, get those turkeys out of your essays!"

Wherever English is spoken, Standard English is the language of educated men and women of the professional, business, and academic communities. Nonstandard English is the language of certain ethnic, minority, and dialect groups within the English-speaking community. Slang, obscenities, colloquialisms, and illiterate expressions are also part of nonstandard English.

Although there are places where, and occasions when, the use of nonstandard English is both appropriate and even quite enjoyable, its use is never appropriate in an expository writing assignment. These assignments should provide training in the kind of Standard English that is the foundation of English-speaking business and professional communities—and those communities can be very unforgiving of people who speak (or write) nonstandard English.

In the 1960s, it was fashionable to speak of Standard English, and the way in which it was taught in our high schools and colleges, as reflecting a "racist society." It was suggested that ethnic and minority students be taught in their own languages, even if it meant that training in Standard English would be sacrificed in the process.

Today, we recognize that this argument created its own form of racial discrimination because it restricted the speakers of nonstandard English to their own ethnic and/or minority groups and denied them access to the larger, more affluent English-speaking society around them. Bob Greene, a Chicago newspaper columnist, suggests that "the world of business, from top to bottom, runs on the correct usage of the English language. . . . Mastery of English usage is one of the few tools that a minority youngster has to make it in a white-dominated society."

The difference between Standard and nonstandard English is illustrated in the following hypothetical responses to the assertion, "By the end of this decade, I hope to be earning at least $100,000 a year."

Nonstandard English

1. Ya gotta be kiddin' me.
2. That's bull cookies.
3. You're jivin'.
4. Something's fishy here.
5. Ah, get off it.
6. You're selling me a shoddy bill of goods.
7. Something doesn't add up here.
8. That's a buncha garbage.
9. Ya, and people will start using Limburger cheese for perfume, too.
10. Whose money do you plan to steal, sucker?
11. Get off my back, Ducknose.

Standard English

1. What are you trying to suggest?
2. How could your financial situation improve so dramatically overnight?
3. The veracity of your seemingly fallacious assertion leaves me highly skeptical of your assumptions. *[Although this frequently passes as Standard English, it, too, should be avoided because it aims to impress rather than communicate. Its lofty, pretentious tone is no more respectable than any of the statements listed under nonstandard English.]*

There are obviously instances in casual conversation when nonstandard English would be preferable to Standard English. For example, if two carpenters were debating how to join a rafter to the wall of a house, it would be perfectly appropriate for one to say to the other, "That's a buncha garbage—I know what I'm doing here!"

In most writing situations, however, Standard English is clearly more appropriate than nonstandard English. For example, a letter to a potential employer could conclude by saying, "I would appreciate any information you could send concerning the availability of job openings in your firm." It would be highly inappropriate and unwise to conclude by saying, "Don't try to kid me, now! I wanta know what kind of work is out there." If there was a job opening, it would be fair to assume that the applicant who wrote his or her letter in Standard English would have the better chance of being hired.

Always keep the audience in mind when selecting the appropriate style, tone, and vocabulary for whatever it is you are writing. Also, use Standard English unless your teacher or professor tells you specifically to do otherwise.

(See also "Identify Your Audience Immediately," pages 5–6, "Bring Your Audience Back into Focus," pages 28–29, "Check for Tone," pages 225–226, and "Avoid Sexist Language," pages 226–228.)

3. Revise Awkward Constructions

> "Awkward constructions contravene the message of which they are
> trying to express."

Every effective English sentence has a rhythm and a meaning that work together to communicate an idea clearly and directly. When the relationship between the rhythm and the meaning of a sentence is undermined in any way, it can result in an awkward construction. Poor phrasing, imprecise or pretentious word choices, word combinations that create discordant sounds, and other grammatical lapses can all create awkward constructions.

An imprecise word choice can create an awkward construction.

Original

The drunk *asserted* himself on just about every person who walked into the cocktail lounge.

Revision

The drunk *harassed* just about every person who walked into the cocktail lounge.

The word "asserted" is used improperly in the above sentence. The drunk can assert *his views* on a given topic, but he cannot assert *himself* on another person. The word "harassed," on the other hand, gives the sentence the precise meaning the writer is attempting to convey—the drunk *pestered* and, perhaps, *insulted* those people who came into the cocktail lounge.

Remember, many words cannot be used interchangeably, even if a thesaurus lists them as having similar meanings. Words take on slightly different meanings in slightly different contexts. The writer who is insensitive to this runs the risk of creating some extremely awkward and confusing sentences.

The problem of awkward constructions is compounded when several imprecise or inappropriate word choices are used in the same sentence.

Original

Whites sometimes *preclassify* blacks, *synthesizing* a list of *properties* defining the role of blacks in a white society.

Revision

Whites sometimes *stereotype* blacks by *exaggerating* both real and imagined racial *characteristics*.

Pretentious words can also create awkward constructions that force the reader to search futilely for the meaning of the sentence. (See also "Eliminate Wordiness," pages 95–97, and "Eliminate Euphemisms," pages 97–99.)

Original

The *aesthetic intent* of this *literary masterpiece* is to stress the *thematic notion of the ecological community existence in conflict with individualism.*

Revision

The *story* stresses the *theme* of the *individual in conflict with society* and its values.

This is not to suggest that a sophisticated vocabulary is inappropriate in effective writing. But words that are selected because they "sound intelligent" inevitably serve only to clutter up the sentence and obscure the meaning. Always search for the word that *best expresses* the thought, not the one that *might impress the reader*.

Some sentences are awkward simply because they do not sound right, even though the meanings of the respective words may be appropriate. (See also "Check for Tone," pages 225–226.)

Original	Revision
The fact that he lacked a new pair of black plaid slacks made my friend Max mighty mad. *[There is obviously too much rhyme and alliteration in this sentence, and they clearly obscure the meaning.]*	My friend Max was angry because he did not own a new pair of black slacks. *[The sentence may be trite, but at least it no longer sounds like a poem that has collapsed under the weight of its rhyme scheme.]*

Through experience, most writers learn that clear prose involves not only the *meanings* of words, but also the *rhythms* and *sounds* of words in various contexts and combinations. (Indeed, this is one of the justifications for utilizing poetry as a teaching device in expository-writing courses; poetry sensitizes the ear to the rhythms and sounds of effective prose.)

As standard editorial practice, read the various drafts of your essay out loud to determine if the flow, rhythm, and meaning of the sentences are affected by inappropriate word choices and/or awkward constructions.

4. Eliminate Coinages

"Students should never feel free to invent new words to avoid complicated sentence structures. That unfreedom is reserved for professors."

Coinages are words writers invent when their existing vocabularies cannot adequately define sophisticated ideas and concepts. There is nothing wrong with using an occasional coinage in the earlier drafts of an essay, especially if the writer is struggling to express sophisticated concepts for which he or she has not yet acquired a suitable vocabulary. In later drafts, however, coinages are to be avoided, primarily because their meanings are limited to an audience of one—the person who created them.

Original

1. The *illiteration* of the American people should be a source of concern for all politicans.
2. This new automobile is advertised by the dealer as featuring the ultimate in *ridability*.
3. Over the past thirty years, the tastes and values of the American people have been *mass-mediated*.
4. This course involves the study of *culturification* of people in diverse ethnic groups.

Revision

1. The *rising illiteracy rate* in America should be a source of concern for all politicians.
2. A *comfortable ride* is one of the many features of this new automobile.
3. Over the past thirty years, the *mass media has had a profound influence* on the tastes and values of the American people.
4. This course involves the study of the ways in which people in diverse ethnic groups *acquire culture*.

Like clichés, coinages tend to make writers sound foolish and uneducated at the very moment when they are attempting to sound most sophisticated and informed.

Coinages should, thus, be eliminated. In addition to confusing the reader, coinages can reduce a serious statement to one that is unintentionally humorous—and the humor can often destroy the writer's credibility.

5. Proofread for Malapropisms

"Check word choices to make sure there are no malapropisms slurping in the shadows of your prose."

Malapropisms are words that sound very much like the words a writer wants to use, but they are often ludicrously different in meaning. The term "malapropos" itself evolved out of an eighteenth-century play (Sheridan's *The Rivals*), in which a character, Mrs. Malaprop, consistently used words humorously and inappropriately. Two centuries later, Archie Bunker popularized malapropisms as a form of humor in the television show, *All in the Family*.

A well-written, logically coherent essay can often survive an inappropriate word choice. Malapropisms that are not edited out of the final drafts, however, can cause serious problems. In the following examples, the malapropisms are italicized and the correct words are in parentheses.

EXAMPLES

1. Human *beans* (beings) have struggled for centuries to eliminate the problems of disease and starvation, and yet these problems persist throughout the world.

2. The young couple was uncertain as to whether they should be married in a church or in a *demagogue* (synagogue).

3. Golf is a very simple game; first, you tee up the ball, then you *fling* (swing) the club at it.

4. The lavish meal prepared for the banquet to honor this year's Nobel Peace Prize winners was a *coronary* (culinary) delight.

5. The *savor-toothed* (saber-toothed) tiger was one of the most ferocious beasts ever to roam the planet earth.

6. Our profit *margarine* (margin) this month is so narrow that we will, unfortunately, have to lay off some of our most dedicated and *conscious* (conscientious) employees.

Proofread carefully for malapropisms that may be concealed in sentences and paragraphs. Malapropisms can seriously distort otherwise perfectly valid arguments.

6. Avoid Double Negatives

"Two negatives in the same sentence are definitely a no, no!"

Whenever possible, avoid using two negatives (no, not, none, never, neither, cannot, and words beginning with the prefix *un-*) in the same sentence. Also avoid cluttering up sentences with multiple negatives.

When too many negatives are used in the same sentence, they can obscure the meaning the writer is trying to express.

Original

1. In some states, tenants do *not* have many rights and *cannot* avoid the authority of their landlords.

2. The idea that parallel lines might conceivably meet in infinity is a concept that is *not unknown.*

3. It was *not uncommon* in the nineteenth century for a suspected horse thief *not* to receive a fair trial before he was hung.

Revision

1. In some states, landlords have unlimited authority to control and evict tenants.

2. The idea that parallel lines might conceivably meet in infinity is a concept that *is known.*

3. In the nineteenth century, it was common for a suspected horse thief to be hung without a fair trial.

[Note: There is nothing grammatically incorrect about the sentences in the left-hand column above, but the ideas are more clearly and forcefully stated when the sentences are rewritten to eliminate the unnecessary negatives.]

The words "neither" and "nor" are acceptable in the same sentence for the purpose of comparison. (Indeed, they work as a team.) However, avoid mixing neither/nor and either/or constructions. (See also "Establish Subject-Verb Agreement," pages 136–137.)

Original

1. *Neither* my mother *or* my father is planning to retire early.

Revision

1. *Neither* my mother *nor* my father is planning to retire early.

Occasionally, two negatives are effective in the same sentence as a way of emphasizing a major point. It is, however, a strategy that should be used sparingly.

EXAMPLE

The idea that slavery can be justified in economic terms is an idea that *cannot* and *must not* be tolerated.

7. Editing Individual Word Choices: All Forms

The following paragraph illustrates a series of problems with individual word choices:

ORIGINAL

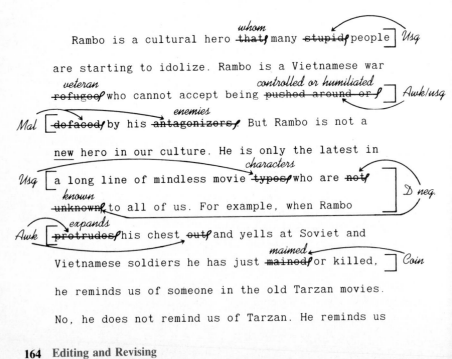

Rambo is a cultural hero ~~that,~~ *whom* many ~~stupid,~~ people ⌉ *Usg*

are starting to idolize. Rambo is a Vietnamese war

veteran
~~refugee,~~ who cannot accept being ~~pushed around or,~~ ⌉ *Awk/usg*
controlled or humiliated

Mal ⌈ ~~defaced,~~ by his ~~antagonizers,~~ But Rambo is not a
enemies

new hero in our culture. He is only the latest in

Usg ⌈ a long line of mindless movie ~~types,~~ who are ~~not,~~ ⌉ *D neg.*
characters

~~unknown,~~ to all of us. For example, when Rambo
known

Awk ⌈ ~~protrudes,~~ his chest ~~out,~~ and yells at Soviet and
expands

Vietnamese soldiers he has just ~~mained,~~ or killed, ⌉ *Coin*
maimed

he reminds us of someone in the old Tarzan movies.

No, he does not remind us of Tarzan. He reminds us

Awk

Like the apes, Rambo has long hair and a primitive
of the apes~~because he wears long hair, has an ape~~
look in his eyes. Furthermore, he knows no fear and is only
~~like stare, has no fear, and cares only about~~
concerned with getting revenge on his enemies
~~getting revenge on everyone over there~~ on the

other side of the world.

REVISION

Rambo is a cultural hero whom many people are starting
to idolize. Rambo is a Vietnamese war veteran who cannot
accept being controlled or humiliated by his enemies. But
Rambo is not a <u>new</u> hero in our culture. He is only the
latest in a long line of mindless movie characters who
are known to all of us. For example, when Rambo expands
his chest and yells at Soviet and Vietnamese soldiers he
has just maimed or killed, he reminds us of someone in
the old Tarzan movies. No, he does not remind us of
Tarzan. He reminds us of the apes. Like the apes, Rambo
has long hair and a primitive look in his eyes.
Furthermore, he knows no fear and is only concerned with
getting revenge on his enemies on the other side of the
world.

Editing End Punctuation

Most writers establish appropriate punctuation quite late in the editing process. The reason for this is very simple; it is a waste of time to punctuate sentences, phrases, and clauses that may very well be eliminated from the final draft.

Punctuation should become an editorial priority only when the writer is reasonably certain that the major problems in sentence structure have been resolved, and the essay is moving toward its completion. That is the point at which most writers establish the necessary end (and, later, internal) punctuation in their essays.

The purpose of end punctuation is not only to clarify the major subdivisions in paragraphs but also to make the relationships between sentences clear to the reader. Most sentences can be either an *extension of* a previous thought or a *response to* a previous thought; it all depends on the end punctuation. But if the end punctuation is incorrect, it can send mixed signals to the reader regarding precisely what the second sentence is supposed to accomplish, thus causing much confusion and ambiguity.

Incorrect

1. Why are so many rock musicians involved in charitable causes. Perhaps they are interested in creating a better public image, but it could also be that many of them are sincerely concerned

Correct

1. Why are so many rock musicians involved in charitable causes? Perhaps they are interested in creating a better public image, but it could also be that many of them are sincerely concerned

Incorrect

about the plight of other people. *[The reader has a right to be confused here as to whether the second sentence is a response to the question raised in the first sentence.]*

2. Many rock musicians are involved in charitable causes? Their efforts have done much to alleviate starvation and disease throughout the world. *[Again, the reader has a right to be confused about the relationship between these two sentences.]*

Correct

about the plight of other people. *[Now it is clear that the second sentence is a response to the question raised in the first sentence.]*

2. Many rock musicians are involved in charitable causes. Their efforts have done much to alleviate starvation and disease throughout the world. *[Now it is clear that the second sentence is an extention of, not a response to, the issue raised in the first sentence.]*

1. Periods

"When you have finished with the thought, always end your sentence with a period"

The period (.) is the end punctuation for most English sentences. The period alerts the reader to the fact that one complete thought has ended and another is about to begin. The period also alerts the reader to the various subdivisions in the paragraph, thus strengthening the flow and movement of the argument.

The period is the appropriate end punctuation for a sentence that makes a statement, gives a mild command or directive, or asks an implied question (one that does not demand a response).

1. Statement

The role of clear writing in the business community is one that has received much publicity in recent years.

J 1

2. Mild command or directive

You should read Mr. Hahn's very timely editorial on business writing in the latest issue of *The San Diego Union.*

3. Implied question

I wonder what motivated Mr. Hahn to write his editorial.

[Note: If this last example was a direct question *(one that demanded a response), the question mark (?) would be the appropriate end punctuation.]*

4. Direct question

What motivated Mr. Hahn to write his editorial?

Never use the period to end an incomplete thought. Remember, it is almost always inappropriate to use the period to separate any part of the sentence from the independent clause. (See also "Avoid Sentence Fragments," pages 112–114.)

Incorrect

1. After next semester. I will take a course in business writing.
2. A new instructor of business writing will be hired soon. One who has a national reputation.

Correct

1. After next semester, I will take a course in business writing.
2. A new instructor of business writing, one who has a national reputation, will be hired soon.

Since the reader has been trained to expect that the period will end a complete thought, writers who use the period to end an incomplete thought will only make their writing difficult to understand.

Through tradition and convention, the period has also been used to punctuate certain abbreviations:

1. Personal titles preceding names

Mrs. Jones, Mr. Thomas, Ms. Carter, Dr. Johnson

2. Countries and states

U.S.A., CA., N.Y.

2. Question Marks

"Use question marks only when appropriate?"

Use the question mark (?) as the end punctuation for a sentence that asks a direct question. Do *not* use the question mark in a sentence that asks an implied or indirect question.

Direct Question

1. Why is there so much poverty in the world?
2. Would you tell me the time, please?

Implied or Indirect Question

1. I wonder why there is so much poverty in the world.
2. I wonder what time it is.

[Note: Direct questions usually demand a response of some kind from another person or group of people. Indirect or implied questions are generally questions that are directed at oneself rather than at some audience.]

In quotations, place the question mark outside the final quotation marks if the entire sentence is a question. If the question is confined to the quotation, place the question mark inside the final quotation marks. (See also "Quotation Marks," pages 193–194.)

Outside Final Quotation Marks

Why did our senator vote against the bill that provided "140 million dollars in supplemental assistance to the underdeveloped nations in Africa"?

Inside Final Quotation Marks

When the senate debated the new relief bill for the underdeveloped nations of Africa, our senator asked, "Why are we providing 140 million dollars in additional aid when most of those countries are allies of the Soviet Union?"

The question mark should be used sparingly in expository writing. However, there are times when the writer can set up an argument or explanation by asking a rhetorical question and then answering it.

EXAMPLE

Why is there so much poverty in the world today? There are many reasons, some having to do with the unstable political climate in many underdeveloped countries. Other reasons include some complicated economic factors and, of course, prolonged droughts and other natural disasters that have raised havoc with the food sources of many third world nations.

3. Use Exclamation Points Sparingly

"Exclamation points are important for emphasis, but remember to use them sparingly!!!!"

The exclamation point (!) is used at the end of emphatic statements.

EXAMPLES

1. As the Japanese airplanes streaked through the skies above Pearl Harbor, Commander Carroll of the *Helm* yelled at a young gunner's mate who had requested keys to open the magazine locks, "Damn the keys—cut the locks!"
2. That was Clint Eastwood who just walked by!
3. The latest statistics on violent crime in this city are extremely frightening. All of us—the police, the public, and the city council—must strive to do everything in our power to make our streets safe once again!
4. Mom, a car just drove into our swimming pool!
5. There are times when it is prudent to remain silent even in the face of overwhelming oppression. But there are other times when one must follow the dictates of one's conscience and speak out against such outrages. This is one of those times!

In expository writing, the exclamation point should be used sparingly. Normally, if a sentence is well-expressed and well-structured, it will be forceful enough without the additional support of an explanation point.

4. Editing End Punctuation: All Forms

The following paragraph illustrates a variety of problems with establishing end punctuation in sentences:

ORIGINAL

Why are so many of today's television

_P_ ⎡commercials directed at teenage audiences. There

are many reasons, but perhaps the most important

one is that teenagers constitute the largest

viewing audience for television. It has been

estimated that teenagers comprise anywhere from 50

to 60 percent of the total television viewing

_P_ ⎡audience. Although one can question the validity

of this statistic, it seems clear that American

advertisers accept it at face value? Otherwise we⎤ _P_

would not see so many commercials for designer

jeans, soft drinks, acne medications, and other

such products during prime-time viewing hours. And

what influence does this have on our society as a

_P_ ⎡whole. Probably, more than anything else, it makes

a youth-oriented culture even more obsessed with

being youthful in both appearance and behavior.

REVISION

Why are so many of today's television commercials directed at teenage audiences? There are many reasons, but perhaps the most important one is that teenagers constitute the largest viewing audience for television. It has been estimated that teenagers comprise anywhere from 50 to 60 percent of the total television viewing audience! Although one can question the validity of this statistic, it seems clear that American advertisers accept it at face value. Otherwise we would not see so many commercials for designer jeans, soft drinks, acne medications, and other such products during prime-time viewing hours. And what influence does this have on our society as a whole? Probably, more than anything else, it makes a youth-oriented culture even more obsessed with being youthful in both appearance and behavior.

K

Editing Internal Punctuation

Internal punctuation (commas, semicolons, colons, and so on) is much like the signs that control traffic on our roads and highways. YIELD signs, STOP signs, and other traffic signals tell us precisely how fast or how slow we can drive so that we do not create absolute chaos and confusion every time we get behind the wheels of our cars.

Similarly, internal punctuation tells readers precisely when to pause in a sentence so that they can understand the flow and subdivisions of the thought. Without these punctuation marks, there would be absolute chaos and confusion on the printed page—and very little communication would take place.

Note what happens, for example, when internal punctuation is removed from the following paragraph:

> The United States Constitution a work of genius in the minds of many political scientists provides for an elaborate system of checks and balances. The executive legislative and judicial branches are cleverly designed to play the role of watchdog over one another. Whereas this can at times create a stalemate at the federal level it nonetheless guarantees that no single branch of government will ever take control of the country. This much-admired much-emulated document has served this country well for over 200 years now.

When the internal punctuation is reinserted into this paragraph, the reader has a much clearer sense of the development of the thought:

> The United States Constitution, a work of genius in the minds of many political scientists, provides for an elaborate system of checks and balances.

The executive, legislative, and judicial branches are cleverly designed to play the role of watchdog over one another. Whereas this can, at times, create a stalemate at the federal level, it nonetheless guarantees that no single branch of government will ever take control of the country. This much-admired, much-emulated document has served this country well for over 200 years now.

Clearly, internal punctuation is an important concern in the final stages of the editing process. Nonetheless, many writers find it difficult to distinguish among the functions of the three major forms of internal punctuation—the comma (,), semicolon (;), and colon (:).

The following is a helpful guide when writers are trying to decide which of these three forms of punctuation is appropriate for establishing the major subdivisions in many English sentences:

1. Independent clause followed by a list

   The Constitution provides for a system of checks and balances between the following branches of government: the executive, legislative, and judicial branches.

2. Independent clause followed by another independent clause

   The Constitution provides for a system of checks and balances; the powers of the executive, legislative, and judicial branches are all limited by this ingenious system.

3. Independent clause followed by a coordinating conjunction and another independent clause

   The Constitution provides for a system of checks and balances, and the powers of the executive, legislative, and judicial branches are all limited by this ingenious system.

4. Independent clause followed by a dependent clause or phrase

   The Constitution provides for a system of checks and balances, thus greatly limiting the powers of the executive, legislative, and judicial branches.

5. Dependent clause or phrase followed by an independent clause

   Greatly limiting the powers of the executive, legislative, and judicial branches, the Constitution provides for a system of checks and balances.

1. Commas

"Proofread your essays carefully to avoid, unnecessary commas."

The comma (,) is one of the most common forms of punctuation in English grammar. Unlike the colon (:) and the semicolon (;)—both of which designate strong internal pauses in a sentence—the comma designates a slight pause that assists the reader in following the flow of the thought. When used correctly, the comma also alerts the reader to the various internal divisions in a sentence so the organization of the thought can be more easily understood.

The question of whether to enclose something in commas can be greatly simplified by asking, "Is the information essential or not essential to the meaning of the sentence?"

Information that is essential to the meaning of the sentence is seldom enclosed in commas:

Faculty advisers *who are never in their offices* make registration very difficult.
[Without the dependent clause, this sentence loses its meaning— hence, no commas.]

Information that is not essential to the meaning of the sentence is almost always enclosed in commas:

My faculty adviser, *who prepares class schedules for well over fifty students,* is never in his office.
[This dependent clause does not substantially affect the meaning of this sentence—hence, it should be enclosed in commas.]

More specifically, the following rules govern the use of the comma in English grammar:

Commas are used to separate long independent clauses when they are joined by a coordinating conjunction ("and," "but," "for," "nor," "so," "or," and others). Always place the comma in front of the conjunction.

Original

1. Sylvia visited Easter island for the first time last year <u>and</u> she plans to return as soon as possible.

2. Sylvia visited Easter island <u>and</u> she plans to return someday.

3. Sylvia visited Easter island <u>and</u> plans to return someday.

Revision

1. Sylvia visited Easter island for the first time last year, <u>and</u> she plans to return as soon as possible. *[The comma is necessary to show the reader that there is a twofold division of this sentence.]*

2. *[This is acceptable. A comma is optional in short independent clauses joined by a conjunction.]*

3. *[This is correct. The two verbs, "visited" and "plans," share the same subject and should <u>not</u> be separated by a comma.]*

Use commas to separate more than two items in a series.

Original

1. My favorite classes this semester were *Biology 3 Psychology 2* and *History 10.*

2. The convict *jumped over the fence ran across the road* and *disappeared* into a grove of trees.

Revision

1. My favorite classes this semester were *Biology 3, Psychology 2,* and *History 10.*

2. The convict *jumped over the fence, ran across the road,* and *disappeared* into a grove of trees.

Commas are used to separate coordinate adjectives. (Coordinate adjectives are adjectives that independently modify the same noun.) Coordinate adjectives are always interchangeable, and they can be joined by the word "and" without creating awkward expressions.

Original

1. The United States Postal Service is sometimes the most *frustrating ineffective* organization in the federal government.

2. The *old country* schoolhouse is about to be torn down and replaced with a more modern structure.

Revision

1. The United States Postal Service is sometimes the most *frustrating, ineffective* organization in the federal government. *[Switch the two adjectives around or replace the comma with the word "and." The sentence is still grammatically correct.]*

2. *[This is correct. Try switching the adjectives "old" and "country" around or replacing them with the word "and." Either test creates an awkward expression.]*

Commas are generally used to separate long dependent clauses or phrases when they introduce or conclude a sentence.

Original

1. *When he returned from Latin America* President Reagan's special envoy drove immediately to the White House for a briefing.

2. *Returning from Latin America* President Reagan's special envoy drove immediately to the White House for a briefing.

3. President Reagan's special envoy to Latin America drove immedi-

Revision

1. *When he returned from Latin America,* President Reagan's special envoy drove immediately to the White House for a briefing. *[The comma is necessary to clarify the twofold division of this sentence. It also informs the reader where the dependent clause ends and the independent clause begins.]*

2. *Returning from Latin America,* President Reagan's special envoy drove immediately to the White House for a briefing.

3. President Reagan's special envoy to Latin America drove immedi-

K 1

Original

ately to the White House *arriving shortly after noon.*

4. *As he drove* he pondered precisely what he would tell President Reagan about his meetings with several Latin American leaders.

Revision

ately to the White House, *arriving shortly after noon.*

4. *[The comma is optional here. The introductory clause, "As he drove," is short enough for the reader to perceive immediately where it ends and the independent clause begins.]*

Commas are used to enclose nonrestrictive clauses. A nonrestrictive clause is a dependent clause that is <u>not</u> essential to the meaning of a sentence.

Original

1. My friend Mark *who has tried unsuccessfully to have his short stories published* does not punctuate everything correctly.

2. A writer *who does not have a literary agent* will find it very difficult to get his or her works published.

Revision

1. My friend Mark, *who has tried unsuccessfully to have his short stories published,* does not punctuate everything correctly. *[The clause is clearly not essential to the meaning of this sentence.]*

2. *[This is correct. The clause, "who does not have a literary agent," is clearly essential to the meaning of this sentence.]*

Commas are almost always used to enclose clauses introduced by the word "which." But commas are almost never used to set off clauses introduced by the word "that."

Original

1. Brenda's senior thesis *which she wrote over a six-month period of time* has finally been completed.

Revision

1. Brenda's senior thesis, *which she wrote over a six-month period of time,* has finally been completed.

Original

Revision

[The clause introduced by the word "which" is not essential to the meaning of the sentence.]

2. The one course, *that Brenda needs to complete her major,* will not be offered this fall.

2. The one course *that Brenda needs to complete her major* will not be offered this fall. *[The clause introduced by the word "that" is essential to the meaning of the sentence.]*

Appositives are almost always enclosed in commas. (Appositives are words or phrases that relabel or rename a preceding noun.)

Original

Herman Melville *the author of Moby Dick* wrote from firsthand experience when he described the life and hardships of the nineteenth-century seaman.

Revision

Herman Melville, *the author of Moby Dick,* wrote from firsthand experience when he described the life and hardships of the nineteenth-century seaman.

[Note: The reason appositives are almost always enclosed in commas is that they seldom contain information that is essential to the meaning of the sentence. Of course, if appositives do contain essential information, they should not be enclosed in commas.]

Absolute phrases are normally separated or enclosed in commas. (An absolute phrase consists of a noun or pronoun followed by a verbal phrase.)

Original

Meg's sister *her hair flowing in the breeze* watched sadly as her husband boarded the train.

Revision

Meg's sister, *her hair flowing in the breeze,* watched sadly as her husband boarded the train.

K 1

Commands

Parenthetical expressions, such as "thus," "however," "finally," "nevertheless," "of course," and "furthermore," are normally set off or enclosed in commas.

Original

1. *However* Judge Parker was quick to remind the defendant that his bond would be forfeited if he failed to appear in court as scheduled.
2. The defendant *nonetheless* failed to appear on the day his trial was to begin.
3. He was of course arrested.

Revision

1. *However,* Judge Parker was quick to remind the defendant that his bond would be forfeited if he failed to appear in court as scheduled.
2. The defendant, *nonetheless,* failed to appear on the day his trial was to begin.
3. *[This is acceptable. To avoid choppiness, parenthetical expressions in short independent clauses need not be enclosed in commas.]*

[Note: The reason parenthetical expressions are almost always enclosed in commas is that they are transitional terms that are not essential to the meaning of the sentence.]

Use a comma whenever one is necessary to avoid confusing the reader. (This is, of course, the purpose of all punctuation.)

Original

1. For *her to* give was better than to receive.
2. *Underneath the* ship's hull was badly in need of repairs.

Revision

1. For *her, to* give was better than to receive.
2. *Underneath, the* ship's hull was badly in need of repairs.

Use commas to separate states from cities, years from days of the month, and nouns in direct address.

1. *Buffalo, New York,* is my hometown.
2. On January *14, 1980,* I moved to Arizona.

180 Editing and Revising

3. How many times must I tell you, *Amanda*, that I will never again put up with one of these cold winters!

Contemporary trends in English grammar are to simplify punctuation as much as possible. The comma, especially, should never be used unless it is necessary for the reader to understand the flow of the thought and the major internal divisions in a sentence. Then the comma functions like a YIELD sign on the highway—it signals the reader to slow down in anticipation of new ideas that are about to merge into the flow of the sentence.

If all else fails, try reading the sentence out loud to determine where slight vocal pauses are necessary to help the reader understand the argument. Those are the places where commas are most likely appropriate.

2. Use Semicolons Sparingly

"A semicolon should never join an independent clause; and a dependent clause or phrase."

The purpose of the semicolon (;) is to join two independent clauses (complete sentences) that share a close relationship. The semicolon also enables the writer to eliminate short, choppy sentence structures, and it alerts the reader to the fact that the sentence contains two thoughts of equal value.

Two Independent Clauses	**Joined by the Semicolon**
Mother Teresa of Calcutta is an authentic twentieth-century saint. She deserved the Nobel Peace Prize. *[The sentences are grammatically correct, but they are also quite choppy.]*	Mother Teresa of Calcutta is an authentic twentieth-century saint; she deserved the Nobel Peace Prize. *[Now the choppiness is eliminated, and the close relationship of the two ideas is emphasized.]*

A semicolon should never be used to join an independent clause and a dependent clause or phrase, even if the two ideas are closely related.

Incorrect

Mother Teresa of Calcutta is constantly trying to focus world attention on the plight of the poor and starving people of India; especially when she is visiting foreign countries.

Correct

Mother Teresa of Calcutta is constantly trying to focus world attention on the plight of the poor and starving people of India, especially when she is visiting foreign countries.

OR

Mother Teresa of Calcutta is constantly trying to focus world attention on the plight of the poor and starving people of India; she is especially effective at doing this when she visits foreign countries.

A semicolon is used when two independent clauses are joined by a conjunctive adverb, such as "also," "hence," "nonetheless," and "finally."

Incorrect

Mother Teresa of Calcutta is someone who has discovered that true happiness comes only to those who dedicate their lives to others, hence, she is a fine example for all of us. *[This is a comma splice.]*

Correct

Mother Teresa of Calcutta is someone who has discovered that true happiness comes only to those who dedicate their lives to others; hence, she is a fine example for all of us.

To avoid confusion, use a semicolon to separate items in a series if any of the items contains commas.

Incorrect

When Mother Teresa arrived in the United States, she was surrounded by a mob of excited, unruly well-wishers, interviewed by discourteous, self-serving journalists, and introduced to the most powerful,

Correct

When Mother Teresa arrived in the United States, she was surrounded by a mob of excited, unruly well-wishers; interviewed by discourteous, self-serving journalists; and introduced to the most powerful,

Incorrect

publicity-seeking members of the
United States Senate.

Correct

publicity-seeking members of the
United States Senate.

Do not substitute a semicolon for a comma or a colon.

Incorrect

1. Oblivious to all the attention she
was receiving; Mother Teresa re-
mained humble and inconspicuous in spite of all the turmoil that
surrounded her.
2. Mother Teresa combines many of
the qualities most of us would like
to have; humility, conviction, integrity, and strong moral purpose.

Correct

1. Oblivious to all the attention she
was receiving, Mother Teresa re-
mained humble and inconspicuous in spite of all the turmoil that
surrounded her.
2. Mother Teresa combines many of
the qualities most of us would like
to have: humility, conviction, integrity, and strong moral purpose.

Although a semicolon is seldom used with a coordinating conjunction, it is advisable to do so if the two independent clauses are very
long. Using a semicolon instead of a comma in such constructions
creates a much clearer sense of the twofold division of the thought.

Acceptable

When Mother Teresa visited New
York City, one local humorist described her as "the only human
being alive today whom Christ himself would have called a Christian,"
and, in retrospect, that remark
seemed to many who had met her
for the first time to contain a certain
element of truth.

Better

When Mother Teresa visited New
York City, one local humorist described her as "the only human
being alive today whom Christ himself would have called a Christian";
and, in retrospect, that remark
seemed to many who had met her
for the first time to contain a certain
element of truth.

[Note: A semicolon is always placed outside of quotation marks.]

The semicolon is one of the easiest marks of punctuation to master.
Yet, next to the comma, it creates more problems for writers than any

other form of punctuation. The best way to avoid problems with the semicolon is, of course, not to use it. (Indeed, many contemporary prose stylists—especially journalists—seldom use the semicolon unless it is the only option available to them.)

Writers should use the semicolon sparingly, primarily because it can create a style that is wordy, stiff, and overly formal. However, when it is necessary to use a semicolon, especially in more complex sentences, remember that it joins two independent clauses—almost never an independent clause and a dependent clause or phrase.

3. Correct Comma Splices

"A comma splice is created when the writer forces the comma to do the job of the semicolon, everyone knows that."

Although the comma (,) and the semicolon (;) perform many of the same functions, at least to the extent that they establish the major internal divisions in most English sentences, they are not interchangeable. The semicolon's major function is to join two independent clauses that have an especially close relationship. A comma, on the other hand, can join two independent clauses only with the help of a coordinating conjunction. Also, a semicolon designates a much stronger pause than does a comma.

A comma splice is created when a comma is used to join two independent clauses without the help of a coordinating conjunction. A comma splice can be corrected by replacing the comma with a semicolon or by placing a coordinating conjunction immediately after the comma. (See also "Correct Run-on Sentences," pages 116–117.)

Comma Splice	Correct
1. Mark Twain was a gifted humorist and a popular folk hero, his major contribution to American fiction was *Huckleberry Finn*.	1. Mark Twain was a gifted humorist and a popular folk hero; his major contribution to American fiction was *Huckleberry Finn*.
	OR

Comma Splice

Correct

2. Mark Twain was a gifted humorist and a popular folk hero, and his major contribution to American fiction was *Huckleberry Finn*.

A comma splice can also be corrected by replacing the comma with a dash or a period.

Comma Splice

1. Mark Twain wrote from personal experience, his many travels took him to the American frontier and later to Europe.

Correct

1. Mark Twain wrote from personal experience—his many travels took him to the American frontier and later to Europe. *[The dash emphasizes the last part of this sentence.]*

OR

2. Mark Twain wrote from personal experience. His many travels took him to the American frontier and later to Europe. *[Be careful, however, when correcting the comma splice with a period; it can lead to some extremely choppy sentence structures.]*

Comma splices are sometimes created when a parenthetical expression (also known as a "conjunctive adverb" or "sentence connective") is used to join two independent clauses.

Comma Splice

Mark Twain was a gifted humorist and a popular folk hero, furthermore, his major contribution to American fiction was *Huckleberry Finn*.

Correct

Mark Twain was a gifted humorist and a popular folk hero; furthermore, his major contribution to American fiction was *Huckleberry Finn*.

The choice of how to correct a comma splice should be based, in part at least, on the meaning and rhythm of the entire sentence in the context of the sentences that precede and follow it.

Do not automatically assume that every comma splice should be corrected by replacing the comma with a semicolon or a period. There may be a better way.

4. Colons

"The colon should only be used: when necessary."

The colon (:) is a formal punctuation mark that is used only when a strong vocal pause is needed to understand the flow and meaning of the sentence. The colon has two major functions in expository writing.

The colon is used primarily to introduce a list of some kind:

1. Donna visited the following cities during her trip through Europe: Paris, Brussels, Dublin, Copenhagen, and London.

OR

2. Donna took several things with her on her trip: two suitcases, a travel bag, and three books of essays.

[Note how the colon always alerts the reader to a strong twofold division of the sentence, the first part of which is an independent clause and the second part a dependent clause or phrase.]

The colon is also used to introduce formal quotations

1. During her travels, Donna found the time to reread George Orwell's "Politics and the English Language." She was especially impressed by Orwell's discussion of the relationship between thought and language:

    It [language] becomes ugly and inaccurate because our thoughts are foolish, but the slovenliness of our language makes it easier for us to have foolish thoughts.

OR

2. Donna was especially impressed by Orwell's discussion of the relationship between thought and language: "It [language] becomes ugly and inaccurate

because our thoughts are foolish, but the slovenliness of our language makes it easier for us to have foolish thoughts."

[Note: A colon always goes outside of the quotation marks.]

It is equally important to know when a colon should *not* be used:

1. Never use a colon in the middle of a prepositional phrase.

During her trip to Europe, Donna rode the train to: Paris, Brussels, and Dublin.

[The colon inappropriately and unnecessarily separates the preposition "to" from its objects.]

2. Never use a colon when a semicolon is the proper form of punctuation.

During her trip to Europe, Donna traveled primarily by train: Paris, Brussels, and Dublin were three of the cities she visited this way.

[A semicolon is required because these are two independent clauses.]

3. Never use a colon in the middle of a dependent or independent clause.

When Donna visited: Paris, Brussels, and Dublin, she traveled by train.

[The colon serves no purpose here except to clutter up the dependent clause.]

OR

Donna visited: Paris, Brussels, and Dublin.

[Similarly, the colon serves no purpose here except to clutter up the independent clause. Note also that there is no strong vocal pause after the verb in either of these sentences.]

5. Know When to Use Dashes

"—The problem with the dash is its versatility—one can use it to replace just about every other form of punctuation—as a result writers tend to overuse it—I mean really overuse it—"

The dash (—) is the most versatile form of punctuation in English grammar. In appropriate contexts, it can be used instead of the comma or the colon.

The primary function of the dash is to emphasize a point—especially at the end of a sentence:

That was the poorest film I have ever seen—absolutely the most hideous!

The dash can be used to indicate a sudden shift in thought:

The sale will feature women's clothing, automobile accessories, furniture, and some food items—just about anything you might want.

The dash, or a pair of dashes, can be used to separate items in a series when commas would cause confusion:

Several books—a bible, a dictionary, and an old philosophical treatise— were damaged by the water that flooded the basement.

The dash can be used to introduce an independent clause that summarizes the words or phrases that precede it:

Balls, bats, gloves, uniforms—everything we needed to compete in the baseball tournament was quickly packed into the back of the van.

Although the dash is a versatile form of punctuation, it is not interchangeable with the semicolon. For example, normally the dash should *not* be used to join two independent clauses.

EXAMPLE

The latest flood control measures have proven to be most ineffective— rains are expected this week that might cause some flooding in the lowlands. [Unless the writer wishes to emphasize the second part of this sentence, the semicolon should be used to join these two independent clauses.]

Know when to use the dash, but use it sparingly. It is self-defeating to emphasize everything one writes.

Use Parentheses Discreetly

K 6

6. Use Parentheses Discreetly

"(Parentheses) (should never) enclose information that is essential to the meaning of the sentence."

Parentheses ( ) are used to enclose information that helps to clarify, but is *not* essential to, the meaning of the sentence. In this respect, parentheses perform the same function as several other forms of English punctuation. Still, there are some important things to consider when making choices between dashes, commas, semicolons, or parentheses.

Dashes and parentheses have opposite functions in English grammar. Dashes emphasize essential information, whereas parentheses de-emphasize information that is *not* essential to the meaning of the sentence.

Dashes Emphasize

The Beatles produced some of the finest popular songs of the twentieth century—indeed, probably the very best songs of this century. *[The dash emphasizes the second part of this sentence.]*

Parentheses De-emphasize

The Beatles (composed of Paul McCartney, John Lennon, George Harrison, and Ringo Starr) produced some of the finest popular songs of the twentieth century. *[The information in parentheses is clearly not essential to the meaning of this sentence.]*

Commas and parentheses both enclose information that is not essential. However, the comma does so in a way that is consistent with the grammatical structure of the sentence, whereas this is not necessarily the case with parentheses. Parentheses, thus, enable the writer to insert words, phrases, and clauses that otherwise would not fit into the natural flow and rhythm of the sentence.

Incorrect

The Beatles, Liverpool, England, have had a profound influence on

Correct

The Beatles (Liverpool, England) have had a profound influence on

Editing Internal Punctuation **189**

Incorrect

many other rock groups for well over twenty years now.

Correct

many other rock groups for well over twenty years now.

Like a semicolon, parentheses can join two independent clauses that have an especially close relationship. However, the semicolon tells the reader that the two independent clauses are of *equal* importance, whereas parentheses tell the reader that the independent clause enclosed in the ( ) is of *less* importance.

With a Semicolon

For years, music critics have debated whether John Lennon or Paul McCartney was the more talented of the Beatles; they agree, however, that both were extremely gifted songwriters.

With Parentheses

For years, music critics have debated whether John Lennon or Paul McCartney was the more talented of the Beatles. (The critics also lamented the fact that the Beatles never reunited.)

[Note: When parentheses enclose a complete sentence, as is the case in the example in the right-hand column above, the end punctuation goes inside *the parentheses. Otherwise, the end punctuation goes* outside *the parentheses.]*

Once writers recognize that parentheses are an easy way to include information that is grammatically inconsistent with the structure of the sentence, there is a natural tendency to overuse them. Commas should normally be used to enclose such information in a sentence. Parentheses are a kind of "last resort" for information that stubbornly resists being expressed in more conventional forms.

Overused

The Beatles (John Lennon, Paul McCartney, George Harrison, and Ringo Starr) were the first British group (Liverpool, England) to attract attention in America (1963).

Better

In 1963, the Beatles (John Lennon, George McCartney, George Harrison, and Ringo Starr) left their homes in Liverpool, England, and became the first British group to attract attention in America.

If you need to use parentheses, use them discreetly and sparingly. Also remember that parentheses always work as a set ( ). They never work individually.

7. Quotation Marks

"As I said earlier, 'The ultimate ego trip in writing is to quote yourself'."

Quotation marks (" ") are used to enclose direct quotations. Do not enclose indirect quotations with quotation marks.

Direct Quotation

Albert Gelpi said of the poet Walt Whitman that "his prophetic presence and his experiments in free verse and organic form have changed the shape of American— and indeed of all—modern poetry."

Indirect Quotation

Albert Gelpi said of the poet Walt Whitman that his experiments with new poetic forms contributed greatly to all modern poetry. *[We are paraphrasing, not quoting Mr. Gelpi; hence, we will need a footnote here, but not quotation marks.]*

Quotations should be used precisely as they appear in the original text. If some words must be omitted, use ellipsis marks (. . .). If the writer adds anything to the quotation, those words should be enclosed in brackets ([ ]). (See also "Ellipses," pages 195–197, and "Brackets," page 195.)

Ellipses

Albert Gelpi said of the poet Walt Whitman that "his prophetic presence and his experiments in free verse and organic form have changed the shape of . . . modern poetry."

Brackets

Albert Gelpi said of the poet Walt Whitman that "his prophetic presence and his experiments in free verse and organic form have changed the shape of [all] modern poetry."

Quotations must be introduced into sentences in such a way as to be compatible with the existing structures. Quotations should never be used as convenient excuses for writing awkward sentences. (See also "Revise Awkward Constructions" pages 158–160.)

Awkward Quotation	Revision
Whitman, in a stanza in one of his poems, "surrounded, detached, in measureless oceans of space," speaks of his soul.	In one of his poems, Whitman describes his soul as "surrounded, detached, in measureless oceans of space."

[Note: To determine if a quotation has created an awkward sentence structure, temporarily remove the quotation marks. The words that were quoted should blend into, and be grammatically compatible with, the sentence in which they appear.]

Do not use too many long quotations in a short essay. If a quotation of more than four typed lines is necessary, introduce it with a colon, indent ten spaces, do *not* use quotation marks, and continue to double-space unless instructed to do otherwise. Also, normally you should explain why the information is essential.

EXAMPLE

Albert Gelpi summarizes the career of Walt Whitman

in the following passage:

> Whitman celebrated himself as the mythic
> American epitomizing and synthesizing the
> variety of his land and the energy of his
> polyglot people; he envisioned an ideal
> America in which love and comradeship created
> an open, free society. (213)

Certainly, Whitman saw himself as ''the mythic

American''; one must question, however, the extent

to which he maintained a vision of ''an ideal

```
America,'' especially much later in his career

when his earlier faith in his country began to

fade.
```

Single quotation marks (' ') can appear within double quotation marks (" ").

EXAMPLE

```
Albert Gelpi concludes his brief synthesis of

Whitman's life and career by saying, ''In Ezra

Pound's words, 'Whitman is to my fatherland . . .

what Dante is to Italy.' ''
```

When punctuating quotations, always remember that periods and commas go inside quotation marks; colons, semicolons, and dashes go outside quotation marks; and question marks and exclamation points go inside or outside, depending upon whether or not they refer to all or only part of the sentence. (See also "Question Marks," page 169.)

Inside Quotation Marks

1. In one of his poems, Whitman refers to President Abraham Lincoln as a "powerful western fallen star."

2. The assassination of President Abraham Lincoln, the "powerful western fallen star," inspired Whitman to write an extremely melancholic poem.

Outside Quotation Marks

1. There are three dominant symbols in Whitman's tribute to the "powerful western fallen star": the lilacs, the hermit thrush, and the star itself.

2. President Lincoln had much in common with the "powerful western fallen star"; he was a beacon of hope for a nation recovering from the Civil War.

K 7

Inside Quotation Marks

3. Whitman asks, "What shall my perfume be for the grave of him I love?"
4. Whitman lamented "the black murk that hides the star!"

Outside Quotation Marks

3. President Lincoln—"a powerful western fallen star"—died suddenly and dramatically.
4. Was that poem the only one in which Whitman compared President Lincoln to a "powerful western fallen star"?
5. It is especially poignant to compare President Lincoln to the "powerful western fallen star"!

Quotation marks are also used to enclose dialogue, words that are used in a special sense, essays, short stories, poems, newspaper and magazine articles, chapters from books, and other short works. (See also "Select the Title Carefully," pages 268–270, and "Underlining," pages 198–199.)

1. Dialogue

   "I don't know if I can read any more of Walt Whitman's poetry," Jane lamented. "It seems awfully wordy to me."

2. Words used in a special sense

   In the eyes of some twentieth-century critics, Walt Whitman is not the "literary genius" many of his contemporaries considered him to be.

3. Titles

   a. Poem: "When Lilacs Last in the Dooryard Bloomed"
   b. Essay: "Whitman and Transcendentalism"
   c. Chapter from a book: "Whitman's Early Life"
   d. Newspaper article: "Walt Whitman, 100 Years Later"

Quotations are frequently the best evidence the writer has to balance and support generalizations. However, be certain to introduce them in such a way that they work with, and not against, the sentences in which they appear.

8. Brackets

"[Brackets should only be used to enclose short phrases or groups of words. They should never be used to enclose two or three sentences.]"

Brackets ([ ]) are used to enclose the writer's own words in the material he or she is quoting. (See also "Quotation Marks," page 191.)

Brackets are commonly used to add a word or words for clarification in quoted material.

EXAMPLE

As one newspaper editorialist has written, "he [Martin Luther King] was the most important figure in the early days of the civil rights movement in this country."

Brackets are also used if the writer must change the wording slightly to make the quotation compatible with the sentence structure in which it appears.

EXAMPLE

Martin Luther King was not only a Baptist minister, but "he was [also] the most important figure in the early days of the civil rights movement in this country."

Try to work quotations into existing sentence structures without using brackets. If brackets are necessary, make sure the material introduced does not alter the meaning of the quotation.

9. Ellipses

"When ellipses are appropriate in the . . middle of a sentence, always use three periods."

Ellipses are used in quotations to indicate to the reader that words have been omitted. Three ellipsis marks (. . .) are used to indicate that words have been omitted within a sentence. Four ellipsis marks (. . . .) are used to indicate that words have been omitted at the end of the sentence or that a complete sentence has been omitted from the quotation. (See also "Quotation Marks," page 191.)

a. Complete Passage

> He was one of the worst writers in modern American literature, but without his writing one cannot imagine modern American literature. That is because, without his writing, we can hardly imagine ourselves. In at least five solid works—*Main Street, Babbit, Arrowsmith, Elmer Gantry,* and *Dodsworth*—the endurable core that followed upon his slow start and preceded his long decline, he gave us a vigorous, perhaps a unique thrust into the imagination of ourselves.
>
> Mark Schorer in *Sinclair Lewis*

b. Omission of Words within a Sentence

In his biography, Mark Schorer describes Sinclair Lewis as follows:

> He was one of the worst writers in modern American literature, but without his writing, one cannot imagine modern American literature. That is because, without his writing, we can hardly imagine ourselves. In at least five solid works . . . he gave us a vigorous, perhaps a unique thrust into the imagination of ourselves.

c. Omission of Words at the End of a Sentence

In his biography, Mark Schorer describes Sinclair Lewis as follows:

> He was one of the worst writers in modern American literature. . . . [But] without his writing, we can hardly imagine ourselves. In at least five solid works—*Main Street, Babbit, Arrowsmith, Elmer Gantry,* and *Dodsworth*—the endurable core that followed upon his slow start and preceded his long decline, he gave us a vigorous, perhaps a unique thrust into the imagination of ourselves.

d. Omission of a Complete Sentence

In his biography, Mark Schorer describes Sinclair Lewis as follows:

> He was one of the worst writers in modern American literature, but without his writing one cannot imagine modern American literature. . . . In at least five solid works—*Main Street, Babbit, Arrowsmith, Elmer Gantry,* and *Dodsworth*—the endurable core that followed upon his slow start and preceded his long decline, he gave us a vigorous, perhaps a unique thrust into the imagination of ourselves.

The purpose of using ellipses is to enable the writer to condense quoted material into manageable segments so the reader will not be burdened with unnecessary words and sentences that contribute little or nothing to the development of the argument.

However, never use ellipses to omit words or sentences that are essential to the meaning of the quotation.

10. Apostrophes

"The apostrophe is such a small, inconspicuous form of punctuation that its awfully easy to overlook."

The apostrophe (') is a small but important punctuation mark in English grammar.

The apostrophe is used primarily to show ownership. Add "'s" to most nouns to show ownership. To show ownership for plural nouns ending in "s," add only the apostrophe. (See also "Avoid Faulty Comparisons," page 150.)

Most Nouns	Plural Nouns Ending in "s"
Mary's house	farmers' crops
anybody's life	musicians' instruments
Ann's career	employees' benefits
nation's destiny	legislators' responsibilities
team's uniforms	

The apostrophe is used to form contractions. (Contractions, however, establish an informal tone and should be avoided as much as possible in expository writing.)

Original	Contraction
will not	won't
did not	didn't
would not	wouldn't
should not	shouldn't

Do not use apostrophes with possessive pronouns such as "their," "your," "his," "hers," and "ours." (It is redundant to use the apostrophe with possessive pronouns because they already show ownership.)

Incorrect	Correct
Is this your' book?	Is this your book?
Is this their' car?	Is this their car?
Yes, this is hers'.	Yes, this is hers.

Know when to use the apostrophe with the words "its" (a possessive pronoun) and "it's" (a contraction meaning "it is.")

Its	It's
The book takes its title from an old Spanish proverb.	It's my favorite book.

11. Underlining

"Certainly not everything you say is so important it deserves to be underlined."

The purpose of underlining (printed as italics in published works) is to draw attention to some word or words in order to clarify the meaning of a sentence.

Underlining can be used occasionally to emphasize an important word or words in a sentence:

Cancer is such a complicated disease that most research scientists have concluded that there will never be <u>a single cure</u> for all malignancies. They argue, instead, that each type of cancer will have to be treated as a separate disease.

Underlining is used to set off the titles of books, magazines, newspapers, films, plays, long poems, works of art, record albums, television shows (but not individual episodes in a series), and most other long works that are separate entities and not part of some other work. (See also "Select the Title Carefully," pages 268–270.)

1. Book: <u>Writer's Market</u>
2. Novel: <u>The Great Gatsby</u>
3. Magazine: <u>Time</u>
4. Newspaper: <u>The New York Times</u>
5. Film: <u>Star Wars</u>
6. Play: <u>Hamlet</u>
7. Long poem: <u>Paradise Lost</u>
8. Painting: <u>The Last Supper</u>
9. Record album: <u>Sargeant Pepper</u>
10. Television show: <u>Sixty Minutes</u>

Underlining can be used to set off words that are being discussed as words:

One must be careful not to use the words <u>except</u> and <u>accept</u> interchangeably.

In the short expository essay, underlining must be used with the same care as one would use the exclamation point. If too many words and phrases are underlined, it is self-defeating because, then, nothing is emphasized. Under these conditions, underlining serves only to clutter up sentences and paragraphs.

Underline important words or phrases only when it is necessary to emphasize a major point or clarify the meaning of the sentence for the reader.

K 12

12. Hyphens

"Now, class, remember that the h-
yphen should never be used to join or separate words that have on-
e syllable. Also, the hyphen should always separate words betwe-
en syllables."

The hyphen (-), which is primarily used to join and divide words, reflects the fact that language is in a constant state of transition. This is not to suggest that words, and the principles that govern their use, are going to be unrecognizable in five or ten years. Rather, it is to suggest that language is in a subtle, but constant, state of evolution as new words and expressions are being created.

The major function of the hyphen is to create new expressions by joining two or more words until time and common usage dictate that they should be one word. Examples of such words are everywhere around us.

Original Usage	Joined by Hyphen	Contemporary Usage
court house	court-house	courthouse
hard ware	hard-ware	hardware
foot ball	foot-ball	football
fire fighter	fire-fighter	firefighter

It is important to remember, however, that words joined by a hyphen are not coinages. Coinages should never be used in the expository essay because their meanings are restricted to an audience of one—the writer who created them. Words joined by a hyphen, on the other hand, are an acceptable part of Standard English, and they can perform some very valuable functions in the expository essay:

1. Hyphenated words give us access to a more extensive, more current, and much livelier vocabulary for the expository essay. Words such as "pro-life," "pro-choice," "self-made," "self-centered," "anti-war," and numerous others are a vital part of the world in which we live, and they can be used very effectively in the expository essay.

2. The hyphen is used to divide words that will not fit at the end of a typed or printed line of prose. It is common practice, however, to divide words between syllables and to avoid dividing words with only one syllable.

Incorrect

"Now, class, remember that the h-
yphen is never used to jo-
in or separate words that have on-
e syllable. Also, the hyphen should always separate words betwe-
en syllables."

Correct

"Now, class, remember that the hyphen is never used to join or separate words that have one syllable.
Also, the hyphen should always separate words between syllables."

Occasionally it is acceptable to join two modifiers with a hyphen if they work as one unit. It is common practice, however, *not* to join adverbs ending in *-ly* this way.

Incorrect

slowly-growing vegetables
commonly-held beliefs

Correct

slowly growing vegetables
commonly held beliefs
fast-food chain
hard-charging fullback
slow-moving train

Some word combinations are, by their very nature, hyphenated to inform the reader that they work as one unit.

1. Numbers

   three-unit course
   two-thirds of a quart
   ninety-two pigeons

2. Political or religious views

   anti-Iranian
   pro-Iranian
   anti-Catholic
   pro-Catholic

3. Relationships

   brother-in-law
   sister-in-law
   ex-wife
   ex-husband

4. Period of time and some historical events

   one-hundredth anniversary
   Mexican-American war
   Lincoln-Douglas debates

Writers should try to use hyphenated words that have become an accepted part of Standard English. They should not use the hyphen to create their own private vocabulary.

Original	Revision
tattered-jean-patches	tattered jean patches
faulty-light-switch	faulty light switch
tuna-sandwich-budget	poverty-level budget
six-figure-man	someone who earns over $100,000
tuna-breath	bad breath
carrot-nose	long, pointed nose
forty-wink-week-end	a relaxing weekend

13. Editing Internal Punctuation: All Forms

The following paragraph illustrates a variety of problems with establishing internal punctuation in sentences. Note how the flow and meaning of the paragraph is improved considerably in the revised version.

ORIGINAL

Most television shows͵ and movies͵ are action *No commas*

Hyphen ͞oriented˳but there are some very good reasons for

this. Psychologists⊙for example⊙have proven

Apostrophe statistically that peoples attention spans have ⊙ ——— *No comma*

Use parentheses been considerably shortened⋏over the past few years.⌒(There is considerable disagreement⊙however⊙ as to why this is the case.) Film producers are⊙ ——— *Use parentheses*

thus⊙placed in somewhat of a dilemma⋏they must ⊙ ——— *Semicolon needed*

try to entertain audiences that will lose interest

in a matter of minutes if something is dull⊙boring⊙

or uneventful. However, some critics say film

producers are merely pandering to a situation⋏ ——— *No comma*

that they themselves have created⸒or at least ——— *Use dash*

promoted! For example, a critic for the San ——— *Und*

Und Francisco Examiner suggested that⋏''it is a ——— *No comma*

Brackets vicious cycle. Films[that have]nonstop action

demand still more and faster-moving films with

still more nonstop action.'' Clearly if this trend

continues⊙eventually there will be no such thing

as character development⊙plot⊙and dialogue. To

avoid this situation⊙it seems clear that film

producers need to do three things⋏seek better ——— *Colon needed*

scripts⊙hire directors who are committed to

quality films⊙and concentrate more on the story= ——— *Hyphen needed*

telling aspects of their craft. If not, it seems
inevitable that films will lose their appeal for
everyone except the sickest, most depraved element
in our society.

REVISION

Most television shows and movies are action–oriented,
but there are some very good reasons for this.
Psychologists, for example, have proven statistically
that people's attention spans have been considerably
shortened over the past few years. (There is considerable
disagreement, however, as to why this is the case.) Film
producers are, thus, placed in somewhat of a dilemma;
they must try to entertain audiences that will lose
interest in a matter of minutes if something is dull,
boring, or uneventful. However, some critics say film
producers are merely pandering to a situation that they
themselves have created––or at least promoted! For
example, a critic for the San Francisco Examiner
suggested that ''it is a vicious cycle. Films [that have]
nonstop action demand still more and faster–moving films
with still more nonstop action.'' Clearly, if this trend
continues, eventually there will be no such thing as
character development, plot, and dialogue. To avoid this
situation, it seems clear that film producers need to do
three things: seek better scripts, hire directors who are
committed to quality films, and concentrate more on the
storytelling aspects of their craft. If not, it seems
inevitable that films will lose their appeal for everyone
except the sickest, most depraved element in our society.

III

Editing, Revising, and Rewriting

A

Writing and Editing:

A Brief Review

1. Writing

A lesson in English grammar is meaningless unless the writer learns how and when to apply grammatical principles to the writing and editing process. Remember, the expository essay develops through four stages—prewriting, writing, editing, and rewriting. Prewriting involves any of several activities (freewriting, brainstorming, and so on) through which the writer generates ideas for the expository essay. Writing is the actual recording of these ideas until one has produced a rough draft. Editing is the process whereby the writer applies the principles of English grammar to the major problem areas in the rough draft. Rewriting, the final stage, can actually involve several new drafts—each one more polished than its predecessor—as the writer rewrites sentences and paragraphs that he or she has identified as grammatically incorrect or inconsistent.

It is important to recognize these stages in the writing process if you are to know how and when to apply the principles of English grammar. Grammar has nothing to do with prewriting and writing. In fact, if you are overly attentive to the rules of English grammar too early in the writing process, you are likely to develop any of several forms of writer's block—anxieties that will make it extremely difficult for you to generate ideas effectively. Furthermore, you will be wasting time and energy editing sentences that might very well be eliminated from the final draft. The principles of English grammar should be introduced only at the editing and rewriting stages, when they can be used most effectively as powerful allies in eliminating the major problem areas in sentence structure and punctuation.

2. Editing

When you enter the editing stage, you must adopt a very different way of looking at the words and ideas you have generated. You must be precise, merciless, and systematic in seeking out the major problem areas in paragraphs, sentence structures, word choices, and punctuation. Most important, you must avoid the tendency to edit haphazardly—adding a comma here, a capital letter there, and so forth. All of this is purely cosmetic work; it might add something to the appearance of the essay, but it will do little to improve the essay's overall effectiveness. Instead, you should learn to *systematically* edit and revise the various drafts of the writing project.

The editing process involves a list of priorities, each of which should be satisfied before you move on to the next stage. This list of priorities (stated as questions you must ask of yourself) is as follows:

a. The Essay as a Whole

1. Does the thesis statement accurately reflect the position I am arguing in the body of the essay?
2. Does the essay have an effective introduction, body, and conclusion?
3. Should some paragraphs be divided or combined?
4. Is the body of the essay sufficiently developed, or should I add another paragraph or two for reinforcement?
5. Are there irrelevant paragraphs that should be eliminated from the body of the essay?
6. Similarly, are the paragraphs in the body of the essay arranged in the most logical sequence?
7. Does the formal outline reflect a solid framework for the essay?

b. Individual Paragraphs

1. Does each paragraph have a topic sentence, and do the topic sentences accurately reflect and reinforce the thesis position?
2. Are the individual paragraphs sufficiently developed?
3. Do the paragraphs have a balance of generalizations and supporting evidence?
4. Are the sentences in the paragraphs arranged in the most logical sequence?
5. Are there sentences that are irrelevant to the topic sentences?
6. Are there sentences that are repetitive?

c. Individual Sentences

1. Have I eliminated all clearly ineffective sentences and expressions (i.e., wordy expressions, repetitive phrases and clauses, clichés, and so on)?
2. Are there sentences that should be combined or divided?
3. Are the sentences complete?
4. Have I corrected all inappropriate word sequences in the individual sentences (i.e., misplaced modifiers, dangling modifiers, passive constructions, and so on)?
5. Are the sentence structures consistent in terms of organization and expression (i.e., subject-verb agreement, pronoun-antecedent agreement, parallel structure, mixed constructions, and so on)?

d. Individual Words

1. Are all word choices appropriate?
2. Have I eliminated all problems with usage, awkward expressions, coinages, malapropisms, double negatives, and other such word choices?

e. Punctuation

1. Have I supplied the appropriate end punctuation?
2. Have I supplied the appropriate internal punctuation?

f. final revision + proofread

1. Is everything spelled correctly?
2. Are there adequate transitions between sentences?
3. Has everything been capitalized correctly?
4. Are there any missing letters or words?
5. Are there any other stylistic lapses?
6. Are there any problems with tone or sexist or other inappropriate language?

g. Manuscript Preparation

1. Does the title accurately reflect the subject of the paper?
2. Have all sources been accurately footnoted?
3. Has a bibliography been affixed to the end of the paper?
4. Have I complied with all other guidelines for manuscript preparation (type of paper, margins, color of typewriter ribbon, and so on)?

In essence, you should focus on the larger units first (the essay as a whole and paragraphs) before moving on to the smaller units (sentences and word choices). This systematic way of editing will eliminate much wasted effort at the same time that it will enable you to avoid mere cosmetic work during the editing stage.

It is also important to emphasize that there will be some occasional overlap and some retracing of the steps outlined above, especially as sentences continue to be divided, blended, and merged throughout the editing and rewriting process. Also, you may feel more comfortable making slight adjustments in the above scale of priorities to suit your personal editorial preferences (i.e., perhaps establishing sentence completeness somewhat later in the editing process).

B

Revising and Proofreading

Although you should *not* be concerned with proofreading in the earlier stages of the editing process, it does become an important concern in the final stages. Whether we like it or not, we live in a world that often judges things by their appearances. For this reason, misspelled words, missing letters, and other editorial oversights can undermine an expository essay, just as in later life they can cause serious problems in an office memorandum, business letter, or any other form of written communication.

Several issues that were discussed earlier in this text must also be incorporated into the final stages of revising and proofreading essays. These issues are basic subject-verb agreement, sentence fragments, word choices, and punctuation. The reason it is important for you to incorporate these concerns into your final editorial strategies is that, through the process of editing and revising sentences, it is very easy for problems in any of these areas to slip back into the essay. And since these concerns are so basic to effective writing, they can create all the wrong impressions for the reader unless they are corrected.

The following discussion suggests other concerns and strategies for writers who are involved in the final stages of revising and proofreading their respective essays.

[Note: The term "final stages of revising and proofreading" refers to the stages prior to *the typing of the final draft, not* after *the final draft is typed. After the final draft is typed, it is too late to make editorial changes, unless, of course, the essay is being typed on a word processor. In this case, it is never too late to make some final adjustments.]*

1. Develop Proofreading Strategies

"Proofread carefully to avoid foolish ears."

One of the paradoxes of the writing and editing process is that you are often the poorest proofreader of your own work. The reason for this is very simple; over a period of time, you become more sensitive to the argument than to the words and letters that are used to express it. Missing letters and words, inappropriate word choices, and misspelled words that might be blatantly obvious to an objective reader can, thus, easily escape your closest scrutiny. Indeed, this is why most publishing companies keep the writing and editing responsibilities as distinct as possible. The writer is one person; the editor is another. However, since most of us cannot afford the luxury of professional editors who can monitor our writing, we must develop certain proofreading strategies of our own.

It is helpful to remember that most successful writers adopt strategies that are similar to those used by professional editors. When they are proofreading, these writers try, in every way, to put the argument out of their minds temporarily while they concentrate on word choices, spelling errors, and missing letters and words. One way to do this is to use a cardboard or plastic cutout that exposes one line at a time while blocking out everything else on the printed page. This enables the writer (now editor) to concentrate more on individual words and letters because the context in which they appear is temporarily out of sight.

Like outlines, proofreading strategies are matters of personal choice. Most professional writers agree that the best strategies are those that work for the person using them—no matter how bizarre or unconventional they might seem to someone else. At the same time, many professional writers have found that they can proofread better when they read everything out loud. Again, the reason is quite simple. The eye is less likely to skip over blatant errors when the voice forces it to slow down as it moves across the printed page. (See also "Check Spelling," pages 213–216, for other proofreading strategies.)

A final point: students often question whether proofreading is really all that important, since the writer is only searching for an occasional misspelled or inappropriate word. Actually, one can make a very strong case that not only are individual word choices important, but individual *letters* are equally important.

For example, some years back I typed up a group of sentence-combining exercises and copied them for my basic writing classes. However, I did not take the time to proofread carefully what I had written, and after I had handed out copies to my students, it became clear that one very blatant error had slipped right past me.

The original group of sentences read as follows:

> The Asian camel is an unusual animal. It can live for days and even weeks without water. It also has two *humps*.

However, when I typed up the final results of the sentence-combining exercise, I failed to notice that the letter *r* had replaced the letter *h* in one of the words. Note what this proofreading oversight on my part did to the meaning of the sentence:

> The Asian camel is a very unusual animal because it can live for days and weeks without water, and it also has two *rumps*.

[A "very unusual animal," indeed!]

2. Check Spelling

"Doubble check all questionable spellings."

Few skills have been so dramatically revolutionized by the new technologies as has the traditional art of spelling. Most word processing systems come equipped with programs that are capable of automatically checking the spelling of 20,000 to 30,000 of the most common English words. Other programs have attendant features that enable the writer to add specialized terms or words that are commonly misspelled. As a result, the drudgery of proofreading for spelling mistakes has been greatly simplified for those writers skilled in these new technologies.

There are, however, limitations to the type of editorial assistance you can expect from word processing systems. For example, even the most modern system probably would not notice that most of the words in the following sentence are misspelled: "Theirs know weigh we should except there word far it." Since every one of these words would be in the computer's memory bank, albeit to be used in very different contexts, most of these gross misspellings would go undetected.

It is important to recognize that spelling skills develop over a long period of time and through constant exposure to the written word. Indeed, the mind tends to spell words as the eye is accustomed to seeing them over a long period of time. So part of the reason there are so many poor spellers today is that people do not read as much as they once did.

The remedy for poor spelling is, thus, to retrain the eye so that it will become more sensitive to misspelled words. Spelling—which properly belongs in any discussion of *proofreading* problems, not *writing* problems—should be one of the last concerns of writers as they move through the editing stage. You can be an average speller and still hand in a final draft that is reasonably free of misspelled words simply by using these standard editorial techniques:

1. Read the essay out loud. This procedure forces the eye to slow down so the mind can concentrate on individual words rather than on entire sentences or paragraphs.

2. Read the essay backward, concentrating on individual word choices rather than on the argument. Granted, the essay will not make much sense if read this way (or at least it shouldn't), but that is the point. There is less chance that your eye will skip over misspelled words if your mind has no argument to distract it.

3. If it is acceptable to your teacher or professor, have a friend proofread the essay for you. Remember, writers are often the poorest editors of their own work, especially when they proofread for misspelled words. After an essay has gone through several drafts, there is a natural tendency for the writer to be somewhat more sensitive to the argument than to the manner in which it is expressed. Misspelled words that go unnoticed by the writer can, however, be blatantly obvious to an objective reader who is proofreading the essay for the first time.

4. Set the essay aside for a few days and forget about it. Like the rougher grains in a newly polished piece of oak furniture, misspelled words tend to become clearer with age.

5. Use a dictionary to check every word that looks the least bit

suspicious. Remember, even professional writers have to use the dictionary occasionally to check the spellings of certain words that are new to them or that suddenly "don't look right." Indeed, you should not be embarrassed if you find it necessary to check the spellings of even the most basic words in the English language. It is simply a matter of common sense. Effective writers learn to use a dictionary for the same reasons that pharmacists read the labels on every bottle two or three times before preparing a prescription they have filled countless times before. It greatly reduces the likelihood of error.

6. Keep lists of words you commonly misspell and either program them into your word processor's memory bank or else keep them on a convenient list. Recognizing the words we commonly misspell is at least 50 percent of the remedy for poor spelling.

7. Use a cardboard or plastic cutout that exposes one line of the manuscript at a time while blocking out everything else on the printed page. This will enable you to concentrate more on the spellings of individual words, because everything else that might distract your eye is out of sight.

Why is an apparently pedantic detail like spelling so important? Actually, many professors and teachers consider spelling the least essential of all writing skills. They may make an occasional comment on misspelled words, but spelling problems will not substantially affect the grades they give on essays (unless, of course, the spelling is so atrocious it is impossible for them to understand the argument).

However, in that ominous place known as "the real world," spelling is frequently equated with intelligence, competence, and basic literacy. If you are a poor speller, society will often assume that you are ignorant and illiterate. It is, no doubt, an unfair and unwarranted assumption, but it is also one of the realities of the world in which we live. For this reason, it is important for all writers—even professionals— to proofread conscientiously for misspelled words, especially in the later stages of the editing process.

At the same time, of course, you should not become too neurotic about words you occasionally misspell. We all have a tendency to commit such oversights, especially when our attention spans have diminished considerably after long proofreading sessions.

Do not be defeated by occasional misspelled words that appear in the final drafts of your essays. Instead, make lists of these words and work to spell them correctly.

3. Provide Clear Transitions

"Therefore, thus, nevertheless, however, and furthermore, it is important to establish bridges between sentences, but be discreet about it."

There is an internal flow and rhythm to effective writing. Readers sense it immediately, and it leads them gracefully and effortlessly from sentence to sentence and from paragraph to paragraph throughout the essay. Much of this is due to "style"—that virtually undefinable, underlying rhythm that one senses in effective writing. But the flow and rhythm of an essay is also due to careful and meticulous attention to transitions.

"Style" and "transitions" are, of course, not synonymous terms. Indeed, transitions are only one aspect of style—albeit perhaps the most important stylistic element in the expository essay. Weak or ineffective expository writing styles are often ones in which the transitions are so poor that each sentence appears to be a self-contained unit without any real connection to the sentences that precede and follow it. The result is a choppy, erratic flow to the argument. A strong expository style, on the other hand, uses transitions effectively so that each sentence is integrally related to the sentences that precede and follow it. The result is a flow and rhythm that reinforce both the communicative and the persuasive goals of the expository essay.

For all of these reasons, it is a sound editorial strategy to devote some time during the final proofreading stage to determine whether or not you have used effective transitions between your sentences. If not, make it a point to incorporate these transitions into your essay prior to typing the final draft. The end result will be an essay with a much more effective style and rhythm.

Try to connect sentences with the following transitional devices:

1. Use key words in topic sentences and repeat them strategically

throughout the paragraph. (Be careful, however, not to repeat the key words in every sentence in the paragraph; transitions should be subtle, not monotonously repetitive.)

2. Place synonyms for the key words strategically throughout the paragraph.
3. Use pronouns that refer back to the key words or to the ideas in preceding sentences. (See "Establish Pronoun-Antecedent Agreement," pages 138–143.)
4. Use parenthetical or transitional expressions (also known as "sentence connectives" and, at times, "conjunctive adverbs") such as "however," "thus," "in addition to," "finally," "similarly," "therefore," "consequently," "on the other hand," and so on.
5. Use parallel structures or phrases that establish the relationships between sentences.
6. Use conjunctions such as "and" and "but" to introduce sentences. Be careful, however, not to overuse conjunctions as transitional devices.
7. Introduce secondary key words after the topic sentence.

Note how these transitional techniques promote greater clarity, coherence, and unity in the following paragraph:

Only rarely do animals communicate with one
another unless they are instructed to do so by
instinct. But animals do not think in terms of God
or the ultimate meaning of life; they can only
deal in the present, concrete aspects of survival.
Humans, on the other hand, have pondered the
mysteries of life for thousands of years. They
have left their queries of immortality, their
search for God and other abstract issues on

written records. *This desire* to write, to record,
³

is unique to *humankind,* and it is the result of
²

their ability to ponder. The very fact that *humans*
³   7

write down anything is proof that *their* realm
³

of thought goes beyond survival. Through

these observations, it becomes apparent that
³

language is the tool that *humans* use to elaborate,
7   7

explain, and transmit *their* thoughts and ideas. *It*
³

is what makes them superior to the *animals.*
3/5   1

It is what makes them distinct from all other
3/5

living things.

   Notice how ponderously and erratically the argument develops
when the writer fails to use a variety of transitions:

   Only rarely do animals communicate with one another
unless they are instructed to do so by instinct. Humans
think in terms of God and the ultimate meaning of life.
The present moment and the concrete aspects of survival
are all that concern most living things. Humans have
pondered the mysteries of life for thousands of years.
Animals do not question whether they are immortal or if
there is a God. Writing and recording are unique to
humans and part of their ability to ponder. Books are
proof that human thought goes beyond survival. Language
is the tool that explains and transmits thoughts and
ideas. Humans are superior to, and distinct from, all
other living things.

   Clearly, each sentence in this paragraph is a self-contained unit that has few, if any, connections to the sentences that precede and follow it.

It is also important to remember that transitional terms do not create logical relationships. They *reinforce* and *emphasize* relationships already inherent in existing sentence structures. Note how these transitional techniques serve only to clutter up paragraphs in which the sentences have no inherently logical relationships:

> *1*
> <u>Words</u> are much more powerful than weapons.
> *4*   *2*
> Hence, a <u>speech</u> to a midwestern audience must take
>
> into consideration the current agricultural crisis
>   *7*   *4*
> in <u>this country</u>. <u>To the contrary,</u> voting patterns
>
> are radically different in different parts of
> *2*   *4*
> <u>America</u>. Politicans must, <u>for this reason,</u> be
>
> careful when they are campaigning. The essence of
> *3*   *4*
> <u>all this</u> is, <u>thus,</u> that candidates who abuse and
>
> distort language are probably unethical and
>   *4*
> immoral to the core. <u>Finally,</u> shouldn't there be a
>
> constitutional amendment to make English the
>   *2*
> official language of the <u>United States?</u>

In this paragraph, the transitional techniques are purely cosmetic. Nothing short of a major rewrite could improve the flow, movement, and logical development of the argument.

During the final stages of the editing and rewriting process, one of your primary responsibilities is to provide clear transitions from sentence to sentence and from paragraph to paragraph throughout the essay. It is a relatively simple task if you know how and when to use the above transitional techniques to reinforce the communicative and persuasive goals of the expository essay.

(See "Paragraphs in the Body of the Essay," page 81, for information on how to establish transitions *between* paragraphs.)

4. Strive to Capitalize Correctly

"remember, the first word in every sentence is always capitalized."

With respect to capitalization, the primary area of difficulty for many writers is in distinguishing between *particular* nouns, which require capital letters, and *general* nouns, which do not require capital letters. By carefully scrutinizing sentences during the editing stage to determine if they contain particular or general nouns, writers can eliminate most problems in capitalization.

Particular Nouns

1. *Senator* Barry Goldwater of Arizona always advocated a policy of peace through strength.
2. My very best friend lives on *Carver Street.*
3. My favorite classes are *Biology 10* and *History 25.*
4. *Point Loma High School* had three class reunions this spring.
5. *Fort Reliance* was a famous nineteenth-century military outpost.
6. *Bleak House* is one of my favorite novels.

General Nouns

1. Many *senators* have advocated a policy of peace through srength.
2. My very best friend lives on one of the *streets* that run parallel to the river.
3. My favorite subjects are *history* and *biology.*
4. Many *high schools* have class reunions in the spring.
5. The military built many *forts* during nineteenth-century skirmishes with the Indians.
6. My favorite *novels* are those that raise serious social issues.

Through convention and tradition, the following words are also capitalized:

1. The first word in a sentence

   The house down the block is now vacant.

2. Official titles when followed by a proper name

   President Abraham Lincoln, Prime Minister Margaret Thatcher, Premier Gorbachev, Senator Paula Hawkins, Mayor Marsha Thomas, *the president*

3. Nations, states, counties, cities

   Norway, Minnesota, Carver County, Indianapolis

4. The first letter of the important words in book titles

   The House of Seven Gables, Bleak House

5. Days of the week, months, holidays

   Monday, January, Christmas

6. Certain historical events and periods

   World War II, the Crimean War, the Middle Ages

7. Schools, political parties, businesses

   University of Miami, Republican party, General Motors

8. First names, middle names or initials, last names

   Joanne B. Fitzpatrick, John David Lowe, Susan A. Carter

9. Proper names of rivers, lakes, oceans, mountains

   Colorado River, Lake Superior, Atlantic Ocean, the Rocky Mountains

10. Nationalities   *Ethnics*

    Japanese, Swedish, Cuban   *Native Americans   Hispanics*

11. Names of deities

    God, Buddha, Jehovah, Apollo, Muhammad

Like spelling, capitalization should be a very late editorial priority. Problems in capitalization can be annoying to the reader, but normally they do not cause serious problems in communication.

Still, you should strive to capitalize everything correctly because, in the world beyond high school and college classrooms, proper capitalization (like spelling) is often equated with intelligence and basic competence.

5. Check for Missing Letters and Words

"It is always prudent to check the final draft of the essay for mising letters and words."

One of the easiest things to overlook during the editing stage is an occasional missing word, missing letter, or letter that does not belong in a word. These oversights can be innocent enough in some sentences, but they can cause serious problems in others.

For example, the underlined letters and words were missing from the following sentences:

EXAMPLES

1. Pawshops (pawnshops) are places where people go to get quick loans or to purchase things that are not always available in other stores.
2. There is some speculation that the latest wave of tax reforms will run (ruin) the nation's economy.
3. It is easy enough to spot missing letters if one learns to go through one's final draft with a fin (fine) tooth comb.
4. This is to inform you that we will (not) be able to meet you in Buffalo, New York, as we previously planned.
5. Our annual marathon run will start at Huntington Beach and end just east of Jupiter (Boulevard).

Sometimes an additional letter in a word can also cause problems:

EXAMPLES

1. Depending upon one's religion, a person can be married by a priest, a minister, or a rabbit (rabbi).
2. Another world wart (war) would probably end life on the planet earth as we know it.

6. Check for Style and Variety in Sentence Structures

"This is not the way to vary sentence structures. This is not the way to convince the reader that your argument is valid. This is not the way to achieve style. This is the way to drive the reader nuts."

In the broadest sense, style involves just about everything discussed in this text. Word choices, transitions, punctuation, sentence structures—everything ultimately contributes to the writer's style.

Still, it is important to make a distinction between style and grammar. "Grammar" involves the use of language in compliance with certain rules that have evolved over the centuries to make communication easier. "Style," on the other hand, involves the range of options and choices available to the writer within the perimeters established by English grammar.

For example, basic problems with subject-verb agreement or sentence fragments are problems with grammar; they are not questions of style. Conversely, the sequence of long and short sentences in a paragraph are stylistic questions; they are not problems in English grammar. In short, the question of style is relevant only after the writer has complied with the basic rules of English grammar.

The most common stylistic problems in student writing involve the movement and variety of sentence structures. The sentences that introduce this section are not, for example, grammatically incorrect. Their repetitive structure will, however, make it very difficult for the reader to understand the writer's intended meaning.

The following examples illustrate several ways to achieve style and variety in sentence structure:

1. Original

   These sentences are dull and monotonous. These sentences will soon bore the reader.

2. With subordination

   Because these sentences are dull and monotonous, they will soon bore the reader.

3. With coordination

   These sentences are dull, monotonous, and boring.

4. With comma, coordinating conjunction

   These sentences are dull and monotonous, and they will soon bore the reader.

5. With a semicolon

   These sentences are dull and monotonous; they will soon bore the reader.

6. By combining essential elements of two sentences

   These dull and monotonous sentences will soon bore the reader.

7. By reversing subject, verb, and predicate

   The reader will be bored by dull and monotonous sentence structures.

8. With an introductory modifier

   Dull and monotonous, these sentences will soon bore the reader.

Other ways to improve style and variety in sentence structures are as follows:

1. Occasionally vary the lengths of sentences to avoid monotonous rhythms.

EXAMPLE

Some sentences end abruptly. Others soar majestically until the reader is enchanted by the liveliness and grace of the prose style.

2. Occasionally ask a rhetorical question or use an exclamatory sentence to vary the rhythms of your prose style.

EXAMPLES

Why are some sentences dull and boring? There are many reasons, some having to do with the personal idiosyncrasies of the writer and others having to do with the nature of language itself.

Dull and boring sentences must be eliminated from essays! Otherwise, we risk losing our audiences.

Prior to typing the final draft of the essay, check to determine if you have adequate style and variety in sentence structures. If not, make the necessary revisions. The end result will be a much more compelling and readable prose style.

(See also "Learn How to Use Subordination and Coordination," pages 114–116).

7. Check for Tone

"I am right! You are wrong! That's all there is to it! So bug off!"

The tone of an essay can often be at least as important as the logic and supporting evidence writers use to present their arguments to the reader. All of us have undoubtedly had the experience of listening to speakers whose tone of voice was too shrill, whose rhythms and patterns of speech were too strident and caustic, and/or whose word choices were offensive. Undoubtedly, we have also listened to speakers who were so self-righteous, intransigent, or prejudiced in their views that we quickly lost interest in what they were saying. Such speakers are seldom successful or convincing, primarily because the tone of what they are saying works against their intended meanings. These speakers also, of course, fail "to sell themselves," something that is essential if they want to convince their audiences that their arguments are valid.

Certainly, tone is at least as important for writers as it is for speakers. If our word choices and methods of presentation are shrill, strident, or self-righteous, we, too, run the risk of losing our respective audiences. At the very least, we certainly make it very difficult, if not impossible, for our readers to pay close attention to what we are trying to say.

Inappropriate Tone

1. The latest attempts to censor certain forms of rock music are *stupid and preposterous. [The italicized phrase is too self-righteous and intransigent.]*

Revision

1. The latest attempts to censor certain forms of rock music are, *in my opinion, unnecessary and unworkable. [This phrasing presents the writer as a fair-minded individual.]*

Inappropriate Tone	Revision

Inappropriate Tone

2. I don't care what anyone else thinks; it is my opinion that *free-loaders, shysters, and other scum* should be dropped from welfare rolls across the country. *[The name-calling here will quickly alienate the reader.]*

3. *The greedy, crass, crude, and craven charlatans of the coffin business are ripping off the American consumer.* *[The rhythm of this entire sentence is much too strident and abrasive.]*

4. I have read everything on that issue, and I consider my position to be *intellectually irrefutable.* *[A tone of smug, intellectual superiority will always alienate the reader.]*

Revision

2. In spite of arguments to the contrary, I believe that *unqualified recipients* should be dropped from welfare rolls across the country.

3. *Unethical morticians should be strictly regulated by law so that they can no longer exploit the American consumer.*

4. Everything I have read on that issue convinces me that my position *is valid.*

Check the final draft of the essay to determine if there are any words or word sequences that might be overly shrill, strident, or otherwise offensive to the reader. If so, make the necessary revisions. (See also "Revise Awkward Constructions," pages 158–160, "Eliminate Logical Fallacies," pages 104–107, and "Avoid Repetition," pages 99–101.)

8. Avoid Sexist Language

"The writer should always try to avoid sexist language. He should know better than that."

Sexist language involves any word choices that unfairly and inappropriately stereotype either men or women. Such language can often be as offensive as certain racial slurs and innuendos.

EXAMPLES OF INAPPROPRIATE SEXIST LANGUAGE

1. Why should secretaries and nurses demand salaries that are equal to those of other professionals? After all, what they do is merely *women's work.*
2. The reason men commit more violent crimes than women is simply that, as everyone knows, most males are *insensitive brutes.*
3. The woman who wrote that newspaper article sounded like another *dumb broad* who couldn't get her facts straight.
4. Men are all alike; they all think of themselves as *irresistible playboys.*

More commonly, the question of sexist language involves the problem of pronoun references, specifically the persistent use of the pronoun "he" to refer to antecedents that could be either male or female. Some writers (and readers) see nothing wrong with using the pronoun "he" as a kind of universal reference to such antecedents. For example, Cheryl Reimold, author of *How to Write a Million Dollar Memo,* dismisses the entire subject when she says, "In the interests of clear and simple writing, I have adopted one pronoun for both sexes. When you read 'he', think 'he/she'. We all know I am referring to both, so why make an unreadable fuss about it?"

In essence, Ms. Reimold's point is that, in business writing especially, it is better to use the simple "he" references than it is to clutter up sentences and paragraphs with persistent "he/she" references. And since the purpose of most forms of business writing is to communicate an idea as clearly, simply, and directly as possible, she believes this is a perfectly acceptable practice.

At the same time, it is important to emphasize that not everyone shares Ms. Reimold's attitudes toward the issue of sexist language. There are, for example, audiences that would be justifiably annoyed by the persistent use of "he" to refer to antecedents that could be either male or female. These audiences believe such a practice not only perpetuates a form of sexual stereotyping but is also quite misleading in many sentences.

When writing for such audiences, it is always wise to convert these pronoun references in one of three ways: by using a "he or she" reference (though avoid doing this too often); by changing both the antecedent and the pronoun to the plural form; or by eliminating the pronoun and replacing it with the antecedent.

(See also "Establish Pronoun-Antecedent Agreement," pages 138–143, and "Case," pages 143–145.)

Sexist Language

A medical student must spend on the average of $40,000 to $80,000 to complete medical school. Still, *he* will eventually enter a profession that has one of the highest standards of living in the country. *[This is sexist language because it creates the mistaken impression that all medical students are males.]*

Revision

A medical student must spend on the average of $40,000 to $80,000 to complete medical school. Still, *he or she* will eventually enter a profession that has one of the highest standards of living in the country.

OR

Medical students must spend on the average of $40,000 to $80,000 to complete medical school. Still, *they* will eventually enter a profession that has one of the highest standards of living in the country.

OR

A medical student must spend on the average of $40,000 to $80,000 to complete medical school. Still, a *medical student* will eventually enter a profession that has one of the highest standards of living in the country.

As with so many other writing problems, the audience should determine precisely how you address the entire issue of sexist language. For this reason, it is always wise to check with your teachers and professors to determine how they want you to handle the question of pronoun references.

Then, if it is appropriate, make the necessary conversions as illustrated above.

9. Take Pride in Good Sentences

"You mean, there are some sentences in this essay that don't need to be edited and rewritten! I can't believe it!"

Since much that we do during editing and rewriting involves the process of identifying and correcting errors, we often become oblivious to those sentences that are extremely well expressed. Protect and cherish those sentences that succinctly and forcefully express or summarize an idea.

The following is, by no means, an exhaustive list of good sentences from student essays, but these examples do illustrate several ideas that were extremely well expressed.

EXAMPLES OF GOOD SENTENCES FROM STUDENT ESSAYS

1. God has given us everything we need to improve on the world—everything, including a sense of humor when the world falls short of our expectations.
2. Humans can reach as high as they can within their limitations. That is the agony of existence. That is the victory within the defeat.
3. A society that destroys its dreamers and its thinkers will soon find itself wandering without direction over drought-stricken plains until it becomes extinct.
4. The only time some people feel truly alone is when they are around other people who make their lives miserable.
5. Helen Keller could neither see nor hear, and yet she became more richly and profoundly human than many people who were blessed with extraordinary talents.

What makes for a good sentence? Obviously, in part, good sentences are structured after the rules of grammar and rhetoric that have been discussed elsewhere in this text. But there is something else that makes a good sentence truly effective.

A good sentence tends to take on a life of its own, one the reader feels instinctively and intuitively, even if it cannot be explained or defined in rational terms. Also, good sentences are often effective simply because they reflect a certain kind of originality (and honesty) in both the idea and the way the idea is expressed. And finally, a good sentence creates the strongest possible impression that there was no other way for that particular idea to be expressed so effectively.

Just because editing and rewriting involve a critical and uncompromising attitude toward everything you have written, there is no reason to assume that you have produced nothing but weak or ineffective sentences. To the contrary, you have undoubtedly produced many sentences that convey the precise meaning with remarkable clarity.

What's more, you have every right to take pride in those sentences!

10. Revising and Proofreading: All Forms

The following paragraph illustrates a variety of final revising and proofreading concerns:

ORIGINAL

No apos [Video cassettes' have become so popular that

Mis word [many movie critics and film historians, *are* predicting

that they will soon command a greater share of the

Word [market ~~that~~ *than* the films that are shown in theaters.

Trans , *Already these* Video cassettes are changing the way the american] *Cap*

people look at the film industry. ~~Video cassettes']~~ *Rep*
Style
~~are having a tremendous influence on all of us~~

Fewer and fewer people are *p* sending their money at] *Miss let*

the theaters; they prefer, instead, to use that

money to either purchase or rent the video

cassettes when they become available. Films such]   *s-v agr*
, For example, have   *trans*
as Sixteen Candles ~~has~~ made almost as much money
rentals (sp)   *in*
through video sales and ~~rentols~~ as they did the]   *Mis word*

s-v agr [movie theaters. This new shift in viewing patterns
has   *its*
~~have~~ not been without ~~it's~~ problems for the film
It has
industry. ~~Having~~ already been estimated that

pirated versions of video cassettes have cost the]   *Frag*
l
Mis let film industry hundreds of milions of dollars in
rental (sp.)
sales and ~~rentel~~ fees. Furthermore, it is

estimated that this figure will approach the one

billion dollar mark before the end of this decade.

[Although the film industry is an extremely
i
affluent business entity, one has to question]   *Mis let*
Good
whether or not even it can afford these staggering

[losses for too many years. But ~~the typical~~
s   are generally so
Hollywood producer ~~is so stupid and~~ out of touch]   *Tone*
they
with reality that one questions if ~~he~~ will do]   *Sxl*

anything about the problem.

REVISION

Video cassettes have become so popular that many movie
critics and film historians are predicting that they will

soon command a greater share of the market than the films that are shown in theaters. Already these video cassettes are changing the way the American people look at the film industry. Fewer and fewer people are spending their money at the theaters; they prefer, instead, to use that money to either purchase or rent the video cassettes when they become available. Films such as *Sixteen Candles*, for example, have made almost as much money through video sales and rentals as they did in the movie theaters. But this new shift in viewing patterns has not been without its problems for the film industry. It has already been estimated that pirated versions of video cassettes have cost the film industry hundreds of millions of dollars in sales and rental fees. Furthermore, it is estimated that this figure will approach the one billion dollar mark before the end of this decade. Although the film industry is an extremely affluent business entity, one has to question whether or not even they can afford these staggering losses for too many years. But Hollywood producers are generally so out of touch with reality that one wonders if they will do anything about the problem.

C

Editing and Rewriting

the Expository Essay

The distinction between editing and rewriting is subtle but significant. "Editing" involves the process of identifying and occasionally revising the major problem areas in essays, paragraphs, and sentences. "Rewriting" involves the actual method that is used to write several new drafts of the essay until the writer has produced a final draft that is grammatically correct and stylistically appropriate.

Certainly there is some overlap between editing and rewriting responsibilities. For example, when sentences are combined, or when supporting evidence is added to individual paragraphs, there is some necessary rewriting that takes place. In fact, it cannot be avoided.

Still, it is wise to attend to as many of the actual rewriting responsibilities as possible *after* the most important editorial work has been completed and the major problem areas have been identified. Once the major problems have been identified, the writer may decide to eliminate some sentences and paragraphs from the essay. So, as always, why waste time rewriting sentences and entire paragraphs if they are not to be included in the final draft?

The following essays represent a range of challenges for writers who are actively engaged in editing and rewriting their respective rough drafts:

1. Violence in America

The following essay, which evolved out of the prewriting and writing stages in Part I of this text, is a relatively simple one to edit and rewrite. The prewriting and writing stages produced an essay with a strong thesis and a solid organization. Furthermore, the paragraphs are well developed and arranged in a logical sequence.

For all of these reasons, this writer does not have to devote too much time and energy to editing either the essay as a whole or its individual paragraphs. Rather, after a few expressions are eliminated or repositioned, this writer can begin immediately to apply the principles of English grammar and rhetoric to individual sentence structures and word choices.

FIRST DRAFT

Jane Morgan

English 10

Violence in America

Going to movies and staying home to watch

pastimes

One word ⎡television are two of America's favorite ~~past~~

⎣~~times~~. They are common ways for many people to

escape from their everyday problems and ~~more in~~⎤   *Awk*

relax through

Awk ⎣~~and out of~~ their fantasies. After a busy day of

more relaxing than lying

work there is nothing ~~easier than relaxing~~ on a⎤   *Clarify words*

234   Editing, Revising, and Rewriting

couch, eating popcorn, and watching an

entertaining movie on television. This may seem

Avoid specific examples in intro

innocent enough, but what happens when ~~one sees~~ *people with psychological and emotional problems watch violent* ~~violent movies, and is affected like John~~ *movies and are affected adversely by them.* ~~Hinckley. He saw a movie about a character trying~~

~~to~~ impress a girl by assassinating the President

and in turn tried to make that fantasy come true

¶ unity. (Eliminate or incorporate into ¶ 4).

for himself. Granted, movies and television can be

great relaxing entertainers, but after the case of

John Hinckley, one is required to believe that

violent shows do effect the people who watch them

often enough adversely. Does the public need to

and movies

fear the effects of television on the minds of

The answer would seem to be, "Yes!" For this reason,

their viewers? Steps must be taken to reduce the

types of violence depicted on television and in

films or else America is doomed.

more serious

Violence on television is probably the ~~larger~~ *Word*

much larger

problem because it reaches a ~~wider range of~~ *Word/awk*

audience. An average American views approximately

Hyphen three and a half hours of television a day. ~~This~~ *Pro*

For

children, this figure is even more alarming.

~~is perhaps best exemplified by children~~ Since

Editing and Rewriting the Expository Essay 235

Pro ~~most of them~~ *many children* have been old enough to watch

television, ~~children~~ *they* have been placed in front of

it by their parents who use this machine as a

No comma babysitter. ¶As ~~they~~ *these children* grow older and come home from

school, what is usually the first thing they do?

They turn on the television set usually to watch

their favorite cartoons. Cartoons can be enjoyable

Awk/usg for ~~most anyone~~ *many children,* but often enough, ~~the violence of~~ *they, too, are extremely*

~~them is ignored~~ *violent.* For example, in viewing the

D mod cartoon Tom and Jerry, ~~it is not uncommon to watch~~ *childen can see*

a tongues being bitten off, or someone's head being

bashed in by a club. Elmer Fudd ~~of Bugs Bunny~~ *Or in Bugs Bunny, they can watch*

Clic trying to gun down a rabbit ~~every spare minute of~~ *in every scene.*

~~his time~~ Also, Bamm Bamm from The Flintstones

Shft tense ~~takes~~ *will take* a person and knock him around on rock

floors. *But* The Roadrunner is perhaps the most violent

of all cartoons. In this cartoon, a coyote is

Awk ~~depicted by trying to catch~~ *constantly trying to catch* and kill a roadrunner

by different methods, ranging from boulders to

Apos dynamite. Obviously, today's ~~youngsters~~ *youngsters* are

spending too much time watching these types of

Right margin notes:
Dev through supporting evidence (examples statistics, etc.)
Awk
Frag
Trans
Sp

programs. Children are very impressionable at such

Pronouns needed a young age, and *they* often mimic what they see. Since

children are especially susceptible to influences

from society, *Something* must be done to limit the

violence depicted on today's television shows.

Frag (Sub the first dep clause.)

As people grow older, they ~~usually switch from~~ *stop*

No apos watching television cartoon's ~~to~~ *and start* watching soap

Trans operas and nighttime television. *However,* The violence on

Awk/word

soap operas is astonishing. On <u>All My Children</u>, a

Underline titles in final draft.

daytime soap opera, one episode showed a woman

hiding from her mother who was trying to kill her.

Nighttime soap operas are no better, ~~and tend to~~ *even though they are*

equally concerned with money and power.

~~focus on the benefits of achieving power.~~ <u>Dynasty</u>,

Clarify

<u>Dallas</u>, and <u>Falcon Crest</u> are three of the nation's

top-rated television shows, and they all focus on

the deviant life styles of the main characters.

Good example For example, J. R. from <u>Dallas</u>, is constantly

No comma

scheming to increase his power and wealth

regardless of who he hurts, and, in one

episode, he was shot down by his mistress. This

one episode ~~drew much attention of the public~~ *received much public attention*

because the ~~media over~~ *network constantly* publicized *the question,* "Who shot

Wordy/ awk

Eliminate (¶ Log. and unity)

J. R.?" ~~No matter how old one is, he can never~~
~~escape from the impact that television has had,~~
~~and again the question is, does television really~~
~~affect the public?~~

Television news also promotes violent forms of behavior.

Awk

~~News is another violence impressionated show~~ On every news station, there is ~~always~~ information about murders, kidnappings, or wars. The news media is also famous for making celebrities out of criminals. Take for example the John Hinckley

Sub/coor

case, ~~He~~ *Hinckley* was just an ~~everyday~~ *ordinary* person until he decided to try to assassinate President Reagan.

However, From the moment he shot his gun and injured three — *Trans*

people, John Hinckley's name ~~was now~~ *became* known around — *Use*

If the people watching had similar problems,

the nation. ~~If a person really had an identity~~

Awk and confusing

what would stop them
~~crisis, and had a lack of norms, what is going to~~
~~stop him~~ from doing the same thing? Because of the

Frag

news has a large audience,
fact that television ~~has a wide audience range.~~
the coverage   *monitored more effectively to protect*
~~The violence~~ needs to be ~~screened out to protect~~ — *Usg*

the general public from the dangers of ~~the~~
over-exposure to violent acts.
~~negative approach of today's television violence~~

Movies, on the other hand, do not reach as large

Awk an audience as television, and ~~they also show more~~ *yet they show even more violence.*
~~sex and violent situations,~~ *For example,* President Nixon, *Trans*

during his term of office, asked sociologists to
perform a series of tests ~~explaining~~ *to evaluate* the over all *Word*
effect of pornographic movies on the public. *Although* The
results were not ~~significant enough to report, but~~ *conclusive, the report strongly suggested*
a correlation between violent movies and violence in real life.
~~this also concluded that people were being~~ *Awk & wdy*
~~influenced, and somebody was in fact trying to~~
~~initiate action against them.~~ As was stated

before, ~~and need not be overstated, was the case~~
Sub/coor ~~off~~ John Hinckley. ~~He enacted his~~ *acted out his* fantasy after *Dev examples or use others that can be dev*
seeing the movie Taxi Driver, which involved a
young prostitute. Another movie, The Wall, depicts
Rep violence, and its theme is violence in a violent
world. ~~This movie is geared on affecting the human~~
~~senses, but what will happen if someone cannot~~
~~handle these reactions. Again the question arises~~
~~will the public have to fear its affects?~~

Necessary steps must be taken to reduce these
types of movies, *or, at the very least,* ~~and~~ critics should try to
discourage the public from viewing them.

*Commas/
word* Violence, as shown in both television and movies
Word must be ~~heavily~~ *greatly* reduced. The screening and rating
Word of such shows must be made ~~harder to pass~~ *more stringent.* It is

up to the reader to answer the previous questions

and decide what should or should not be done about

*Dev
con* such shows. The last thing to be stated is, does

the public really need to be afraid of the *e*ffects   *Word*

of violence on the minds of ~~it's~~ *its* viewers (that is

depicted in movies and on television)?   *M mod*

Sub/coor

After some careful proofreading, this essay can now be considered a very effective final draft. Note, however, that even as this writer makes the final revisions, she adds a few ideas (and deletes a few others) that had not occurred to her previously.

Remember, successful writers seldom *record* anything. They are almost always *discovering and clarifying* new meanings about what they have written, right up to and including the final drafts of their respective writing projects. When writers begin to merely *record* their ideas on paper, it generally indicates that their writing has become dull, mechanical, and unconvincing.

Jane Morgan

English 10

American Violence and Media Violence

Going to movies and staying home to watch

television are two of America's favorite pastimes.

They are common ways for many people to escape from their everyday problems and relax through their fantasies. After a busy day of work, there is nothing more relaxing than lying on a couch, eating popcorn, and watching an entertaining movie on television. *Although* ~~This~~ may seem innocent enough, ~~but~~ what happens when people with psychological and emotional problems watch violent movies and are

Word [*a* ~~e~~ffected adversely by them? Does the public need to fear that such unstable personalities will try to imitate the violent acts they see in movie theaters and on television shows? The answer to this question *is* ~~seems to be~~ an unequivocal, "Yes!" For this reason, steps must be taken to reduce the

Good thesis!

types of violence depicted on television and in *will suffer a serious loss of values.*

Clarify [films, or else America ~~is doomed~~

Violence on television is probably the more serious problem because it reaches a much larger audience. It has been estimated that the average

Cap [*A* ~~a~~merican views approximatly three-and-a-half hours] *Sp*

Footn? [of television a day. For children, this figure is even more alarming. Many children, since they have been old enough to watch television, have been

placed in front of it by their parents, who use

this machine as a baby-sitter. It has been

Comma ⌈ estimated that‸by the time these children are
①

*Good
evidence
(footnote!)* ⌈ ready for kindergarten, they will have spent

"twice as much time in front of the television set

as they have with their parents."

Once these same children start school, what

happens to them? As soon as they get home, they

turn on the television set, usually to watch their

favorite cartoons. Cartoons can be enjoyable for

many children, but often they, too, are extremely

violent. For example, in the cartoon Tom and

Jerry, children can see tongues being bitten off

or heads being bashed in by a club. Or in Bugs

*Miss
word* ⌈ Bunny, they can watch Elmer Fudd trying‸kill a
to

rabbit in almost every scene. Also, Bamm Bamm from

The Flintstones will pound people on rock floors.

But of all the cartoons, perhaps The Roadrunner is

the most violent. In this cartoon, a coyote is

Comma ⌈ constantly trying to catch and kill a roadrunner⊙
②

either by dropping a boulder on its head, blowing

it to bits with dynamite, or destroying it in some
other way. Obviously, judging by these programs,
children today are exposed to far too much
violence on television. And, since children are
very impressionable, these violent cartoons could
cause them to mimic these patterns of behavior.
Surely, for these reasons, something must be done
to limit the violence depicted on television
cartoons.

As people grow older, they usually stop watching
television cartoons and start watching soap operas
and nighttime television. However, the violence on
soap operas is astonishing. On All My Children, a
daytime soap opera, one episode showed a woman

Miss word ☐ hiding *from* her mother who was trying to kill her.

Nighttime soap operas are equally violent, even

Rep ☐ though they are ~~equally~~ *more* concerned with money and
power. Dynasty, Dallas, and Falcon Crest are three
of the nation's top-rated television shows, and

Word ☐ they all focus on the ~~deviant~~ *bizarre and twisted* lifestyles of the
main characters. For example, J. R. from Dallas is
constantly scheming to increase his power and

Comma

Rep

wealth, regardless of whom he hurts, and, in one
episode, he was shot ~~down~~ by his mistress. This
one episode received much public attention,
primarily because the network constantly
publicized the question, "Who shot J. R.?"

The television news services also promotes
S-v agr

violent forms of behavior. On every news station,
there is information about murders, kidnappings,
or wars. The news ~~media is~~ *services are* also famous for making
Word

celebrities out of criminals. Take, for example,
the John Hinckley case; Hinckley was just an
ordinary person until he tried to assassinate
President Reagan. However, from the moment he
Sp

shot his gun and injured three people, John
Hinckley's name became known across the nation. If
the people watching had similar problems,
television gave them a way to gain both publicity
and psychological help—but at the cost of someone

Apos

elses life! Certainly, the violence on the news
services needs to be more carefully monitored so
that unstable personalities do not imitate the
actions of people like John Hinckley.

Violent movies do not reach as large an audience as does television, but, at the same time, they seem to have an even greater influence on the people who watch them. For example, during his term in office, President Nixon asked a group of sociologists to perform a series of tests to evaluate the overall effects of pornographic movies on the public. Although the results were not conclusive, the report strongly suggested a correlation between violent movies and violence in real life. John Hinckley, for example, was influenced by the movie Taxi Driver, a film that involved a young prostitute and an insane taxi driver who falls in love with her and who resorts to violence to gain her attention. Based on this incident, it seems clear that movies can and do motivate people to commit violent acts. At the very least, critics should warn the public about such films.

Violence, as shown in both television and movies, must be greatly reduced, and the screening and rating of such shows must be made more

Quote? (Direct quote would be better evidence.)

Footn?

stringent. Although we may disagree on precisely

how to do this, we must acknowledge that movie and

television violence does affect certain people

adversely. For this reason, the <u>public</u> should put

pressure on ~~their~~ *its* elected officials to pass laws

                                              Pro/agr

to control the violence that is depicted in movies

and on television.

2. An Examination of Homer's *The Life Line*

The following essay presents a much more challenging test of a writer's editorial and rewriting skills:

1. The thesis, "This painting is very well composed, and the artist created a very poignant scene with the use of color," is too broad to provide a clear focus for the essay. The thesis could, in fact, apply to just about any painting.
2. The introductory paragraph introduces specific examples much too early, and the movement from generalizations to specifics is haphazard and illogical.
3. The last paragraph in the body of the essay is blended into the conclusion, suggesting that the essay is both insufficiently developed and ineffectively concluded.
4. One paragraph in the body of the essay goes off on a tangent and begins to discuss the woman's "religion" and "ethnic race."
5. There are numerous problems with subordination and coordination, word choices, comma splices, subject-verb agreement, and the other principles of English grammar.
6. Some words are misspelled, and some words have missing letters.

When confronted by such a range of editorial and rewriting challenges in the rough drafts, the writer is always wise to go back to the basics of thesis development, organization, and paragraphing before attending to the details of sentence structure, punctuation, and spelling. It is also wise to do such editing and rewriting over at least two drafts, rather than to try to incorporate all of the revisions into one draft.

FIRST DRAFT

Howard Carter

English 10

An Examination of Homer's <u>The Life Line</u>

<u>The Life Line</u> is an emotional painting. The artist uses color to communicate this emotion. The colors used in the painting are the first thing the observer sees. The use of grey to color the torentous ocean and the ominous sky suggest how wretched the situation is. Particularly noticible is the use of bright red in the center of the painting. This suggests life and determination. Red is a rich color and it contains strength and hope. The use of this color is also effective in attracting the observer's attention to the main subject of the painting. Contrast also comes into play here--while the ocean looks bleak and colorless, the people look tenacious and swarthy.

Intr moves too quickly to specifics. (Instead, dev the more universal statement about the relationship between people and nature in this painting.)

Move discussion of color to new ¶ 5.

Thesis is too broad.

Homer presents a powerful theme. That theme involves a person's stubborn ~~This painting is very well composed and the artist~~ will to survive—and to help others survive—even when confronted ~~created a very poignant scene with the use of~~ by certain destruction. ~~color~~

The observer's attention is directed to the people on the life line. These people are in the center of the painting and they are the most important element. The two are placed at midpoint between the unseen ships. This causes the observer to feel the urgency of the situation. "En media res," in the middle of things, this is always the most important point in any progression of scenes or events. The artist also places the actors far out at sea, far from the security and strength of the cliffs in the background. The actors are dangling directly above the torrent with nothing to cling to but their own physical strength and their innate stubbornness.

The people are well portrayed in this painting. A man is depicted trying to save his own life and the life of a woman. A woman is unconscious but still the man does not let go. Again the tenacity is evident. The strength of the man is shown in the way he holds the woman's body with one great arm. The man in this painting is not thinking about trivial matters: he is not concerned with the woman's religion or whether she is of the right ethnic race. He is only concerned with the task at hand. He keeps moving and he doesn't let go. He is a person stripped of vanity, left only with a willingness to survive.

Upon observance of this painting, it is noticed that the face of the man cannot be seen, only his dangling legs and the resoluteness of his ruddy hand are visable. But why is the man's face hidden? It is not necessary to see the face. A frightened countenance would detract from the over-all mood portrayed in the rest of the man's body, and a determined, strong visage would add nothing. No, to expose the face of the man would be a mistake. The meaning behind this painting deal with the sould of all people and of the universal nature of the human heart. So it could be any person, with any face, and the scene would be unchanged.

New ¶: discussion of color from ¶ 1

At rock bottom, in the souls of all people, be

they criminals or entrepeneurs, lies the undaunted

will to survive and the tendency to be altruistic.

Surely the man here would have a better change of

surviving if he wasn't trying to also save the

woman. But he has to give of himself, to be a hero

for the sake of someone else, someone he may not

even be acquainted with.

There are obviously still many sentences that will need to be edited and rewritten in the second draft of this essay. But now that we have the foundations for an introductory paragraph, a stronger thesis, a logical arrangement to the paragraphs, and a concluding paragraph, we are ready to focus more effectively on the principles of sentence structure, word choices, punctuation, and spelling.

SECOND DRAFT

Howard Carter

English 10

An Examination of Homer's The Life Line

The Life Line is an emotional painting through

which the artist Winslow Homer makes a universal

statement about human perserverance when

confronted by the powerful forces of nature.

Through the dramatic situation, colors, and other

details in the painting, Homer presents a powerful

Good thesis

theme. That theme involves a person's stubborn

will to survive—and to help others survive—even

when confronted by certain destruction.

The observer's attention is directed to the

people on the life line. These people are in the

suspended between two

Sub/coor

center of the painting, ~~and they are the most~~

~~important element. The two are placed at midpoint~~

~~between the~~ unseen ships. ~~This causes the observer~~

Wdy

~~to feel the urgency of the situation. "En media~~

~~res," in the middle of things, this is always the~~

~~most important point in any progression of scenes~~

~~or events~~ The artist also places the actors ~~far~~   *Rep*

where they are far removed

out at sea, ~~far~~ from the security and strength of

the cliffs in the background. The actors are

violent waves,

Awk

dangling directly above the ~~torrent~~ with nothing

sustain them except their innate determination to survive.

to ~~cling to but their own physical strength and~~

~~their innate stubbornness~~

Other details are equally important in depicting this grim struggle for survival. — *Topic sentence is weak*

∧ ~~The people are well portrayed in this painting.~~

desperately

A man is ~~depicted~~ trying ∧ to save his own life ~~and~~

as well as   *The*

Sub/coor — ∧ the life of a woman. ~~A~~ woman is unconscious, but

allow for her to slip into the

still the man does not ~~let go. Again the tenacity~~

thrashing waves.

~~is evident,~~ ∧ The strength of the man is shown in

the way he holds the woman's body with one great

arm. The man in this painting is not thinking

Θ

about trivial matters; he is ~~not concerned with~~

totally preoccupied with the task at hand.

~~the woman's religion or whether she is of the~~

Stripped of all vanity, he acts only to survive and to help

~~right ethnic race. He is only concerned with the~~

others survive.

~~task at hand. He keeps moving and he doesn't let~~

Wdy/rep — ~~go. He is a person, stripped of vanity, left only~~

~~with a willingness to survive~~

— *¶ Unity/log*

closer observation, one can see that Homer has

Trans — Upon ~~observance of this painting, it is noticed~~ — *Awk*

deliberately concealed the man's face from the observer.

~~that the face of the man cannot be seen.~~ Only his

dangling legs and the resoluteness of his ruddy

hand are visable. But why is the man's face

The reason might be that a

Chop — hidden? ~~It is not necessary to see the face. A~~

frightened countenance would detract from the

over-all mood portrayed in the rest of the man's

A   *determined*

body, ~~and a determined~~ strong ∧ visage would add

because the

nothing, ~~No, to expose the face of the man would~~ ⌐   *Rep*

~~be a mistake. The~~ meaning behind this painting

deal with the souls of all people and of the

universal nature of the human heart. So it could

be any person, with any face, and the scene would

be unchanged.

Trans ⌐   The artist *also* uses color to communicate this

emotion. ~~The colors used in the painting are the~~

~~first thing the observer sees~~ The use of grey to   *Rep*

color the torentous ocean and the ominous sky

suggest how wretched the situation is.

¶ Unity (move to end of this ¶)

Particularly noticible is the use of bright red in

the center of the painting. *Suggesting life and determination,* ~~This suggests life and~~   *Sub/coor*

~~determination~~ Red is a rich color and it contains

strength and hope. The use of this color is also

effective in attracting the observer's attention

, *the people trapped on the life line.*

to the main subject of the painting. Contrast also

comes into play here while the ocean looks bleak ⌐   *Wrong punc*

and colorless, the people look tenacious and

swarthy.

Homer's painting thus presents the idea that,

Clic ⌐ ~~At rock bottom~~ in the souls of all people ~~, be~~ ⌐   *Log*

Log [~~they criminals or entrepeneurs~~ *there*] lies the undaunted

will to survive and the tendency to be altruistic.

Surely the man here would have a better chan*c*e of] *Wrong word*

surviving if he wasn't trying to also save the

woman. But he has to give of himself, to be a hero

for the sake of someone else, someone he may not

Wdy [even ~~be acquainted with~~ *know*].

Now this essay is ready for some final proofreading and editorial polish. (Note, again, how this writer is still making changes even as he transcribes his handwritten revisions from the second to the third draft. He is constantly writing and discovering the meaning of his essay; he is never merely recording.)

THIRD DRAFT

Howard Carter

English 10

An Examination of Homer's The Life Line

The Life Line is an emotional painting through

which the artist Winslow Homer makes a universal

statement about human perserverance when

confronted by the powerful forces of nature.

Through the dramatic situation, colors, and other

Miss word ⎣details ^in^ the painting, Homer presents a powerful theme. That theme involves a person's stubborn will to survive—and to help others survive—even when confronted by certain destruction.

The observer's attention is directed immediately to the people on the life line. These people are in the center of the painting, suspended between two unseen ^s^ships. *Trans* The artist ^also^ places the actors out⎦ *No cap* at sea, where they are far removed from the security and strength of the cliffs in the background. The actors are dangling directly above the violent waves, with nothing to sustain them except their innate determination to survive. Undoubtedly, Homer incorporated all of these

Rep ⎡details into the scene to reinforce the deep sense
⎣of urgency that pervades the ~~scene~~ ^mood^ depicted in the painting.

Other details are equally important in depicting this grim struggle for survival. A man is trying desperately to save his own life as well as the life of a woman. The woman is unconscious, but the

man clings to her with one arm and will not allow
her to slip into the thrashing waves. The man in
this painting has no time to think about selfish

Cs or trivial matters, he is totally preoccupied with
the task at hand. Stripped of all vanity, he acts
only to survive and to help someone else survive.

Upon closer observation, one can see that Homer
has deliberately concealed the man's face from the

Apos observer. The man's dangling legs and powerful arms
are all that the observer can see. But why would *Sp*
Homer omit such an important detail as the
expression on the man's face? The reason might be
that a frightened countenance would detract from
the overall mood portrayed in the rest of the
man's body. A strong determined visage, on the *Coor adjs*
other hand, would probably be redundant because

Good summary the action speaks for itself. But most important,
this painting deals with the souls of all people
and the universal nature of the human heart. So,
to universalize this theme, Homer cleverly keeps
the man's identity anonymous.

Homer also uses color to reinforce the major

theme of his painting. The rich red clothing of the characters on the life line is contrasted with the grays that dominate the ocean and the ~~strange~~ *ominous* sky. The color red immediately attracts the observer's attention to the plight of the figures on the life line, but it also represents strength and hope. The people are trapped in a wretched situation; nonetheless, their tenacity is reflected in the color red that surrounded them. At the same time, of course, nature's indifference is reflected in the color gray that pervade the background of the painting.

Wrong word [margin note]

Shft [margin note]

S-V agr [margin note]

Homer's painting thus presents the idea that every person has the inherent will to survive. But beyond that, it also suggests an altruistic need to help others survive. Surely the man in the painting would have a better chance of surviving if he was not struggling to save the woman. But something in his character forces him to give of himself, to be a hero for the sake of someone he may not even know—someone who appears to be an innocent victim of the capricious forces of nature.

Miss letter [margin note]

Editing and Rewriting the Expository Essay   257

The following essay has potential, but there is still much editorial work that needs to be done:

1. The thesis and organization are fairly effective, although some development is needed in the body of the essay. The essay could also use a stronger conclusion.
2. More work is needed with the specific language of the two poems, especially by integrating shorter quotations into existing sentence structures.
3. First-person pronoun references ("I") should probably be edited from the final draft of the essay.
4. The sentence structures need strengthening, especially in such areas as subordination and coordination, style, pronoun references, passive constructions, transitions, faulty comparisons, and so on.
5. Some attention to spelling and proofreading would also add much to the effectiveness of the essay.

FIRST DRAFT

Marsha Thomas

English 10

The Dying Season

The two poems "After Apple-Picking" and
"Reluctance" develop similar themes. ~~One of them~~ *"Reluctance,"* ⨍
as its name implies, describes the reluctance of the narrator to let ⨍
~~is not too sure what he has accomplished with his~~ ⨍
go of life; he is perhaps ready to die physically but surely not in
~~life though the other does not have those worries~~ ⨍
spirit. A different perspective on death is found in "After Apple-Picking."
Awk/   ~~He simply does not want to give up. This speaker~~ ⨍
pro   *In this poem Frost allows one to see how death could be looked upon,*
refs   ~~the one who does not want to give up, is tired~~ ⨍

Clarify word choices

even looked forward to as a kind of necessary respite at the end
~~physically but not mentally. His life has been a~~
of life's constant toil.
~~long and troubled journey, and yet it has never~~

~~been tedious.~~ The theme of the two poems involves

two narrators who are confronted by the

inevitability of death, and yet they confront this

adversary in two very different ways.

The details of the two poems are noteworthy.

Looking around himself the speaker in "Reluctance"

M mod sees everywhere subtle hints that since everything

else is dying, he too should be prepared to die:

Dev through specific evidence from the poem.

    And the dead leaves lie huddled and still,

      No longer blown hither and thither;

    The last lone aster is gone;

      The flowers of the witch-hazel wither.

Perhaps work shorter quotes into sentences and ¶

New ¶ In contrast, "After Apple-picking" describes the melancholic state
~~Even more aware of this is the speaker in "After~~
of mind of an old apple picker in late fall. As this old man
~~Apple Picking." As he~~ looks through a thin sheet

Run of ice he skimmed from a drinking trough he begins

to see reality fade around the area where he is

standing. Something moves him though to wonder

Good point— dev it! what this all means. Is it a sign for him to start

thinking about more important things than just

picking apples? Maybe he should have been more

Good use more short quotes like this.

sensitive to these things all his life--since the

ladder's always been "sticking through a tree/
Nonetheless, he accepts the fact that he is about
Toward heaven." ~~Whatever the case, the dilema is~~
to die, for he has no desire to pick the apples that still remain   *Awk*
~~not so much that he wants to go on but rather that~~
on the tree.
~~he wants it all over with./~~ He is "done with apple

picking now."

    The choice of whether to live life to the

fullest or give up becomes the central concern of
                           In "Reluctance," the
both poetic works. ~~The one~~ speaker climbs to the   *Trans*
                                    he
top of a hill and looks out over the world. ~~He~~   *Sub/coor*

knows in his heart that it is time to "go by the
                        Still, although he realizes that his body is dying,
highway home." ~~Still he concludes that it would be~~
he questions the undeniable treason of those men who can accept so
Sub/coor ~~"treason" to give up. He will search in spirit if~~
easily and effortlessly the end of something they hold dear.
~~not with his body. He will live life mentally even~~

Divide and develop the issues raised in this ¶.
~~as his physical being persists out of existence.~~
New ¶ In contrast,
~~Not so~~ the speaker in the other poem, ~~He~~ is ready   *Trans*
                                        O
for the release of death. ~~He is~~ "Overtired of the   *Sub/coor*
                                         he
Great Harvest" he once pursued so diligently. ~~He~~
Sub/coor
becomes somewhat uneasy when he compares himself   *Cite specific lines from*

to the apples that have fallen from the tree to be

the poem as supporting evidence.

turned into cider. These apples make him think

that maybe the cellar where the cider is pressed

is a symbol of hell. ~~The~~ *Still, although* The thought frightens him,

~~but~~ more than anything he just wants to sleep.

In writing these two poems, Frost thus presents two unique perspectives on the way two old men view death. ①~~think the two poems start from much the same~~ ~~idea. But they are very different in the end.~~

Avoid first person "I" in con, since it hasn't been established earlier in the essay

There is a force and a restless spirit in the one

speaker. The spirit in the other man though faded

away like the reality on the other side of the

sheet of ice. The body lies down to rest knowing

that the spirit has already ceased to be a part of

the planet earth. It has moved into that world

only pointed at by the ladder sticking through the

tree. "Essence of winter sleep is on the night,"

he thinks before falling asleep.

Tighten up both language and focus of this con

Students occasionally ask, "So what if I can't write. Aren't my ideas valid?" One answer to this question is, "The idea and the expression of the idea are inseparable. If the expression is confused for any reason whatsoever, including a failure to follow the basic rules of English grammar, the thought will also be confused." When this happens, it is the writer who has failed—not the reader.

In the following essay, however, the ideas and the expression of the ideas fuse into an organized, lucid prose style that effectively explains this writer's views of the two poems. There may be some minor grammatical lapses, but they do not cause serious problems in communication.

SECOND DRAFT

Marsha Thomas

English 10

The Dying Season

In the poems "Reluctance" and "After Apple-

Comma   Picking," Robert Frost presents two unique*(,)*but

Comma   comparable*(,)*views of death. "Reluctance," as its

name implies, describes the reluctance of the

narrator to let go of life; he is perhaps ready to

Comma   die physically*(,)*but surely not in spirit. A

different perspective on death is found in "After

Apple-Picking." In this poem*(,)*Frost allows one to   *Comma*

see how death could be looked upon, even looked

Comma   forward to*(,)*as a kind of necessary respite at the

end of life's constant toil. Both poems, thus,

present narrators who are confronted by the

Good thesis!   inevitability of death, and yet they view this

conflict in their lives in two very different

ways.

*Good
use of
quotations
as sup-
porting
evidence!*

*(Establish
general
foot note
after
title or
sentence
containing
first
quotation.)*

No caps

Comma

In "Reluctance," the narrator sees unmistakable
signs of death everywhere. The last of the
summer's flowers have withered away and died, and
the leaves, "No longer blown hither and thither"
by the wind, lie dead and scattered on the ground
where they await the first snowfall. Indeed, the
only leaves that are left are "those that the oak
is keeping. . . . [to send] / Out over the crusted
snow / While others are sleeping." But even the
pervasive presence of death cannot extinguish the
narrator's restless, searching spirit. He is
determined not to give up on life without a
struggle, a point that is reinforced when he says
passionately, but with some anxiety, that his
"heart is still aching to seek, / But the feet
question 'Whither'?"

In contrast, "After Apple-Picking" describes the
melancholic state of mind of an old *a*pple
*h*arvester in late fall after he has looked at the
world through nature's magnifying glass—a slab of
ice he "skimmed [that] morning from the drinking
trough." He seems surprised, but not upset, that

the season has changed, perhaps a sign that he was anticipating the "Essence of winter sleep" as a long-awaited end to a weary existence. What's more, he clearly accepts the fact that he is about to die, for he expresses no desire to pick the apples that still remain on the tree. These apples, life's final experiences, are no longer of any interest to him ① *he* ̶H̶e̶ is "done with apple-picking now."

Again, nice balance of generalizations and supporting evidence!

Sub/coor

This dilemma—the choice of whether to live life to the fullest or simply to give up altogether—becomes the central conflict in both poems. In "Reluctance," the speaker admits his life is coming to an end; he has "climbed the hills of view/ And looked at the world, and descended." Still, although he realizes that his body is dying, he questions the undeniable treason of those people who can accept so easily and effortlessly the end of something they hold dear. To the contrary, he concludes that one must never "yield with a grace to reason,/ And bow and accept the end/ Of a love or a season[.]"

Good analysis and summary!

The narrator in "After Apple-Picking," on the other hand, seems ready for the release of death. He is "overtired / Of the great harvest" he once pursued so diligently. Yet, he becomes somewhat *Comma* uneasy when he subconsciously compares himself to the apples that have already fallen from the tree. These castoffs, "No matter if not bruised or spiked with stubble," are worthless except to be thrown into the cellar and squeezed into apple cider. The implications of this temporarily leave the narrator apprehensive, for he foresees the possibility of a troubled sleep as he ~~ponders the~~ *Rep* *wonders if* ~~possibility that~~ his life may have been equally worthless. Nonetheless, in the last few lines of the poem, he seems to give up almost willingly, as *Commas* he falls asleep and dreams about what comes "After Apple-Picking."

In writing these poems, Frost thus presents two unique perspectives on the way two old men view death. By developing a common autumn scene in "Reluctance," and by using apple-picking as a metaphor for life in "After Apple-Picking," he

Excellent con

manages to make a very forceful poetic statement

about death itself. Depending upon how one chooses

to look at it, Frost suggests the prospect of

death can be either a challenge to live life more

Comma meaningfully⌒or a signal that it is time to give

up altogether.

4. Understand the Importance of Editing and Rewriting

Never complain when your teachers and professors ask you to edit and rewrite the rough drafts of your essays. Editing and rewriting are the heart and soul of effective writing.

In many respects, the difference between effective and ineffective writers is very simple. Effective writers understand the importance of editing and rewriting, whereas ineffective writers either do not understand those responsibilities or tend to ignore them altogether.

D

Preparing the Manuscript

The final draft of your manuscript should be properly prepared and neat in appearance. After all, what have you accomplished if you have written flawless sentences and paragraphs, but your typewriter ribbon is so worn that the type is virtually illegible, or the paper you used is soiled and smudged, or your footnoting procedures are so haphazard that your readers are likely to question your integrity and credibility? Any of these (and other) problems with manuscript preparation can create all of the wrong impressions in the minds of your readers. And if your readers cannot read what you have written, or if they are misled or confused by other problems in manuscript preparation, then they have every right to reject your arguments—no matter how valid and compelling they might otherwise be.

For all of these reasons, you must devote some time and conscientious attention to the actual preparation of your manuscript. And even if it seems unreasonable that teachers and professors insist on cleanly typed, well-documented final drafts, remember that business executives, publishers, and professionals in a variety of fields will seldom read anything that is illegible or poorly prepared. The best example of this is the advice that one professional résumé service regularly gives its clients: "If, for any reason whatsoever, your résumé is difficult to read, then you can rest assured that it won't be read by potential employers!"

This being the case, students are well-advised to learn how to prepare a manuscript properly during classroom writing assignments. Years later, it might be too late; many opportunities could be lost simply because a poorly prepared résumé or letter of inquiry created all of the wrong impressions about the writer's competence and intelligence.

1. Select the Title Carefully

"Titles are the Only Expressions in English Grammar in which the First Letters of the Important Words are Capitalized."

Most instructors require a title for the expository essay. If the title is selected carefully, it serves at least two very valuable functions. It catches and focuses the reader's attention, and it reflects (but does not repeat) the thesis position—thus preparing the reader for the argument.

Keep the title of the expository essay short (generally no more than from three to six words), do *not* underline or enclose it in quotation marks, and capitalize the first letter of the important words.

Incorrect	**Correct**
"The Art of Cinema"	The Art of Cinema
THE ART OF CINEMA	
THE ART OF CINEMA	
The Art of Cinema	
"The Art of Cinema"	

Also, do *not* use a title page unless the essay is quite long. It is a waste of paper to introduce a two- or three-page essay with a one-page marquee. Instead, center the title of the expository essay at the top of the first page.

Like thesis statements, titles can be effective or ineffective for a variety of reasons:

Title	**Comment**
1. My Paper	*[Too bland]*
2. My Title	*[Still too bland]*
3. THE GREATEST PAPER EVER WRITTEN	*[Too pretentious]*

Title	Comment
4. my feeble attempt	*[Too humble]*
5. The Mystery of the Pyramids: Solved at Last	*[Catchy, but can you deliver?]*
6. Sewing Pot Holders	*[Too dull]*
7. A HISTORY OF THE UNI-VERSE	*[Too broad]*
8. a speck of dust	*[Too narrow]*
9. America's Ridiculous Foreign Policy	*[A bit too blunt]*
10. A Statistical Analysis of the Psychological and Emotional Ramifications of Debilitating Vehicular Confrontations	*[Too long, too euphemistic]*
11.	*[Too short]*
12. Gone With The Wind	*[Belongs to someone else]*
13. Hamlet	*[Still belongs to someone else]*
14. Jay Gatsby and the American Dream	*[Very good]*
15. Jane Austen's Social Satire	*[Again, very good]*
16. The Effect of Media Violence on American Life	*[Also very good]*

During the proofreading stage, it is also wise to double-check to make sure the titles of works other than your own are properly punctuated.

The titles of works other than your own are either enclosed in quotation marks or underlined. In general, longer works are underlined and shorter works are enclosed in quotation marks. Titles of paintings and most other works of art are also underlined. Unpublished works are, however, always enclosed in quotation marks.

Enclosed in Quotation Marks

"Dover Beach" (a short poem)
"The Lottery" (a short story)

Underlined

Paradise Lost (a long poem)
Flowering Judas and Other Stories (a book of short stories)

Enclosed in Quotation Marks	**Underlined**
"Civil Disobedience" (an essay)	In Defense of Reason (a book of essays)
"The White Whale" (a chapter from a novel)	Moby Dick (a novel)
"The Rose" (a song)	Sargeant Pepper (a record album)
"Two Airliners Almost Collide" (a newspaper article)	The New York Times (a newspaper)
"The Town Cryer" (an unpublished novel)	Hamlet (a play)
	Christina's World (a painting)
	Statue of Liberty (a monument)
	Rambo (a movie)
	Dynasty (a television series)

(See also "Underlining," page 199, and "Quotation Marks," page 194.)

2. Make an Effort to Document Sources

"According to one disillusioned writer, 'Footnotes are often used by the unscrupulous to create the illusory appearance of scholarship and research that never took place'."

"*There is no such person. I just made him up because I needed a quote."

Although there is seldom sufficient time to work extensively with footnoting and bibliographical procedures in many basic writing courses, there are, nonetheless, several reasons why you should use footnotes when they are appropriate:

1. Footnotes enable the reader to distinguish between ideas and language that belong to the writer and those that belong to the writer's sources. Should the reader want more detailed information on the subject, he or she then knows precisely where to look for it.

2. Footnotes give credit to those who deserve it and not to those who are only using their ideas and language.
3. Footnotes, when appropriate, enhance the credibility and integrity of the writer in ways that add considerable strength to the position that is being advocated in the essay itself. Conversely, the absence of footnotes, when they are clearly required, raises questions in the reader's mind as to the writer's sense of integrity and fair play.

Since footnoting and bibliographical procedures are primarily the concern of practicing scholars, they are generally kept as simple as possible in short expository writing assignments. Direct quotations, paraphrased ideas, and statements that are outside the general public knowledge must, however, be footnoted. When such documentation is necessary, you are well-advised to do the following:

1. Always follow the footnoting and bibliographical procedures recommended by the instructor. Remember, documentation that may be appropriate for one class may very well be inappropriate for another.
2. If the instructor does not recommend any specific procedures for documentation, use the procedures outlined in either the *MLA Handbook* (for papers in the humanities) or the *APA Publication Manual* (for papers in the social sciences).
3. Ask the instructor if the footnoting and bibliographical procedures are to be informal or formal.

[Note: Formal footnoting and bibliographical procedures are covered in "Appendix A" of this text, pages 285–288]

In basic writing courses, where the emphasis is on writing and not on research skills, it is frequently acceptable to place an Arabic numeral following the title and supply a corresponding explanation at the bottom of the first page. This is especially true if the essay assignment is based on a single work or a limited number of works. Subsequent references can then appear in parentheses in the body of the essay, or else they can be dispensed with altogether, depending upon the length of the work or works being cited.

EXAMPLE 1

The Dying Season[1]

---

[1]All references in this essay are to Robert Frost's "Reluctance" and "After Apple-Picking" in The Selected Poems of Robert Frost (New York: Holt, Rinehart and Winston, 1963) 21–22 and 52–53.

Since this essay involves two short poems that are easily located in their entirety, no further footnotes or bibliographical entries are necessary.

EXAMPLE 2

The Small-Town Hero[1]

---

[1]All references in this essay are to Sinclair Lewis's Babbitt (New York: Harcourt, Brace and Company, 1922).

Since this essay involves a longer work, subsequent page references should appear in parentheses in the body of the essay.

George F. Babbitt, the main character in Lewis's novel, is described as a man who "made nothing in particular, neither butter nor shoes nor poetry, but he was nimble in the calling of selling houses for more than people could afford to pay"(2).

EXAMPLE 3

Two Small-Town Characters[1]

---

[1]All references in this essay are to Sinclair Lewis's Babbitt (New York: Harcourt, Brace and Company, 1922) and to Main Street (New York: Harcourt, Brace and Company, 1921).

Since this essay involves two or more books by the same author, subsequent references in the body of the essay should include the page number or numbers and one key word from the title.

George F. Babbitt is described as a man who "was nimble in the calling of selling houses for more than people could afford to pay" (Babbitt 2). Carol Milford, on the other hand, is said to represent "that bewildered empire called the American Middlewest" (Street 1).

EXAMPLE 4

Two Views of Small-Town America[1]

---

[1]All references in this essay are to Sinclair Lewis's Babbitt (New York: Harcourt, Brace and Company, 1922) and Frank Norris's The Octopus (New York: Doubleday, Page and Company, 1901).

Since this essay involves books by two different authors, subsequent references in the body of the essay should include the respective authors' last names and the page number or numbers:

George F. Babbitt is described as a man who "was nimble in the calling of selling houses for more than people could afford to pay" (Lewis 2). Presley, on the other hand, is described in Norris's novel as a graduate of "an Eastern college, where he had devoted himself to a passionate study of literature, and, more especially, of poetry" (Norris 9).

[Note: Informal documentation does not give the writer the right to pillage any available source once the general footnote is established on page 1 of the essay. Any quotations, ideas, or paraphrased materials that are not adequately covered by the general footnote, and that are

cited later in the essay, must be documented. Of course, if there are many such sources, then the writer would probably be wise to use formal documentation. (Again, see "Appendix A" of this text, pages 285–288.]

When in doubt, footnote. It is better to be wrong in terms of procedures than it is to be guilty of plagiarism. Most instructors will honor an honest attempt at documentation, no matter how botched the details might be. Few, however, will look very kindly on essays where the writer has made little or no effort to document sources that contributed significantly to the final draft.

3. Basic Manuscript Requirements for the Expository Essay

> "Maybe if I
> use 3-inch
> margins at
> the top and
> bottom of
> the page,
> and 4-inch
> margins on
> the sides, I
> can complete
> the essay
> assignment
> in one long
> sentence."

Unless your instructor specifies otherwise, the basic manuscript requirements for the short expository essay are as follows:

a. Titles

1. Do not use a title page. Center and double-space the title at the top of the first page of the essay.

2. Capitalize the first, last, and all the important words in your title.
3. Do not underline or enclose your title in quotation marks.
4. Do not put a period at the end of your title.
5. (See also "Select the Title Carefully," pages 268–269.)

b. Name and Course Number

1. Put your name in either the upper left-hand or upper right-hand corner of the first page.
2. Put the course name and number immediately below your name.

c. Margins, Pagination, and Spacing

1. Use 1¼- to 1½-inch margins at the top, sides, and bottom of each page.
2. Indent all paragraphs.
3. Do not number the first page. Number subsequent pages in consecutive order. Normally, page numbers should be placed at the top right-hand corner or centered at the top of each page.
4. Double-space the entire essay, including title, block quotations, footnotes (or endnotes), and bibliography.

d. Other Requirements

1. Use a good black typewriter ribbon. Avoid ribbons that are red, green, purple, or faded beyond recognition.
2. If you are using a computer printer, avoid dot-matrix printers that create fuzzy, faded, or otherwise unrecognizable letters. Remember, most publishers, newspapers, and many businesses will *not* read materials printed by such printers. Such printers are generally used to produce the rough drafts of a writing project—but never, unless they are very high-quality dot-matrix printers, are they used to produce the final drafts.
3. Similarly, if you are using a word processing system, ask your instructor if he or she prefers justified (block print) or unjustified margins.
4. Write on one side of the paper only.

5. Avoid erasable papers that smudge and become unreadable.

[Note: There are several major differences between the basic manuscript requirements for the expository essay and for the research or term paper. See "Appendix A" of this text, page 289–290, for further information on the basic manuscript requirements for the research and/or term paper. See also "A Sample Research Paper," pages 292–308.]

E

In Conclusion

In conclusion, let's not get too snobbish about the whole thing. Although this text has tried to demonstrate that a basic knowledge of English grammar is an essential part of the writing and editing process, it is now time to acknowledge that much powerful prose has been written or spoken by men and women who had no formal training whatsoever in this area. Of course, these people were not writing for the business community or the academic community or any other audience for whom a knowledge of Standard English is a necessity. Still, some of these men and women used language in ways that were deeply moving.

One such person was Sojourner Truth, an uneducated former slave who spoke out defiantly at the 1851 Women's Rights Convention in Akron, Ohio. Her speech remains one of the most moving passages in all of English or American prose:

> That man over there say that a woman needs to be helped into carriages, and lifted over ditches, and to have the best place everywhere. Nobody ever helped me into carriages, or over mud puddles, or gives me a best place. . . . Ain't I a woman? Look at me. Look at my arm! I have plowed and planted and gathered into barns, and no man could head me. . . . And ain't I a woman? I could work as much and eat as much as a man when I could get it, and bear the lash as well. . . . And ain't I a woman? I have borned thirteen children and seen them most all sold off into slavery. And when I cried out

with a mother's grief, none but Jesus heard. . . . Ain't I a woman?

It would be easy to dismiss this as illiterate prose. And, indeed, in some ways it is. There are problems with word choices, shifts in tense, and improper agreement of subject and verb; and yet, it is a deeply moving prose passage.

Why? In part, the answer might be that Sojourner Truth had an intuitive sense of the essential rhythms of language, of parallel phrasing and structure, and of certain other strategies discussed more formally in this text. But, above all else, the power of this passage is that it comes sincerely and unpretentiously from the heart.

And isn't that, ultimately, the definition of all good writing?

APPENDIX A

The Research Paper

1. Defining the "Research Paper"

The "research paper" is a long essay based on several outside sources. Like the expository essay, the research paper is written in Standard English, and it is both explanatory and persuasive in nature. Furthermore, the research paper takes a position and tries to demonstrate the validity of that position through clear prose, logic, and supporting evidence. All of the guidelines for effective writing and editing that have been discussed elsewhere in this text also apply to the research paper.

The process of writing the research paper should also be divided into four separate stages: prewriting, writing, editing, and rewriting. Prewriting, in this case, generally involves more extensive research in a library or libraries. The goals of this research are threefold: to develop a thesis position, to establish an outline, and to gather supporting evidence to develop the body of the paper. Once the writer has moved beyond the "prewriting" (research) stage of the project, the system of writing, editing, and rewriting is precisely the same as the one used in the expository essay.

2. Selecting the Topic

There are several things to consider when you are selecting the topic for a research paper:

- If at all possible, select a topic that is of interest to you. It will be much easier to write with purpose and conviction (and to remain motivated throughout the research and writing stages) if you are genuinely interested in the topic of your research paper. (See also "Write with Purpose and Conviction," page 6.)
- Select a topic for which there is readily available material in local libraries. Most undergraduates have neither the time nor the money to travel long distances to complete their research projects.
- At the same time, try to select a topic that is somewhat original. For one thing, it is much easier to remain motivated if you find that you are making an original contribution to the area you are research-

ing. Conversely, if your research reveals that you are merely repeating what several hundred scholars have already discovered about the topic, it will be almost impossible to remain motivated throughout the research project.

- Select a topic that is related to, or was inspired by, classroom discussions or lectures. Generally, you will have a context within which to address such a topic, and this background information will greatly simplify both the research and the writing of the paper.

- Of course, once you have selected a topic for the research paper, always check with your instructor to see if he or she thinks it will work. Your instructor is in a much better position to determine whether or not there will be problems with available sources, originality, and other research-related activities.

3. Narrowing the Topic

The longer and more extensive the writing project, the more essential it is to narrow the topic and develop a specific focus. For this reason, establishing a preliminary thesis is at least as crucial for the research paper as it is for the short expository essay. The preliminary thesis will help you establish a direction for the research, thus guaranteeing that the time you (the researcher) devote to the project will be used efficiently.

Of course, this is not to suggest that the thesis will remain constant throughout the research project. Rather, the thesis will generally change subtly, and sometimes dramatically, as you continue to discover the meaning of the research project throughout the writing and editing stages.

(See also "Clarify Your Thesis Statement and Preliminary Outline," pages 25–27, and "Establish a Thesis Statement," pages 51–53.)

4. Freewriting and Brainstorming

If you have difficulty generating a thesis for the research project, remember what you learned earlier in this text about freewriting and brainstorming. Freewriting exercises are some of the best ways to develop thesis possibilities, topic sentences, and supporting evidence. Similarly, brainstorming activities can help writers clarify their thesis statements and prepare strategies for responding to opposing views.

(See also "Try Freewriting," pages 6–11, and "Try Brainstorming," pages 11–12.)

5. Using the Outline

Whereas a preliminary or sketch outline is often sufficient for the short expository essay, it is rarely sufficient for the longer research paper. Generally, a fairly extensive formal outline will greatly simplify every stage of the research project.

Like thesis statements, formal outlines provide immediate direction and focus for the research paper, thus guaranteeing that there will be less wasted time and effort. Of course, you should feel free to depart from the outline occasionally as the meaning of the project becomes clearer.

Still, a formal outline is a necessary part of a "game plan," one that may have to be adjusted occasionally, but one that will greatly simplify the way you use the library, write the earlier drafts, and complete the project in an orderly fashion.

(See also "Clarify Your Thesis Statement and Preliminary Outline," pages 25–27, and "Formal Outlines and Organization," pages 65–72.)

6. Using the Library

Libraries can often be terribly intimidating places for people who are unaccustomed to using them. To those who know how to use libraries, however, they can be the most enjoyable, challenging, and informative places imaginable.

There are several ways to learn how to use a library effectively:

■ Most libraries offer weekly (and sometimes daily) tours of their facilities. Take advantage of these tours even before your instructors begin to assign research projects. If you have developed a general sense of everything a good library has to offer, you will be far less overwhelmed and intimidated once you start to do your own research.

- Similarly, acquaint yourself with the reference librarians whose job it is to facilitate your research and introduce you to library resources that are not always available to, or understood by, the general public. Reference librarians are, on the whole, the most helpful and congenial people in the entire academic world. Learn to seek them out, even in the very earliest stages of the research project.

- If you are the least bit uncertain as to how to use a library's card catalog, ask for assistance from the reference librarian. (In most libraries, a book is listed on at least three cards: a subject card, a title card, and an author card.) Without a working knowledge of a library's card catalog, however, even experienced researchers find it difficult, if not impossible, to locate their sources.

- Find out whether the library you are using has any kind of interlibrary loan system through which you can order the books and other materials necessary to complete your research paper.

- It is also important to know *when* to use a library. As a general guideline, go into the library and check out your sources as soon as you have a preliminary sense of your research topic. This early detective work is necessary to determine whether or not the library you plan to use has sufficient resources to develop this particular research paper.

- Once you have determined that the library has sufficient materials to develop the research topic, your subsequent research will be somewhat more methodical. Prior to engaging in these research ventures, carefully study your outline to determine what precisely you will need in the way of primary and secondary sources. (Primary sources are works of literature, other books, autobiographies, and so on; secondary sources are generally shorter works that comment on, or analyze, these primary sources.) Then, once you have determined what you will need to complete your research, carefully "block off" the segments you can realistically hope to complete during any subsequent visit to the library. (Although this procedure may appear somewhat mechanical, it can save much time, primarily because it discourages haphazard and undisciplined research.)

7. Taking Notes

The process of taking notes for the research paper is somewhat more systematic than the one used in the short expository essay. (See "Keep a Notebook Handy," pages 18–19.) Although notes for the short expository essay can easily be recorded in a notebook and later grouped and arranged into a logical sequence, this is not quite so simple a task with the research paper. Often the research paper will involve a hundred (or several hundred) individual notes. For this reason, the method you use to take notes must be flexible enough to allow for subsequent reorganizations.

Use 3 x 5 or 4 x 6 inch cards to record the notes you take during your research. On your note cards, include the information you will need to complete both your footnote and bibliographical references. This information is as follows:

1. The author's name
2. The title of the work cited
3. The publisher
4. The place of publication
5. The year of publication
6. The page numbers you are quoting, paraphrasing, and so on
7. The precise quotation you are using

Of course, you can abbreviate much of this information in subsequent notes you take from the same source.

Also, be sure to include only one note per card. Most research papers involve several different attempts at organization and reorganization as the meaning of the project is clarified. And individual note cards will provide greater organizational flexibility in the later stages of the research project.

Finally, be sure to place quotation marks around directly quoted materials in order to avoid potential problems with plagiarism. Later, after your research has taken you through a variety of different books and journal articles, it may be impossible to remember what is a paraphrase, what is a quote, and what is your own summary of a source.

In time, your individual note cards will be grouped and arranged in the sequence that best develops the specific thesis of your research project. This process is very similar to the one discussed in "Prewriting Strategies." (See "Group and Arrange Ideas," pages 20–24.)

8. Preparing Formal Footnotes and Formal Bibliography

a. Formal Footnotes

In formal footnotes, each direct quotation and each paraphrased idea or statement receives its own individual footnote. Similarly, each source cited in the footnotes receives a separate entry in the bibliography. Formal documentation is always preferable to informal documentation when one is writing a long expository essay, research paper, or term paper that involves several different sources. (See also "Make an Effort to Document Sources," pages 270–274, for more information on informal documentation.)

Depending upon your instructor's preference, footnotes can appear at the foot of pages or on a separate page at the very end of the essay. (In the latter case, they are properly referred to as "endnotes.") Always check with your instructor to determine which system of footnoting he or she prefers.

The following are some of the more common footnote and endnote entries, although the list is by no means complete. (It is always wise to have a copy of the *MLA Handbook* available for convenient reference if you are doing a research paper in the humanities, or the *APA Publication Manual* if you are doing a research paper in the social sciences.)

1. A book by one author

   ¹Robert Frost, *The Poems of Robert Frost* (New York: Modern Library, 1946) 44.

2. A book by two or more authors

    ²Robert A. Greenberg and James G. Hepburn, *Robert Frost: An Introduction* (New York: Holt, Rinehart and Winston, 1961) 13–14.

3. A selection from an anthology

    ³Robert Frost, "After Apple-Picking," *Selected Poems of Robert Frost* (New York: Holt, Rinehart and Winston, 1968) 52–53.

4. A preface, introduction, or afterword

    ⁴Robert Graves, introduction, *Selected Poems of Robert Frost* (New York: Holt, Rinehart and Winston, 1968) xii.

5. An edited book

    ⁵Robert Frost, *The Letters of Robert Frost to Louis Untermeyer,* ed. Louis Untermeyer (New York: Holt, Rinehart and Winston, 1963) 29.

6. An article in a journal, periodical, or magazine

    ⁶Malcolm Cowley, "Frost: A Dissenting Opinion," *New Republic* 11 September 1944: 312.

7. An article in a daily newspaper

    ⁷Paul J. Martin, "Robert Frost: America's Poet," *Los Angeles Times* 20 July 1960: C9.

8. An unpublished dissertation or thesis

    ⁸Phillip Conway, "The Puritan Origins of Frost's Poetry," diss., Ann Arbor: U of Michigan, 1965, 123–124.

9. A subsequent reference to the same source

    ⁹Radcliffe Squires, *The Major Themes of Robert Frost* (Ann Arbor: U of Michigan, 1963) 11.

    ¹⁰Carlos Baker, "Frost on the Pumpkin," *Georgia Review* Summer 1957: 118.

    ¹¹Squires 12.

    ¹²Baker 120.

[Note: The MLA Handbook *recommends that subsequent references of the type illustrated in footnotes 11 and 12 above, and 15 and 16 below, appear* not *at the foot of the page or at the end of the paper, but rather* in parentheses *in the body of the paper. See the "Sample Research Paper" for specific examples of how this is done.]*

10. A subsequent reference when you use two or more sources by the same author

[13]James Melville Cox, *Robert Frost* (New York: Prentice-Hall, 1962) 46.

[14]James Melville Cox, "Robert Frost and the Edge of the Clearing," *Virginia Quarterly Review* Winter 1959: 81.

[15]Cox, *Robert Frost* 67.

[16]Cox, "Robert Frost and the Edge" 86.

[Note: Latin abbreviations such as "ibid" and others are no longer recommended by the MLA Handbook *and should be avoided.]*

b. Formal Bibliography

The bibliography ("Works Cited") should appear on the last page of the expository essay, research paper, or term paper, and it should contain only entries cited in the footnotes. If your instructor wants you to include *all* of the sources you consulted during your research, call it "Works Consulted." Also, the bibliography is alphabetized, and its form and contents differ somewhat from the footnote entries.

Works Cited

Baker, Carlos. "Frost on the Pumpkin." *Georgia Review* XI Summer 1957: 117–131.

Conway, Phillip. "The Puritan Origins of Frost's Poetry." Ann Arbor: U of Michigan: 1965.

Cowley, Malcolm. "Frost: A Dissenting Opinion." *New Republic* CLI September 11, 1944: 312–313.

Cox, James Melville. *Robert Frost.* New York: Prentice-Hall, 1962.

——."Robert Frost and the Edge of the Clearing." *Virginia Quarterly Review* XXXV Winter 1959: 73–88.

Frost, Robert. *Selected Poems of Robert Frost.* New York: Holt, Rinehart and Winston, 1968.

——. *The Letters of Robert Frost to Louis Untermeyer.* Ed.

Louis Untermeyer. New York: Holt, Rinehart and Winston, 1963.

——. *The Poems of Robert Frost.* New York: Modern Library, 1946.

Graves, Robert. Introduction. *Selected Poems of Robert Frost.* New York: Holt, Rinehart and Winston, 1968. ix–xiv.

Greenberg, Robert A. and James G. Hepburn. *Robert Frost: An Introduction.* New York: Holt, Rinehart and Winston, 1961.

Martin, Paul J. "Robert Frost: America's Poet." *Los Angeles Times* 20 July 1960: C9.

Squires, Radcliffe. *The Major Themes of Robert Frost.* Ann Arbor: U of Michigan, 1963.

9. Avoiding Plagiarism

Plagiarism occurs when writers do not acknowledge that they have used words or ideas from one of the sources consulted. Plagiarism is a particularly troubling problem for both teachers and students, primarily because it takes up much time and emotional energy.

When teachers suspect plagiarism, they are required to protect both the academic integrity of their courses and the integrity of the vast majority of students who do *not* plagiarize. Furthermore, students who are suspected of plagiarism must be given every opportunity to present their cases to an instructor or to some committee set up to deal with such problems. Needless to say, because of the investment in time and emotional energy, both teachers and students agonize over potential plagiarism cases.

Most problems with plagiarism, however, are unintentional, caused either by the student's ignorance of footnoting procedures or by haphazard research techniques. There are at least three ways to avoid problems with unintentional plagiarism:

■ During the note-taking stage of the research process, carefully distinguish between direct quotations and paraphrased materials, which require footnotes, and your own observations, which do *not* require footnotes.

- If you are uncertain as to whether or not something should be footnoted, check with your instructor prior to typing the final draft. Most instructors consider potential plagiarism problems so troubling and so time-consuming that they will welcome your attempts to avoid the issue altogether. Furthermore, by raising the issue with your instructor prior to handing in the final draft of the research paper, you will have demonstrated good faith—and that will go a long way toward resolving any potential plagiarism issues. (This does not, of course, mean that once you have raised the issue with your instructor, you can feel free to ignore all footnoting and bibliographical procedures.)

- If you have any doubts whatsoever, footnote! It is better to insert a footnote occasionally where one is not needed, than to omit it where it is clearly required.

10. Preparing the Manuscript

There are some significant differences between the guidelines for preparing the final manuscripts of the short expository essay and the research paper. The following are the *MLA Handbook*'s guidelines for preparing the sequence of materials to appear in the final manuscript of the research paper. (See also "A Sample Research Paper," pages 292–308.)

1. The research paper normally requires a title page. The title page should list the author's name, the class, the date, and other information required by your instructor.
2. A formal outline
3. The body of the paper
4. Endnotes, unless your instructor requires that you place footnotes at the foot of the pages or in parentheses in the body of the paper
5. A list of works cited

The other basic manuscript requirements for the research paper are precisely the same as those for the short expository essay. (See also

"Basic Manuscript Requirements for the Expository Essay," pages 274–276.)

11. Avoiding Some Common Problems in the Research Paper

- Avoid the extremes of footnoting too much or footnoting too little. You should, of course, footnote all the words and ideas you either cite directly or paraphrase in the body of the paper. But do not sprinkle footnotes in just to remind your reader that you "are now doing a research paper."

- Similarly, do not pad the bibliography with every book you checked out of the library. In the bibliography, cite only those works you have referred to in the footnote references. If your instructor requires that you list not only works cited in the footnotes, but also works consulted, label the list "Works Consulted."

- Be sure to narrow the topic. Often when writers are assigned long research projects, they think it is no longer necessary to establish a specific focus. However, a well-defined thesis position is at least as important to the research paper as it is to the expository essay.

- Avoid wordiness. Because the research paper is, by its very nature, longer than the expository essay, many writers tend to avoid editing and cutting the words, phrases, and sentences that merely clutter up the argument. Be as vigilant in eliminating wordiness from the research paper as you are in eliminating it from the expository essay. (See also "Eliminate Wordiness," pages 95–97.)

- Avoid using too many long quotations as supporting evidence. Certainly long quotations are acceptable in the research paper; in fact, they are often essential to the development of the argument. But do not get into the habit of dropping them into the middle of each paragraph just to create the impression that "this is a research paper." Also, when you use long quotations, be sure to indent, double-space, and discuss the significance of the quotations at some length. (See also "Quotation Marks," pages 192–193, and "Colons," pages 186–187.)

- Similarly, introduce quotations in such a way that they are compatible with the sentence structures in which they appear. Do not use them as convenient excuses for writing awkward sentences.

- Editing and rewriting are at least as important in the research paper as they are in the short expository essay. Although the research paper is a longer project, it, too, needs to be meticulously edited and proofread. "A Sample Research Paper," for example, is *not* a first draft. It is, rather, the fifth draft of this particular research project.

A SAMPLE RESEARCH PAPER

The Meaning of the Frontier in Kesey's
One Flew Over the Cuckoo's Nest

by
Robert Jenkins
English 36, Section 4
April 3, 1985

Outline

Thesis: Ken Kesey's <u>One Flew Over the Cuckoo's Nest</u> has its roots in the American frontier ethic to the extent that its central themes involve the issues of escape and challenge.

I. A definition of the frontier ethic
   A. Historians and literary critics
      1. Frederick Jackson Turner
      2. Henry Nash Smith
      3. R. W. B. Lewis
   B. Others who helped define the frontier ethic
      1. Thomas Jefferson
      2. Henry Adams
      3. Henry David Thoreau

II. Kesey's definition of civilization
   A. The "combine"
   B. Chief Bromden, Nurse Ratched, and the "combine"

III. R. P. McMurphy—the frontier hero
   A. McMurphy and the frontier ethic
      1. No home
      2. Outside the law
      3. Bigger than life
      4. His masculinity, individualism, and non-conformity
   B. McMurphy's influence on the other patients
      1. The gift of laughter
      2. Restores their sexuality
      3. His persistence
      4. The fishing trip

IV. McMurphy's demise—Bromden's rebirth

    A. The final confrontation with Nurse Ratched

    B. Bromden as the new McMurphy

    C. Bromden's escape

The Meaning of the Frontier in Kesey's
<u>One Flew Over the Cuckoo's Nest</u>

Then they crossed the moon—a black, weaving
necklace, drawn into a V by that lead goose.
For an instant that lead goose was right in the
center of that circle, bigger than the others,
a black cross opening and closing, then he
pulled his V out of sight into the sky once more.[1]

Ken Kesey's <u>One Flew Over the Cuckoo's Nest</u> addresses
itself to the meaning of the frontier in American life,
and eventually to the crisis that arises in the twentieth
century when the restless spirit of the frontiersman
lingers on in our culture long after the frontier itself
has vanished. Within this context, the central characters
in Kesey's novel are R. P. McMurphy and his Indian
companion, Chief Bromden. Together they confront the
conformity-minded values of the community in the insane
asylum, a kind of last frontier, for it is the last place
where a person can be different. Significantly, R. P.
McMurphy and Chief Bromden reflect two fairly traditional
attitudes toward the meaning of the frontier. For
McMurphy, the insane asylum is a <u>challenge</u>, a place where
he can prove his masculinity and individuality. But for
Chief Bromden, the insane asylum is an <u>escape valve</u>
wherein he can retreat from the encroaching forces of
civilization. The frontier as challenge or the frontier
as escape--this issue is the thematic center of Kesey's

novel, just as it was one of the fundamental issues involved in the nineteenth-century frontier experience.

With the publication of Frederick Jackson Turner's The Frontier in American History (1893) and later works such as Henry Nash Smith's Virgin Land (1950) and R. W. B. Lewis' The American Adam (1955), it has become axiomatic to argue that the frontier experience had a profound effect on American life and values. It is equally self-evident that the frontier had many ideological manifestations, including variations on the themes of escape and challenge.[2] Still, it is important to establish Kesey within the frontier tradition. Kesey is neither concerned with the political, economic, and social ramifications of the frontier experience (which were, of course, Turner's primary focus),[3] nor does his notion of the frontier parallel Henry Nash Smith's definition that the frontier offered "every man an opportunity to acquire a farm and become an independent member of society."[4] Kesey is working, instead, within the romantic tradition of the frontier experience.

Kesey's definition of the frontier has its roots in the myths, legends, and romantic preconceptions surrounding Daniel Boone, Davy Crockett, Buffalo Bill, and others. This tradition stresses the more mythical qualities of the frontier experience: the way the frontier provides an area where a man can prove his masculinity and find his individual identity, where he can laugh uproariously at the absurdities of life without fear of social reprisals, and where he can confront the unknown and strive for the unattainable.

According to R. W. B. Lewis, the romantic tradition also saw the frontier as an escape route opening up onto a vast wilderness that was located in space but outside of time altogether (91). Kesey's attitude toward the frontier ethic is an extension of this idea, for through the character of Chief Bromden he denies the frontier not only its temporal, but also its spatial, dimensions. The reason for this, of course, is that the physical frontier had long since vanished by the time Kesey was writing his novel. Indeed, all that was left was the memory of a vanishing frontier ethic, held in timeless and spaceless suspension in Chief Bromden's subconscious mind. This frontier provides Bromden with a schizophrenic escape valve into which he can escape whenever he is threatened by the forces of civilization.

Civilization, in this novel, is appropriately defined as a "combine," a vast machine that seeks to make every member of society conform to a single, mechanistic standard of behavior--the very standard of behavior the rugged individualists of the earlier century had sought to avoid by fleeing to the frontier and the open land beyond. That Kesey should choose the machine to represent the values of civilization is quite appropriate within the larger context of the American frontier experience, for it was industrialization that posed the greatest threat to the agrarian ideal Jefferson envisioned on the edge of the American wilderness.[5] It was the railroad whistling in the background that disturbed the tranquility and repose of the sanctuary Thoreau had established at Walden Pond.[6] And for Henry Adams, it was

the dynamo that destroyed the serenity of the nineteenth-
century agrarian landscape and led this country into the
twentieth century.[7] In other words, the machine and what
it represents was recognized by many earlier writers as
the single greatest threat to the frontier ethic. Kesey's
novel merely reflects what happens when not only the
landscape, but also its inhabitants, become totally
mechanized.

The ultimate goal of the "combine" is to create a
world in which everyone is precisely the same—a world in
which there is no individuality. Chief Bromden describes
this world in the following passage:

> All up the coast I could see the signs of what
> the Combine had accomplished since I was last
> through this country, things like, for example—
> a train stopping at a station and laying a
> string of full-grown men in mirrored suits and
> machined hats, laying them like a hatch of
> identical insects, half-life things coming pht-
> pht-pht out of the last car, then hooting its
> electrical whistle and moving on down the
> spoiled land to deposit another hatch. Or
> things like five thousand houses punched out
> identical by machine and strung across the
> hills outside of town. (203)

However, the "combine" has some parts that simply
cannot conform to this mechanized standard of behavior,
and so there is a need for the super mechanic, Nurse

Ratched, who makes the necessary adjustments on the mental patients. Nurse Ratched's name itself suggests many analogies and obvious puns: "wretched," "rat shit," and, perhaps most importantly, "ratchet." For like the wrench after which she is named, Nurse Ratched is an essential tool for performing the necessary maintenance work on the malfunctioning members of society, the mental patients who insist on being different. Indeed, the wicker bag she carries with her every day is compared to a "tool box [full of] wheels and gears, cogs polished to a hard glitter, tiny pills that gleam like porcelain, needles, forceps, watchmaker's pliers, [and] rolls of copper wire" (10).

In addition to her role as super mechanic, Nurse Ratched is also the vanguard of those civilized values that have thrust their way into the last frontier of the insane asylum. She dominates the men on the ward by denying them their individuality and their masculinity, the two qualities that were necessary for survival on the original frontier. She also takes away their manhood by psychologically emasculating them during the group therapy sessions and, occasionally, by performing the ultimate castration—the lobotomy. Thus, she perpetuates a principle of complete sterility wherein the model patient is the one who has become a psychologically and physically emasculated robot whose movements are directed by "powerful magnets in the floor [that] maneuver personnel through the ward like arcade puppets" (32). This principle of sterility is further evidenced in the color white found throughout the ward, especially in the black orderlies who have submitted to Nurse Ratched's rules and who wear "snow-white pants and white shoes with metal snaps down one side and white shoes polished like ice" (32).

Confronted by Nurse Ratched and the forces of civilization, the majority of the patients give in to the "combine." But some, like Chief Bromden, instinctively react to the intrusion of the "combine" into their lives by searching for some escape valve. Bromden, the narrator of this novel and a man who pretends to be deaf and dumb, holds in a kind of timeless and spaceless suspension the memory of the vanishing frontier ethic that still existed in the Pacific Northwest during his youth. Whenever Bromden is threatened by the "combine," he blurs the edges of reality by projecting a psychological smoke screen (the result of his World War II experiences when he was involved with the fog machines that camouflaged Allied airstrips in England), and then he escapes into the fog.

Bromden's periodic retreats into this inner frontier seem an acceptable enough way of coping with the "combine" until R. P. McMurphy enters the ward and teaches him that the frontier should be more than just an escape valve. It should be a place to prove, not avoid, one's manhood and individuality, a place permeated "by the man smell of dust and dirt from the open fields, and sweat, and work" (91).

McMurphy is, in every way, the archetypal frontiersman. He has no permanent base, preferring instead to drift from place to place without ever establishing roots. Later in the novel, we learn that he had a home, but he seems almost to be without a family. He is a physical man who is terribly skeptical of book learning or any intellectual approach to life, a fact made explicit in his confrontations with Harding. And like the classic frontier hero, McMurphy exists just outside of the law, having come directly from the Pendleton Work Farm.

But most important, R. P. McMurphy is in every way bigger than life. He is a man of many identities—— lumberjack, ex-Marine, brawling Irishman, con man, and motorcylist. In fact, he is so much bigger than life that the reader comes to question whether he exists at all, or whether he is an alter ego fabricated by Chief Bromden to help him do battle with the "combine." Indeed, Bromden suggests at the outset that the story "is the truth even if it didn't happen" (13). Also, the relationship between Bromden and McMurphy is a curious one, for McMurphy diminishes in size at precisely the moment that Bromden regains a sense of his manhood and individuality. This, of course, implies that Bromden may be feeding on the strength of his alter ego, R. P. McMurphy.

Although the question of McMurphy's existence is an interesting one, the important point is unchanged either way, for his significance is that he embodies a system of values that is in opposition to the "combine." He represents masculinity, individualism, nonconformity, and the frontier spirit of adventure, just as Nurse Ratched and the "combine" represent sterility, group consciousness, conformity, and the spirit of caution.

McMurphy recognizes at the outset that the men on the ward have abdicated their manhood to Nurse Ratched, and he attributes many of their psychological problems to this abdication.[8] He tells dirty jokes, plays cards with a deck illustrating fifty-two positions for sexual intercourse, and brags freely about his own sexual escapades. McMurphy does this, not necessarily because he is a hedonist, but rather because he recognizes that the mental patients must accept their sexuality before they can regain their sanity.

At the same time that McMurphy teaches the patients to accept their sexuality, he also strives to instill in them the gift of laughter. Nurse Ratched, of course, forbids laughter on the ward, just as she forbids discussions of human sexuality, for she knows that the kind of humor McMurphy brings with him will enable the patients to regain their manhood and their individuality. Nonetheless, McMurphy perseveres; he celebrates the leg-slapping, earthy humor of the frontier, which exaggerates the absurdities of life, because he knows "you have to laugh at the things that hurt you just to keep yourself in balance, just to keep the world from running you crazy" (212).

The spirit of the frontier is evident in McMurphy in other ways as well. Like the lead goose that pulls its "V" out of sight and into the sky, McMurphy, the self-proclaimed "Bull-Goose Looney," is a migratory spirit who refuses to remain stationary. Cuckoos build nests; geese keep moving. As Richard Blessing has suggested in an essay entitled, "The Moving Target: Kesey's Evolving

Hero," R. P. McMurphy's initials (RPM) suggest a character who is constantly on the move, for he knows the best way to avoid the "combine" is to be a moving target.[9] However, the significance of his perpetual motion goes well beyond this, for it is the kind of movement that is associated with the frontier experience. Throughout the story, McMurphy refuses to take a step backward, no matter what the predicament, and he also refuses to go around objects (Blessing 617). Rather, he is always building up momentum, whether it be in the fight with Washington, where he circles once and then plods determinedly forward, or in the basketball game, where he is an advocate of the fast break. Furthermore, he is always smashing through doors, windows, and glass-enclosed rooms, either to get a pack of cigarettes or, at the end of the novel, to attack Nurse Ratched. Hence, McMurphy's relentless progression through life is an extension of the ethic of an entire nation that pushed stubbornly from frontier to frontier, through natural obstacles if necessary, eventually to conquer this continent.

In time, McMurphy realizes that it is not enough merely to bring the spirit of the frontier ethic into the ward; ultimately the patients must be tested on the physical frontier if they are to regain their manhood and their individuality. Significantly, they find all of this, plus a renewed ability to laugh, when they escape from the insane asylum to go fishing far to the west of "the sports boats trolling up and down the coast" (208). Later, their manhood and individuality secure, they have

the confidence to laugh at themselves and their
predicament. They send out a chorus of "laughter that
rang out on the water in ever-widening circles, farther
and farther, until it crashed up on the beaches all over
the coast, on beaches all over all coasts, in wave after
wave" (212).

McMurphy is, for all practical purposes, exhausted and
his demise predictable after the fishing trip. When the
men return to the ward, the "acutes," who had not gone
along on the fishing trip, wonder why "McMurphy looked so
beat and worn down where the rest . . . looked red-
cheeked and full of excitement" (216). Thematically,
either McMurphy has served his purpose as Chief Bromden's
alter ego, or else the effort of trying to restore
meaning to the lives of the patients has exhausted him.
In either case, he has accomplished what he set out to
do; he has instilled in the minds of the mental patients
the frontier ethic that he himself represents.

The confrontation between McMurphy and Nurse Ratched
at the end of the novel involves the elements of the
classic frontier shoot-out. In the second chapter of the
novel, McMurphy had entered the mental ward like the
western gunfighter, his heels ringing "on the floor like
horseshoes . . . thumbs in his pockets, boots wide apart"
(16). Later, when he decides he will not play by Nurse
Ratched's rules, he is again described as "the cowboy out
of the TV set walking down the middle of the street to
meet a dare" (172). So it is appropriate that he should
confront Nurse Ratched for the last time like the western
gunfighter "with horsehide chaps . . . a ten-gallon

Stetson [and] bare heels ring[ing] sparks out of the
tile" (267). Through the final confrontation with Nurse
Ratched, he makes the frontier ethic a permanent part of
the ward. Then, like some wild animal dying without being
tamed, he falls back, not caring "any more about anything
but himself and dying" (267).

Although McMurphy dies at the end of the story, the
novel does not necessarily end on a depressing note—
especially if his character is viewed as an alter ego.
Throughout the novel, McMurphy has been "reaching into
the fog and dropping down and dragging men up by their
hands, dragging them blinking into the open" (124). Now
Chief Bromden becomes the new McMurphy, a transformation
made explicit when he tries on McMurphy's cap, busts out
of the ward through a window, and cons a Mexican truck
driver into giving him a leather jacket and 10 dollars.
But, most important, Bromden speculates that perhaps he
will go to Canada after he has visited his hometown:

> I might go to Canada eventually, but I think
> I'll stop along the Columbia along the way. I'd
> like to check around Portland and Hood River
> and The Dalles to see if there's any guys I
> used to know back in the village who haven't
> drunk themselves goofy. I'd like to see what
> they've been doing since the government tried
> to buy their right to be indians. (272)

The frontier ethic that R. P. McMurphy embodied is now
alive in Chief Bromden. But Bromden is no longer

concerned with simply <u>escaping</u> from the "combine." With his manhood and sense of individuality restored, he is now ready for the <u>challenge</u> of this new Canadian frontier.

Notes

[1]Ken Kesey, One Flew Over the Cuckoo's Nest (New York: New American Library, 1962) 143.

[2]R. W. B. Lewis, The American Adam (U of Chicago, 1955) 98–105.

[3]Frederick Jackson Turner, The Frontier in American History (New York: Henry Holt and Company, 1920) 1–4.

[4]Henry Nash Smith, Virgin Land (New York: Vintage Books, 1950) 293.

[5]Gilbert Chinard, Thomas Jefferson, the Apostle of Americanism (Ann Arbor: U of Michigan, 1975) 492.

[6]Henry David Thoreau, Walden, ed. Sherman Paul (Boston: Houghton Mifflin, 1960) 79.

[7]Henry Adams, The Education of Henry Adams (Boston: Houghton Mifflin, 1961) 379–390.

[8]Richard Maxwell, "The Abdication of Masculinity in One Flew Over the Cuckoo's Nest," Twenty-Seven to One, ed. Bradford Broughton (New York, 1970), 203–205.

[9]Richard Blessing, "The Moving Target: Ken Kesey's Evolving Hero," Journal of Popular Culture IV Winter 1971: 615–618.

Works Cited

Adams, Henry. The Education of Henry Adams. Boston: Houghton
    Mifflin Company, 1961.

Blessing, Richard. "The Moving Target: Ken Kesey's Evolving
    Hero," Journal of Popular Culture IV Winter 1971: 615–627.

Chinard, Gilbert. Thomas Jefferson, The Apostle of American-
    ism. Ann Arbor: U of Michigan, 1975.

Kesey, Ken. One Flew Over the Cuckoo's Nest. New York: New
    American Library, 1962.

Lewis, R. W. B. The American Adam. Chicago: U of Chicago,
    1955.

Maxwell, Richard. "The Abdication of Masculinity in One Flew
    Over the Cuckoo's Nest," Twenty-Seven to One, ed. Brad-
    ford Broughton. New York, 1970: 203–211.

Smith, Henry Nash. Virgin Land. New York: Vintage Books,
    1950.

Thoreau, Henry David. Walden. Boston: Houghton Mifflin Com-
    pany, 1960.

Turner, Frederick Jackson. The Frontier in American History.
    New York: Henry Holt and Company, 1920.

Index

Commas (*Cont.*):
 with coordinate adjectives, 176–177
 in dates, 180
 in direct address, 180–181
 essential and nonessential information, 175
 for independent clauses with coordinating
  conjunctions, 114–115, 174–176
 after introductory word groupings, 174, 177–178
 for items in a series, 176
 with nonrestrictive clauses, 178–179
 with parenthetical and transitional expressions,
  180
 for places and addresses, 180
 in quotations, 193–194
 and semicolons, 182–186
 to separate dependent clauses, 174–175, 177–178
 with subordinating conjunctions, 174–176
Comparisons:
 essays of comparison and contrast, 54–64, 68–71,
  258–266
 faulty, 149–150
 including necessary words in, 149
Complex sentences, 92
Compound sentences, 93
Compound subjects, verbs with, 135
Compound verbs and comma usage, 176
Compound words and hyphens, 200
Computers, writing with, 36–37
 manuscript requirements in, 275
Concluding paragraphs, 81–84
Conjunctions:
 coordinating, 91, 115
  to correct run-on sentences, 116
  to introduce sentences, 217
  semicolon with, 183
 subordinating, 114–115
  with commas, 174–176
Conjunctive adverbs, 182, 217
Consistency in sentences, 133–153
Constructions, sentence:
 active vs. passive, 127–129
 awkward, 158–160
 mixed, 151
Contractions, 197–198
Coordinating conjunctions (*see* Conjunctions,
  coordinating)
Coordination in sentences, 114–116
 proper vs. faulty, 115
Criticism, using, 35–36

Dangling modifier, 89, 121, 125–127
Dashes, use of, 185, 187–188
Dependent clauses, 92
 and comma use, 117, 174–175, 177–179
 vs. independent clauses, 92
 parallelism of, 147–149
 as sentence fragments, 112–113
Development of essay, 53–64
 examples of, 54–64
Development of paragraph:
 evidence in, use of, 78–79
 length in, appropriate, 78–79
Dictionaries, 214–215

Direct vs. implied question, 168–169
Direct vs. indirect quotation, 191
Direct address, comma in, 180–181
Direct object, 90, 128
Documentation of sources:
 examples of end notes and works cited, 307–308
 formal footnotes and bibliography, 285–288
 informal footnotes and bibliography, 270–274
 primary vs. secondary sources, 283
 (*See also* Paraphrases and summaries of sources;
  Parenthetical documentation of sources)
Dot-matrix printer, 275
Double negatives, 163–164

Editing:
 prematurely, 31–32
 vs. rewriting, 233
 strategies for, 45
 vs. writing, 46–49, 207–209
Editing and writing process, xvii–xix, 3–4, 207–210
Ellipsis marks, use of, 191, 195–197
Emotionalism, avoiding, 75–76, 82, 106
End notes or footnotes (*see* Documentation of
  sources)
End punctuation, 166–172
 exclamation points, 170–171
 periods, 167–168
 question marks, 168–170
Essays:
 comparison and contrast, examples of, 54–64, 68–
  71, 258–266
 development and unity of, 53–64
 editing, as a whole, 50–72
 examples of, 234–266
 formal outlines for, 65–72
 paragraphs in, 53–61, 77–81
 preliminary or sketch outlines for, 20–24
Euphemisms, avoiding, 97–99, 108–109
Evidence, use of, 78–79
Examples, use of, 75, 78–79
Exclamation points, use of, 170–171
Expository writing, 50
 examples of, 234–266

Faulty comparisons, 149–150
Faulty logic, 104–107
Faulty parallelism (*see* Parallel structure)
First-person singular pronouns, use of, 33–34
Footnotes (*see* Documentation of sources)
Formal outlines, 65–72
 examples of, 66–72
 in research paper, 282, 293–294
Fragmentary sentences (*see* Sentence fragments)
Freewriting, 6–11, 281–282

General nouns, 220–222
Generalizations:
 balancing with evidence, 78–79
 in introductory paragraphs, 75
Glossary of grammatical terms, 88–93
Goals:
 of prewriting, 25
 of writing, 37